THE TIMES

COMPACT HISTORY OF THE WORLD

THE TIMES

COMPACT

HISTORY

OF THE

WORLD

Edited by Geoffrey Parker

Grafton

Times Books, London
77-85 Fulham Palace Road,
Hammersmith, London W6 8JB

First published by Times Books (as *The Times
Compact Atlas of World History*) 1995
Second edition 1997
Third edition 2001

Printed and bound in Italy

British Library Cataloguing in Publication Data
A catalogue record for this book is available
from the British Library

ISBN 0 0076 5080 9

EDITOR

GEOFFREY PARKER
Andreas Dorpalen
Distinguished Professor
of History
The Ohio State University

Editorial Consultants
Chris Scarre
McDonald Institute
University of Cambridge

Richard Overy
Professor of Modern History
King's College
University of London

Editorial Direction
Philip Parker

Cartographic Direction and Design
Martin Brown

Cartographers
Cosmographics, Watford
Bartholomew Mapping Services,
Glasgow

Designer
Colin Brown

Place-names Consultant, Index
Pat Geelan

Contents

PART THREE

The Rise of the West

PART FOUR

The Modern World

Introduction

This volume, like *The Times History of the World*, first published in 1978 and now in its fifth edition (and available in 16 languages), attempts to cover the whole story of humankind from its origins, when our ancestors first emerged from the tropical forests of Africa, to the complex, highly articulated world in which we now live.

It differs, however, from the original *History of the World* in three important ways. First, as its name makes clear, it presents the data in a more compact form. Although it includes 80 spreads each contains fewer, simpler maps and (proportionately) more text. Second, every map has been reviewed in order to highlight the salient trends and facts it features. Third, the topics selected for treatment include far more material from the modern period: 24 spreads concentrate on the period since 1914 and no fewer than 17 of them cover the world since 1945.

Nevertheless, although the present volume incorporates new material and differs in other important ways from its predecessor, it rests upon the same principles. Above all, it tries to break away from a concentration on Europe and to offer instead a view of history that is world-wide in conception and presentation and which does justice, without prejudice or favour, to the achievements of all peoples, in all ages and in all quarters of the globe. It thus remains true to the vision of Geoffrey Barraclough, who planned and edited the *History*.

'When we say this is an atlas of world history, we mean that it is not simply a series of national histories loosely strung together. In other words, it is concerned less with particular events in the history of particular countries than with broad movements – for example the spread of the great world religions spanning whole continents... In singling out topics for inclusion we have adhered to the principle of selecting what was important then rather than what seems important now'

The essence of history, as Geoffrey Barraclough realized, is change and movement over time; and the historian's principal mission is therefore to discern the static from the dynamic, the aberration from the trend, and the contingent from the constant. So instead of presenting a series of individual snapshots, *The Times Compact History of the World* emphasizes change, expansion and contraction. It aims to convey a sense of the past as a continuing process and thus to provide a fresh perspective on today's world which will meet the requirements and interests of present-day readers in all parts of the globe.

This revised edition incorporates several new features. First, all the later spreads – both maps and text – have been updated to cover events since the original edition went to press and four new spreads have been added. Second, many other maps have been revised provided with physical bases. Third – a totally new feature – over 80 images and more tables have been included. Finally, errors brought to our attention by readers have been corrected and major developments down to February 2002 have been added.

GEOFFREY PARKER
February 2002

ONE

The Ancient World

About 6000 years ago, in a few areas of particularly intensive agriculture, the dispersed villages of Neolithic peoples gave way to more complex societies. These were the first civilizations, and their emergence marks the start of a new phase of world history. They arose, apparently independently, in four widely dispersed areas (the early civilizations of America emerged considerably later): the lower Tigris and Euphrates valleys; the valley of the Nile; the Indus valley around Harappa and Mohenjo-Daro; and the Yellow River around An-yang. The characteristic feature of them all was the city, which now became an increasingly dominant social form, gradually encroaching on the surrounding countryside, until today urban civilization has become the criterion of social progress. But the city possessed other important connotations: a complex division of labour; literacy and a literate class (usually the priesthood); monumental public buildings; political and religious hierarchies; a kingship descended from the gods.

Statue of the pharaoh Ramesses II
Great Temple of Abu Simbel, c. 1257 BC

Human origins

The earliest known hominine fossils come from the Afar region of Ethiopia and are 4.5 million years old. Between three and four million years ago, skeletal and fossilized footprints of *Australopithecus afarensis* indicate a serviceable if not fully bipedal gait, hands still partly adapted for specialized tree climbing and a brain approximately one-third the size of ours. This species is the probable ancestor both of the robustly built Australopithecines ('southern apes'), all with large teeth and herbivorous diets, and of our genus *Homo* ('man'). These

closely related but nonetheless distinct species not only lived at the same time but side by side in the same habitats.

About three million years ago, *Homo* began to undergo important evolutionary trends, acquiring a larger brain and full bipedalism. As larger brains need better diets to sustain them, the increase in

1 Human origins and colonization of the world

dates of first human occupation

- 5 million to 1.8 million years ago
- 1.8 million years ago
- 1.5 million years ago
- 500,000 years ago
- 100,000 years ago
- 50,000 to 5000 years ago
- 5000 years ago to AD 1492

fossil sites

- more than 4 million years old
- Australopithecines
- early *Homo* ergaster / rudolfensis
- Asian *Homo erectus*
- *Homo heidelbergensis* / African archaic *Homo sapiens*
- Neanderthals
- late *Homo erectus*
- *Homo sapiens sapiens*

NORTH AMERICA

ARCTIC

GREENLAND

Bering Strait

SIBERIA

North Atlantic Ocean

EUROPE

ASIA

Swanscombe
Pontnewydd
Pavilard
Boxgrove
St Césaire
Cro Magnon
La Chapelle Aux Saints
Atapuerca
& La Ferrassie Zaffaraya
Gibraltar
Sidi Abderrahman
Salé
Steinheim
Krapina
Grimaldi
Bilzingsleben
Mauer
Dolní Vestonice
Vértesszöllös
Saccopastore
Petralona
Sunghir
Kostenki
Kiik Koba
Dmanisi
Teshik Tash
Shanidar
Amud/Zuttiyeh
Qafzeh
Skhul/Tabun
Kebara
Dar Es Soltan
Ternifine
Jebel Irhoud

Sahara Desert

1.8 million years ago: first hominine migration to Asia

INDIA

Narmad

Bahr El Ghazal

AFRICA

SOUTH AMERICA

South Atlantic Ocean

Hadar
Aramis
ETHIOPIA
Bodo/Gona/ Middle Awash
Omo
West Turkana
Nariokotome
Koobi Fora
Kanapoi
Rift Valley
Ndutu
Olduvai
Laetoli/ Ngaloba

SOUTHERN AFRICA
Kabwe
Kromdraai
Sterkfontein
Taung
Makapansgat
Elandsfontein
Border Cave
Swartkrans
Klasies River Mouth

12

brain size must have been accompanied by a move towards an energy-rich diet including animal proteins. And indeed the earliest-known stone tools, found in Gona, Ethiopia, suggest that 2.5 million years ago meat was a central part of hominines' diet. The sharpened stones were used to cut flesh and pound marrow-rich bones from carcasses either scavenged or hunted and then defended against other carnivores. Burnt bones found in southern Africa indicate that by 1.5 million years ago hominines had learned to cook their food, a development which would have aided digestion by breaking down animal proteins before eating.

This pattern of development was the basis for the colonization by *Homo erectus* of areas outside sub-Saharan Africa around 1.8 million years ago. Then, a million years ago *Homo heidelbergensis* migrated into North Africa and the Near East, reaching northern Europe about 500,000 years ago. Both *erectus* and *heidelbergensis* probably shared a common African ancestor,

A hand-axe from Olduvai Gorge, Tanzania. Handaxes, which are more efficient butchery tools than stone flakes, began to appear around 1.5 million years ago. This probably coincided with an increase in active hunting – as opposed to scavenging – for meat.

Homo ergaster, best known from the Nariokotome skeleton. All three had brains of about 1,000 cubic centimetres and an adaptable stone technology: the weight and careful shaping of the edges of their distinctive handaxes, whether pointed or oval, made them effective butchery tools.

Stone technology in itself did not play a part in the evolutionary pressures that led to larger brains. The importance of *Homo*'s larger brain had less to do with the food quest than with allowing hominines to remember, to manipulate, to support and to organize others in more complex ways. This in turn allowed them to colonize harsher barrier habitats such as the Sahara at the margins of their homelands from where they could spread into more temperate areas beyond.

From about 500,000 years ago, this early burst of colonization came to a halt. There followed a period during which, through many dispersals of populations and much intermingling of genes, regional populations such as the Neanderthals developed, living side by side with other groups. But from 100,000 years ago, a second major dispersal began when anatomically modern people – *Homo sapiens sapiens* – emigrated from sub-Saharan Africa. By 50,000 years ago, Australia had been reached by boat; 33,000 years ago, the western Pacific islands were colonized; 15,000 years ago, the Americas were reached. Major expansion into the Arctic began about 4500 years as the continental ice sheets retreated. Finally, 2000 years ago, humans began to settle the deep Pacific islands from where they reached New Zealand around 1200 years ago, 1000 years before the island's discovery by Captain Cook.

2 Hominine development

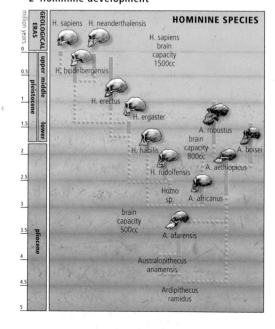

13

The spread of modern humans

DNA studies have revealed that the first anatomically modern humans (*Homo sapiens sapiens*) arose in Africa between 200,000 and 140,000 years ago. The earliest modern-looking human skulls yet found are about 130,000 years old and come from the Omo basin in Ethiopia and Klasies River Mouth in southern Africa. Around 100,000 years ago, these early populations began to migrate northwards out of Africa.

Archaeological and genetic evidence then point to a further rapid expansion of modern human populations and settlements about 50,000 years ago. There is evidence of lighter, multi-component weapons and of textiles and baskets. Camp sites became more orderly and included cold-weather dwellings and underground food stores. Trading networks also expanded dramatically and raw materials, particularly stone, which had previously been traded over distances of less than 50 miles, were now traded over many hundreds of miles.

Human colonisation of the Old World took place against the background of the Ice Ages. There have been eight Ice Ages in the last 800,000 years, alternating with warmer periods of about 10,000 years known as interglacials. During the Ice Ages, ice sheets advanced across the frozen wastes of the northern hemisphere and temperatures fell by up to 15 degrees centigrade. With so much of the earth's water locked into the ice sheets, sea levels fell,

opening up land bridges, but half the area between the tropics became desert as rainfall diminished. Animals withdrew to warmer latitudes during cold phases and humans, too, must have migrated with these changing climates, although they could also adapt to the cold through the mastery of fire, the invention of clothing, and new social and communication skills.

For many thousands of years, *Homo sapiens sapiens* shared the world with *Homo erectus* in East Asia and with Neanderthals in Europe and West Asia, both groups in many ways as sophisticated and successful in their mastery of their environments as *Homo sapiens sapiens*. The similarities between these contemporary hominine species are in most respects more striking than the differences. Nonetheless, the greater social sophistication of *Homo sapiens sapiens* proved decisive in allowing them to colonize a much wider range of habitats than any previous hominine.

By 12,000 years ago, the last Ice Age was drawing to a close. As temperatures rose, vegetation spread and animals re-colonized the cold northern wastes. With them went hunters and gatherers. Meanwhile, in South-West Asia, people had begun to move beyond their existing resources and to investigate new ways of producing food and manipulating plants and animals in the first experiments in farming.

2 The spread of Homo sapiens

maximum extent of ice caps
mammoth steppe
savannah
tropical deserts
tropical forest refuges
forest steppe
grassland scrub
temperate desert
loess
ancient coastline
modern coastline
cave art site
other sites

Arctic Ocean

Kanto Plain
Sokchang-Ni
SIBERIA
Zhoukoudian Upper Cave
Salawusu
Tongliang
Malta
Buret
Shlenka
Shestakovo
Anyi
A S I A
SUNDA
Laharia-Dih
ngia land-bridge

Pacific Ocean
Sokchang-Ni
Kanto Plain
SUNDA
SAHUL
Nawamoyn
Puritjarra
AUSTRALIA
Koonalda
Lake Mungo
Murray
Kutikina

Pushkari
Kostienki
Amvrosievka
Krakow Spadzista
EUROPE
WEST ASIA
INDIA

Grotta dei Fanciulli
Lascaux
Kastritsa
Altamíra
Paglicci
va Morin
Kebara Cave
Wadi Al-Hammeh
Wadi Jilat
Parpalló
Tamar Hat
Haua Fteah
Taforalt
Wadi Kubbaniya
Nile

Indian Ocean

Sahara
AFRICA
Omo
Ishango
Nasera

A bison from the caves at Altamíra, near Santander in northern Spain. This 14,000-year-old masterpiece comes from the painted ceiling of a chamber covered with depictions of animals. The painters used more than one colour and exploited the natural contours of the ceiling to give a number of the creatures three-dimensional form. It remains among the most potent and vivid images created by the artists of the late Ice Age in Europe.

Depression Cave
Sehonghong
Klasies River Mouth
Boomplaas
Nelson Bay Cave

The origins of agriculture

The period 10,000 to 4000 BC witnessed three critical developments: the origins of settled life; the first farming; and the first cities. The origin of agriculture is often termed the 'Neolithic revolution', but archaeology reveals only gradual changes in techniques of food acquisition over thousands of years until present-day climatic conditions began to prevail, around 8000 BC.

Until then, humankind consisted of bands of hunters and gatherers who, although more numerous than ever before, pursued a lifestyle that differed little from that of their predecessors. In China and west Asia, however, new lifestyles began to develop, based on cultivation rather than collecting plant foods. Within the next 2,000 years substantial villages appeared in certain regions; and 5,000 years later there were towns and cities.

This decisive quickening in the pace of human development stemmed largely from the beginning of agriculture: the deliberate alteration of natural systems to promote the abundance of an exploited species or set of species. Many parts of the globe, especially those between latitude 10° South and 50° North, have contributed to the present-day repertory of domesticated plants and animals (map 1). Among the earliest and most important centres of cereal cultivation were South-West Asia, where the wild ancestors of wheat and barley grew; China and South-East Asia, where millet and rice thrived; and Mesoamerica, which developed maize as a staple crop. In Africa, people in the lands south of the Sahara and in the high grasslands of North-East Africa domesticated a wide variety of native plant species. Generally, cereal cultivation characterized temperate regions while root or tree crop cultivation – potatoes, yams, bananas – predominated in tropical zones.

At the same time, useful local animal species were domesticated to provide meat, milk, hides or wool, and (except in the Americas, which lacked suitable animals) an important source of power for ploughing and other agricultural tasks. On the steppe-lands of central Eurasia, animal-keeping prevailed over plant cultivation, and the domestication of the horse facilitated a specialized life-style based on nomadic herding.

The exact origins of agriculture remain unknown, but once chosen, farming developed a momentum of its own: there was no easy turning back, and the very success of the new lifestyle induced other fundamental changes. The ensuing increase in food resources made possible a spectacular growth of human population between 8000 and 4000 BC. It also required cooperative effort, particularly after the introduction of

MESOAMERICA

Cereals	Pulses
Maize	Common bean
Teosinte	Runner bean
	Tepary bean

Fruits	Other Crops
Avocado	Chilli pepper
Tomato	Squashes

NORTHERN SOUTH AMERICA

Pulses	Root Crops
Common bean	Manioc
	Potato
Lima bean	Sweet Potato
	Yam

Fruits	Other Crops
Guava	Cashew
Pineapple	Chili pepper
Soursop	Cocoa
Sweetsop	Peanut
	Quinoa
	Squashes

Turk

MESOAMERI

ANDES

LOWLAN

Guinea pig

Llama

Alpaca

African rock art painting
From around 9000 BC to 3000 BC the climate in the Sahara was much more favourable than today. Rock art paintings depict a great variety of plants and animals such as elephant, lion and buffalo as well as, from about 6000 BC, domesticated cattle.

irrigation led to the establishment of settled organized societies, at first in villages and later in towns and cities, and the development of new technologies, social systems and ideologies.

The transformation from hunting and gathering to agriculture, from a migratory to a sedentary life, was a decisive event in world history. Hunters and gatherers survived but, as farming spread, they retreated to the marginal world environments where agriculture could not secure a foothold (map 2). Both absolutely and relatively, their numbers declined until today their representatives survive only in hot deserts (the Kalahari and central Australia), in the dense rain forests of the Amazon basin, central Africa and South-East Asia, and in the frozen Arctic. Even there, traditional lifestyles – followed by mankind for millennia – now face the threat of extinction.

2 The decline of hunting and gathering

world distribution of hunter-gathering peoples

15,000 BC
world population: 10 million
% hunters: 100

world population: 350 million
% hunters: 1.0

AD 1500

1960
world population: 3 billion
% hunters: 0.001

1 The origins of domestic plants and animals to 4000 BC

the origins of domestic plants and animals to 4000 BC

NORTH AMERICA

Pacific Ocean

Atlantic Ocean

SOUTH WESTERN STEPPES

Reindeer

Pig

Horse

Cattle

Bactrian Camel

CENTRAL ASIA

Yak

CHINA

Chicken

Pig

Cattle

Goat

Sheep

Yak

INDUS

Water Buffalo

SOUTHEAST ASIA

Ass

SOUTHWEST ASIA

Zebu

Pig

SAHARA

Dromedary

NORTHERN TROPICAL AFRICA

CHINA AND SOUTHEAST ASIA

Cereals	Pulses	Root Crops
Asian rice	Mung bean	Taro
Common millet	Soybean	Yams
Foxtail millet		

Fruits	Other Crops
Apricot	Aubergine
Banana	Coconut
Citrus fruits	Sago palm
Mango	Tea
Peach	

SOUTHWEST AND CENTRAL ASIA

Cereals	Pulses	Root Crops
Barley	Broad bean	Carrot
Oats	Chickpea	Parsnip
Rye	Grasspea	Radish
Wheats	Lentil	
	Pea	

Fruits	Other Crops
Apple	Garlic
Date	Onion
Fig	Safflower
Grape	
Olive	
Pear	

NORTHERN TROPICAL AFRICA

Cereals	Pulses	Root Crops
African rice	Cowpea	Yams
Finger millet	Pigeon pea	
Pearl millet		
Sorghum		

Fruits	Other Crops
Tamarind	Coffee
Watermelon	Oil palm
	Sesame

The first farmers of Asia

The first economies to be based on the husbandry of animal and plant staples came into being in South-West Asia. In the upland areas around the Zagros and Taurus mountains, and in Palestine, moister conditions led to the spread of large-seeded grasses – the ancestors of modern wheat and barley – which early hunters quickly appreciated for their nutrition and ease of storage. By 10,000 BC small villages of circular stone-walled huts developed, whose inhabitants lived from both the hunting and herding of gazelle and the harvesting of wild wheat. About 9000 BC, in northern Syria, some communities began to cultivate cereals outside their natural habitat while sheep were domesticated in Mesopotamia. By 7000 BC wheat and barley cultivation was established, as was the herding of goats, from Anatolia to the Zagros mountains, and this agricultural revolution spread shortly afterwards to Greece.

In the 7th and 6th millennia BC, developed Neolithic villages appeared over much of the landscape. Their economies depended on domesticated plants and animals, and on technological developments. Excavations at Çatal Hüyük, 32 acres in area, revealed extensive evidence of wealth (obsidian and semi-processed stones) and house fittings bore elaborate ornaments (including wall paintings and the plastered skulls of wild cattle). Much of the lowland area, however, remained too dry for cultivation. Only the development of irrigation – by spreading water from the rivers that drained from the mountains – allowed settlements to extend to the Mesopotamian plain in the 6th and 5th millennia. Sedentary farming began in South Asia on the Kachi Plain of Pakistan around 7000 BC. The early settlers cultivated barley and wheat, domesticated sheep, cattle and goats, and buried their dead with elaborate grave goods. From 6000 BC onwards, mud-brick storehouses divided into small compartments served as the focal point for food, tools and trade goods.

Plants and animals were independently domesticated in many other parts of the world. In northern China the cultivation of millet, another cereal, began on the great loess plain around the Yellow River and its tributaries around 7000 BC. It remained the staple crop of the region for many centuries. Further south the principal cereal was rice, first cultivated in the Yangtze valley before 6000 BC (map 2). Villages acquired defensive walls, from 8000 BC in the Near East (the first fortified community being Jericho) and from around 3500 BC in China.

Terracotta figurine
Characteristic products of the earliest farming villages are small terracotta figurines of women, with emphasis on their sexual characteristics. This small cult statuette, only 6.5 inches high, came from Çatal Hüyük in south-central Turkey.

In addition, the ox-drawn plough began to be adapted throughout much of Eurasia, enlisting animal traction to increase the efficiency of farming.

The greater size and permanence of farming settlements stemmed from three major factors: firstly, the exceptional productivity of the principal cultivated species could feed large concentrations of people all year round – something hunting and gathering can never do; secondly, plant foods could survive storage over many months, allowing the community to stay in one place and live off the previous harvest while a new crop grows and ripens. Finally, farmers need to live near their fields, both to protect them against human and animal predators and to minimize the travel and transport involved in preparing the ground, in weeding, and in harvesting.

Hunters and gatherers keep their possessions to a minimum, since they must carry everything around; but sedentary communities can produce and accumulate a wide range of items, both utilitarian and for ritual and pleasure – pottery and tools, ornaments and display items. Village farming communities became larger and more differentiated, with specialist craftspeople producing fine ceramics and metalwork. As complexity increased, new forms of social organisation developed, leading around 3000 BC to the first cities.

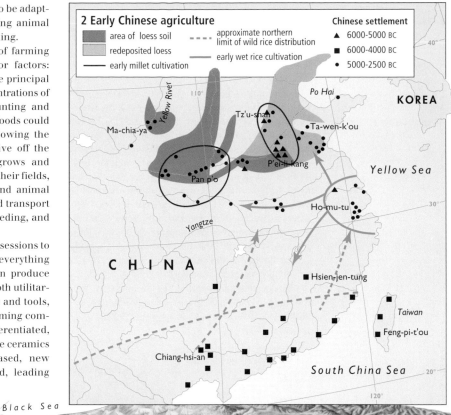

2 Early Chinese agriculture

- area of loess soil
- redeposited loess
- early millet cultivation
- approximate northern limit of wild rice distribution
- early wet rice cultivation

Chinese settlement
- ▲ 6000–5000 BC
- ■ 6000–4000 BC
- • 5000–2500 BC

1 The ancient Near East, 12,000–3100 BC

- natural habitat of wild emmer
- natural habitat of wild einkorn and emmer
- southern limit of rain-fed agriculture (300mm average annual rainfall)

ancient sites:
- epipalaeolithic, 12,000–9000 BC
- ▲ pre-pottery Neolithic, 9000–6500 BC
- • pottery Neolithic, 6500–5500 BC
- Chalcolithic
  'Ubaid period, 5500–4200 BC
  Uruk period, 4200–3100 BC
- □ multi-period Neolithic-Chalcolithic sites

The rise of civilization

The first civilizations arose in the alluvial basins of four major rivers which drain from the mountain fringes where agriculture began: the Tigris and Euphrates in Mesopotamia, the Nile in Egypt, the Indus in India, and the Yellow River in China. Each proved capable of supplying the high, regular yields needed to support large urban populations. Cities of thousands, and then tens of thousands, evolved. In Mesopotamia, cities already existed by 3500 BC. Egypt adopted urban civilization in about 3200 BC and the Harappan civilization arose in the Indus plain from about 2500 BC. Civilization in north China appears to have developed, again wholly or largely independently, around 1800 BC.

These societies shared many common features: the development of cities; writing; large public buildings; and the political apparatus of a state. The large agricultural surpluses produced by irrigation – some Mesopotamian communities harvested 60, 70 or even 80 grains for each grain sown – made it possible to employ a significant segment of society in activities other than farming, such as manufacture and trade. This in turn led to the emergence of a ruling class which accumulated wealth through the exploitation of labour and the imposition of taxes. In Mesopotamia the ruler was also the chief priest and the temple centre provided a vital element of the political system, its monumental structure

1 The rise of civilization
- fertile land
- centres of urban civilization
- areas of pastoral nomadism

forming a visual reminder to all citizens of the power that governed their daily life. The centralized control found in these societies fostered a special legal system, a standing army, a permanent bureaucracy, and the division of society into distinct classes. The state also supported scribes, who were usually trained and employed within the temples and palaces. The earliest writing was used as a means of keeping track of commodities, wages and taxes; but it soon served other purposes: to preserve religious traditions, which thereby became sacred books; to register social customs, which thereby became codes of law; and to record myths, which thereby developed into history and literature.

Since, apart from agricultural produce, the alluvial plains lacked most other natural resources, an extensive trading activity exchanged luxury goods and raw materials from other areas with the textiles and other manufactured goods of the cities and thus helped to develop other trading centres in a great arc from the eastern Mediterranean to the Indus valley and in China. The cities therefore exercised an influence out of all proportion to their comparatively small geographical extent. True, not all areas were affected: Australia, Africa, Europe and large parts of Asia had no cities; the first civilizations of the Americas did not emerge until about 1500 BC (and, when they did, owed nothing to ideas introduced from outside). Nevertheless the growth of the first urban centres, with their technology, literacy, and class divisions began a new phase in the development of human society.

The Royal standard of Ur from the largest of the royal tombs at Ur. It has panels on each side depicting the activities of the king in peace and war. The war side shows helmeted infantry, four-wheeled battle wagons pulled by asses or onagers, and prisoners being presented to the king.

Ocean

Ob

Yenisey

L.Baikal

NOMADS

L.Balkhash

Atlai Mts

MONGOLIA
hunting fishing and gathering replaced by mounted nomadic pastoralism from the west

Amur

AMUR VALLEY
sedentary village communities supported by salmon fishing and millet farming

Takla Maka

Gobi Desert

Kaocheng

Singtai

Lo-yang

Anyang

Erh-li-t'ou

Chengchow

T I B E T

Yellow Sea

Rupar

Alamgirpur

C H I N A

Panlungchen

ibangan

Brahmaputra

Ganges

GANGETIC PLAIN
colonization of flood plain by rice-farming villages

Wucheng

I N D I A

90°

DECCAN
temporary hunting camps and cattle-herding pens replaced by farming villages

Bay of Bengal

INDO CHINA
rice farming villages with domestic animals and bronze tool technology

South China Sea

West Asia and Egypt

The earliest of all known civilizations, Sumer, rested upon some 12 city-states in southern Mesopotamia, the largest of them covering about 100 hectares, defended by a wall, and housing perhaps 30,000 people. At first, pre-eminence passed from one city to another, but towards the end of the 3rd millennium powerful leaders established hegemony over ever-wider areas. The first was Sargon (c. 2296-2240 BC), who created a new political centre at Agade (also known as Akkad) before conquering the cities of southern Mesopotamia and claiming authority as far west as Byblos. Sargon's grandson Naram-Sin (2213-2176 BC) enlarged the empire further, but within a generation it disappeared as subject cities asserted their independence. The rise of Agade had long-lasting effects on the region, with Akkadian (whose variants included Babylonian and Assyrian) replacing Sumerian as the main language of Mesopotamia.

Around 2000 BC, a new empire arose around Ur, its hegemony stretching from the Persian Gulf to Nineveh, but Ur also fell after about a century, and a kaleidoscope of shifting alliances brought new cities to prominence, most notably Mari and Babylon on the Euphrates. Under its powerful king Hammurabi (1728-1686 BC), Babylon created another empire that covered the whole of southern Mesopotamia; but, once more, it did not long survive the death of its founder (map 1).

Even before Sargon unified Mesopotamia, Egypt

came under the sway of a single ruler. The harnessing of the Nile's annual floods to irrigate the fields on its banks made possible a civilization that lasted for over 25 centuries. Around 3000 BC an Upper Egyptian ruler conquered the Nile delta and established a new capital at Memphis, which for almost 2000 years served as the administrative centre for a densely

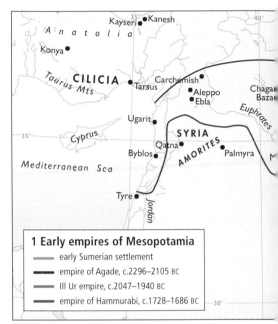

1 Early empires of Mesopotamia
- early Sumerian settlement
- empire of Agade, c.2296–2105 BC
- III Ur empire, c.2047–1940 BC
- empire of Hammurabi, c.1728–1686 BC

3 Kingdoms and empires, c. 1500–1100 BC
- Hittite empire established by Suppiluliuma I, 1344–1322 BC
- Mitanni territory at its greatest extent, c. 1480–1340 BC
- Mitanni after c. 1340 BC (under Hittite and Assyrian control)
- Assyrian territory gained by Ashur-uballit I, 1353–1318 BC
- Babylonia under Burnaburiash II, 1347–1321 BC
- Elam under Tepti-ahar, c. 1353–1318 BC
- Egypt under Amenophis IV and Tutankhamun, 1352–1335 BC

populated region of some 15,000 square miles running from the first cataract at Aswan to the Mediterranean coast (map 2). At about the same time, writing in hieroglyphic script commenced. During the 'Old Kingdom' period (2685-2180 BC) the rulers of Egypt built a series of massive pyramid-tombs along the desert edge opposite Memphis which emphasised their power and prestige. Then, after a century of invasion and anarchy, the Egyptian state entered a second period of cultural achievement under the able rulers of the Middle Kingdom (2040-1783 BC); and another era of expansion under the XVIIIth and XIXth dynasties (1570-1200 BC). At home they undertook vast building projects, like the rock-cut temple at Abu Simbel created by Ramesses II (1290-1224 BC); abroad they advanced through Palestine into Syria and created an empire that extended almost to the Euphrates.

The continuity of Ancient Egyptian language, religion and culture stood in marked contrast to developments in Mesopotamia. The two civilizations also differed in other respects. First, because of the annual Nile flood, Egypt did not depend to the same extent on irrigation canals and dams; second, although it possessed some cities, they lacked the geographical concentration found in southern Mesopotamia, so that Egypt was more a territorial unit than an agglomeration of city-states. Third, and most important, Egypt rarely suffered foreign invasion. Admittedly the Hyksos, an Asiatic people, overran most of the country in the 18th century BC, but a new native dynasty expelled them c.1570 BC and then pursued the invaders northwards to the upper Euphrates. Egypt's Asiatic empire lasted until about 1200 BC when the 'Sea Peoples', marauders from the Aegean and Asia Minor, attacked all the major powers of the East Mediterranean and initiated a 'Dark Age', concerning which very few historical sources survive, until about 900 BC and the emergence of Assyria.

Babylon and Assyria weathered the storm of the 12th and 11th centuries with greatly reduced territory, and the 10th century saw the beginnings of an Assyrian recovery. In the following century Ashurnasirpal II (883-859 BC) sent his armies north and west and used the wealth they gained to build a spectacular new palace at Nimrud. Even greater gains were made by Tiglath-pileser III (744-727 BC) and Sargon II (721-705 BC) who annexed Babylonia and conquered the Phoenician cities on the Mediterranean coast. Egyptian weakness allowed Esarhaddon (680-669 BC) and Ashurbanipal (668-627 BC) to capture Memphis and Thebes, although the Assyrians did not attempt to formalize their control over Egypt.

To the Old Testament prophets, the Assyrians appeared invincible; yet their control over Babylonia was never secure: the Babylonian king Nabopolassar (626-605 BC) rebelled and, aided by the Medes, sacked the major Assyrian cities including Ashur and Nineveh. The Babylonians then inherited the Assyrian empire, but they too had to fight to keep it. In 605 BC the Egyptians attempted to annex Syria, but were defeated at Carchemish and Hamath. Nebuchadnezzar (604-562 BC) consolidated Babylonian rule, but his successors were unable to maintain their gains and Babylon fell to the Persians in 539 BC.

2 Old Kingdom Egypt, c.2685–2180 BC

- town or city, c.3250–2000 BC
- royal tomb, c.3250–2650 BC
- pyramid, c.2650–2000 BC
- fertile land

A Limestone stela, now in the Louvre, of Naram-Sin of Agade (2213-2176 BC) depicting his victory over the Lullubu of the Zagros mountains. Naram-Sin led many successful campaigns in his reign, leaving rock-reliefs commemorating his achievements near Diyarbakir in Turkey and in the Zagros.

The Americas

The Americas were colonized from Asia late in the last Ice Age, when lowered sea levels turned the Bering Strait into dry land. The subsequent melting of the ice cut off the continent from Eurasia (page 14). It is one of the remarkable facts of human history that despite their geographical separation, development in Old and New Worlds followed much the same path: the adoption of agriculture; the creation of cities and empires; the invention of writing. These two geographical zones continued on parallel paths until the New World was invaded by Europeans after 1492 (page 86). The New World civilizations were highly inventive in their own right, and in some ways in advance of their western counterparts. They produced – quite independent of the Old World – magnificent art, remarkable mathematical and astronomical skills, and monumental architecture.

The inhabitants of Mesoamerica and the central Andes began to experiment with plant cultivation around 7000 BC and farming soon allowed a rapid increase in population. By 800 BC the Olmec on the Gulf of Mexico, the Zapotec at Monte Albán, and the people of Chavín in Peru had developed complex societies with populations that numbered tens of thousands, boasting a hierarchy of social classes, an efficient civil service, a professional priesthood, and specialists in all kinds of tasks, from manufacturing to commerce and government.

Around and between these civilizations, other communities remained at the chiefdom level. Maize, beans and squash cultivation spread from Mexico to north America, and their arrival initiated a period of rapid development. In Ohio and Illinois, between 300 BC and AD 550, Hopewell chiefs built elaborate burial mounds and maintained trade contacts from Florida to the Rockies. Most American chiefdoms were agricultural, based on plant cultivation, but along the north-west coast rich fishing grounds and an abundance of whales and seals supported large villages and a complex ceremonial life by hunting, fishing and gathering alone. Towards the extremities of the continent, however, harsh conditions precluded farming, settlement remained sparse, and nomadic lifestyles persisted (map 1).

The sudden rise of Teotihuacán about AD 100 eclipsed earlier developments in Mesoamerica. Laid out in a precise grid plan and covering 8 square miles (20 km^2), its population grew eventually to some 200,000. The nature of the city's economy remains uncertain but the centre, with two mighty pyramids, was planned for rites that included human sacrifice. Whether or not in association with trade, the Teotihuacanos' influence spread widely. They colonized some neighbouring districts and possibly sponsored new towns further afield.

At the same time, the powerful lowland kingdoms of the Maya flourished. Their capitals were

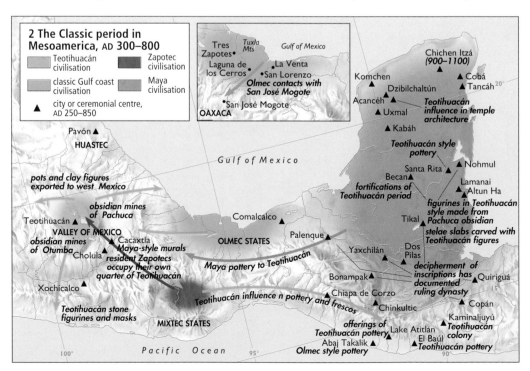

2 The Classic period in Mesoamerica, AD 300–800

- Teotihuacán civilisation
- classic Gulf coast civilisation
- Zapotec civilisation
- Maya civilisation
- ▲ city or ceremonial centre, AD 250–850

pyramid-studded ceremonial centres with extensive suburbs. Voluminous inscriptions in a distinctive hieroglyphic script reveal a sophisticated concern with astronomy and astrology: their experts calculated the exact length of the solar year and the lunar month, and predicted eclipses. However, whether on account of the chronic wars that their carved stones also recorded, or of popular discontent, or of environmental degradation by excessive population – or of all three factors – most of the towns were abandoned between 790 and about 860. Many districts revived in what is known as the 'Post-Classic' period, but the Maya never regained their grandeur (map 2).

A separate group of interrelated civilizations grew up in the central Andes, supported by spectacular irrigation systems in the lowlands and by ingenious terraced fields in the highlands. The Andean peoples developed sophisticated skills in working gold, silver and copper, and used these metals for tools as well as for jewellery. The coast of the central Andes is best known for the graphic pottery of the Moche, dating from AD 100 to 600, which reveals much about the daily life and religion of his makers.

Although its vast distances and harsh topography made this region difficult to unify, the centuries between AD 600 and 1000 saw the rise of a truly imperial power based on Huari in the Peruvian Andes. Many elements of Huari religion and art originated at Tiahuanaco, further south, but were quickly adopted by Huari and then spread by force to many parts of the coast and highlands. For a short time Huari was the capital of a state embracing most of Peru, but around AD 800 the city was sacked and abandoned for ever. The fragile unity soon collapsed and not until the Inca conquests of the 15th and 16th centuries would the central Andes be reunified under a single government (page 72).

The king of Yaxchilán (on the left above) prepares for battle against another Maya kingdom in AD 724. The hieroglyphs above the figures record that one of his wives (on the right above) helped him prepare.

1 Peoples of the Americas, 300 BC to AD 1300

- farming peoples
- chiefdoms
- civilized states
- hunters and gatherers
- ■ site first occupied before AD 600
- ■ site mainly occupied after AD 600

25

Prehistoric Africa and Australasia

TIMELINE

c.50,000 BC
Settlement of Australia from southeast Asia

c. 6000 BC
Earliest cereal cultivation in Africa

c. 4000 – 3000 BC
Desiccation of Sahara begins; population moves south and east

c. 2000 BC
Settlement of Melanesia begins

c.1300 BC
Settlement of Fiji

c.900 BC
Kingdom of Meroe established

c.550 BC
Iron use begins in sub-Saharan Africa; southwards expansion of Bantu speakers

c.AD 750
Settlers reach New Zealand

Both Australia and Sub-Saharan Africa have been largely isolated from the rest of the Old World for the last 10,000 years, the former by sea, the latter by desert. Although the inhabitants of North Africa began the transition from hunting and gathering to farming around 8000 BC, the desiccation of the Sahara after about 4000 BC cut off Africa south of the Equator for centuries.

In Australia, the aborigines mostly remained hunters and gatherers adapted to living in a large range of environments from tropical forest to harsh desert. They enjoyed a rich symbolic life, as evidenced by the marking of their sacred places with rock art from at least 25,000 years ago. The colonization of the Melanesian islands occurred considerably later, when settlers from New Guinea, associated with the distinctive Lapita pottery, reached Fiji around 1300 BC and then made their way into Polynesia via Tonga and Samoa, reaching the Marquesas islands in about 150 BC (map 1). From there they spread north to Hawaii (c. AD 400)

and south-west via the Cook islands to New Zealand between AD 750 and 1300. When the Europeans arrived in the 18th century, at least 750,000 aborigines inhabited Australia and up to 150,000 Maoris lived in New Zealand

The geographical isolation of southern Africa was never complete. In the east settlers spread down the Rift Valley from Ethiopia during the first millennium BC, while trans-Saharan trade increased in importance after the introduction of the camel from Asia, around 100 BC. Iron came into use in parts of sub-Saharan Africa after 750 BC. Aided by the new technology, Bantu-speaking farmers and cattle-herders began to colonize southern Africa in the early centuries AD. By the 13th century powerful Bantu chiefdoms had emerged, such as that centred on Great Zimbabwe, and on cattle-raising communities. These engaged in long-distance trade, long before the Portuguese arrived off both the south-east and south-west coasts of the continent at the close of the 15th century

Rock art became common in Australia 25,000 years ago. This more recent painting shows the two 'Lightning Brothers', ancestral spirits of the Wardaman Aboriginal people from northwestern Australia.

M e d i t e r r a n e a n   S e a

PHOENICIA

ARABIA

Atlantic Ocean

Utica
Carthage
Capeletti
Mogador
Leptis (Homs)
Cyrene
Greek colonies from 700 BC
Naucratis
Sais
Memphis
Merimde 4200 BC
Fayum 4300 BC
EGYPT
Thebes
Zemmour
S
Meniet
Adrar Tiouiyne
Immidir
Adrar Bous
Arlit
Hoggar Massif
Tassili Massif
Tibesti Massif
Uan Muhaggiag
6000–5000 BC
a
h
a
r
a
Nile
Iron
NUBIA
Napata
Nuri
KUSH
Meroe 500 BC
Adulis
Aksum
KINGDOM OF AKSUM
AD 100–1000
Tichitt
Iron
2000 BC
3000 BC
Air
Karkarchinkat
Gao
Jenne-jeno
proto-urban settlement by 1st century AD
Adrar
KINGDOM OF GHANA
1st millennium AD
S
a
h
e
l
Jebel Uweinat
Ennedi
KINGDOM OF MEROE
900 BC–AD 400
Kadero
Shaheinab 3200 BC
Jebel Moya
Ethiopian Highlands
Red Sea
Ntereso 1400 BC
Kintampo
1500 BC
Taruga
Ife
Nok
Atwetwebooso
Igbo Ukwu shrines AD 800–900
Niger
Daima
Iron-working widespread north of equatorial forest by c. 500 BC
Sudanic Belt
Gulf of Guinea
500 BC
iron and cattle
Batalimo
possible spread of cultivation to lower Congo 1st millennium BC
Congo forests penetrated by pottery-using peoples late in 1st millennium BC
Funa River 270 BC
Congo
iron and cattle
Namib Desert
Lake Victoria
Katuruka 5th century BC
Urewe
Elmenteita
Narosura
Crescent Is.
Sandawe
Kwale
Ileret
east African 'pastoral neolithic' sites
Manda & Shanga
ports involved in overseas trade by AD 800
Rift Valley
Lake Tanganyika
Sanga
late 1st millennium AD cemetery
Kalambo
Kamnama
Lake Nyasa
Nkope
Kilwa
Lubusi
Salumano
Zambezi
Kapwirimbwe
Kalundu
iron and cattle
iron and cattle
AD 200
Ziwa
Gokomere
Great Zimbabwe
Mabveni
Malapati
AD 800
Madagascar
Austronesian settlement
Snake Rock Falls Rock
Mirabib
Kalahari Desert
Broederstroom
Lydenburg
Phalaborwa
Silver Leaves
AD 1100
Equus
Witkrans
Limerock
Dikbosch
Blackburn
Doornfontein
Blinkklipkop
domestic sheep herded by 1st century BC
Tortoise Cave
Steenberg
Hawston
Eland's Bay
Diepkloof
Kasteelberg
Die Kelders
Byneskranskop
Nelson Bay

1 Initial settlement of Polynesia and island Micronesia

rock art styles:
- paranamittee engravings
- complex figurative
- simple figurative

the Lapita potters:
- Lapita pottery area
- sites with Lapita pottery
- other contemporary Melanesian pottery traditions
- settlement of Eastern Polynesia, 150 BC–AD 1000

Hawaiian Islands
c. AD 400
Fanning Island
Line Islands
Marquesas Islands
c. 150 BC
Tahiti
to Easter I. c. AD 400
Cook Islands
to Pitcairn I. c. AD 1000
Tuvalu (ce Islands)
Tokelau Islands
Samoa
P O L Y N E S I A
Fiji
Tonga
Kermadec Is.
c. AD 950
c. AD 750
North Island
NEW ZEALAND
uth Island

South Pacific Ocean

2 Africa: the Stone Age to the Iron Age

- ▲ fishing harpoon site
- area of Saharan rock painting, c. 6000–1000 BC
- areas of rock painting in southern and eastern Africa
- – – – approximate extent of cattle herders, 6000–500 BC
- ● site of cattle domestication
- ▲ early agricultural site
- ▼ sites of southern African Stone Age herders
- – – – approximate extent of iron-using farmers, AD 200–1100
- ● important metal workers' sites
- → possible arrival of iron technology
- ○ Greek colonies
- ● Phoenician or Punic colonies

South and South East Asia

The first great Indian civilization emerged in the Indus valley in the 3rd millennium with complex urban societies at Harappa and Mohenjo-Daro, which developed a pictographic writing system (as yet not definitively deciphered) and traded as far afield as Mesopotamia (map 1). Around 1500 BC, for reasons that remain obscure, the major Indus valley cities suddenly collapsed

When the picture becomes clear once again the population of northern India had been transformed, with a Hindu religion, a Sanskrit literature, a caste system and (by about 800 BC) iron working, which enabled the spread of farming communities eastward into the rich plain of the Ganges. By 600 BC at least 16 political units had grown up along the Ganges, the subcontinent's new centre of gravity. By 400 BC war had reduced the states to four, and no doubt the resulting social tensions helped to spread new ethical and religious systems, for in the 6th century Gautama (Buddha), founder of Asia's most pervasive religion, was born in one of these states (see

page 34), while in another Mahavira formulated the teaching of Jainism.

A further turning point came in 320 BC when Chandragupta Maurya seized the state of Magadha on the lower Ganges, and occupied large parts of central India, and in 305 BC annexed the province of Trans-Indus from the successors of Alexander the Great (see page 32). Chandragupta's grandson Ashoka (273-232 BC) expanded this Mauryan empire southwards, bringing the greater part of the sub-continent under his rule and inscribing edicts on pillars and rock-faces all over India as a permanent reminder of his power (map 2). Ashoka's death introduced a troubled period, punctuated by invasions of both Greeks and nomads who founded states in the north-west, such as the Kushan empire, where Hellenistic and Indian influences mingled. Further south, the Satavahanas of the Deccan ruled a state that straddled the peninsula by AD 150. Then, in the 4th century, the Gupta dynasty, created an empire which by AD 400 extended from the Indus to the bay

1 The Indus civilizations of Harappa and Mohenjo-Daro, c. 2500–1750 BC

○ pre-Harappan settlements

● principal sites of Harappan civilization

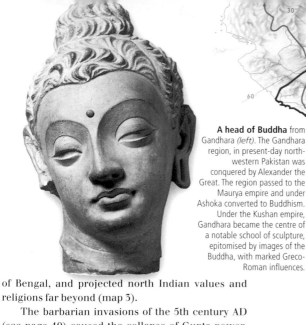

A head of Buddha from Gandhara *(left)*. The Gandhara region, in present-day north-western Pakistan was conquered by Alexander the Great. The region passed to the Maurya empire and under Ashoka converted to Buddhism. Under the Kushan empire, Gandhara became the centre of a notable school of sculpture, epitomised by images of the Buddha, with marked Greco-Roman influences.

of Bengal, and projected north Indian values and religions far beyond (map 3).

The barbarian invasions of the 5th century AD (see page 40) caused the collapse of Gupta power, but it was precisely during this period that Hindu and Buddhist influences began to spread to South-East Asia. The cultivation of rice in this area, beginning as early as 3000 BC, allowed the development of prosperous farming villages. Bronze came into use after about 1000 BC, reflected in distinctive bronze Dong Son drums, and iron followed after about 500 BC (map 4). By AD 300 trading links with India had burgeoned, and Buddhist images appeared by AD 500, notably in Burma, Cambodia, and Java. By AD 700 the construction of Hindu temples in the same three areas had begun.

2 The formation of the Mauryan empire

→ Alexander the Great's eastern campaign, c. 329–325 BC

— Mauryan empire under Chandragupta, c. 297 BC

— Mauryan empire under Ashoka, c. 260 BC

■ ancestral home of the Mauryas

● site of Ashokan inscriptions

● site of Mauryan-age Buddhist stupa

ANGA regions   *CODAS* dynasties
(place names in brackets are Prakrit forms)

3 The Gupta-Vakataka imperial formation, AD 300–550

▓ Gupta core area   ▓ Vakataka core area

— maximum extent of Gupta empire   — limit of areas at some time under Vakataka rule

4 Prehistoric sites in Southeast Asia

● Neolithic/Bronze Age settlements

● Dong Son drums

● Early Iron Age and urn burial sites

Early Europe

Farming spread from West Asia to Europe about 6500 BC, beginning with the Balkans. Agriculture in these regions involved wheat and barley, sheep and goats, just as in western Asia; but as farming spread beyond into more temperate zones, major adjustments became necessary. New, more robust types of cereal developed, and cattle and pigs became the dominant livestock. By about 5500 BC agricultural communities had developed along the Danube valley, and their descendants spread northwest from there until they reached the Paris basin around 4750 BC. After a brief pause, the final phase saw the spread of farming to the northern fringes of Europe, including Scandinavia and the British Isles, where existing hunter-gatherer communities adopted it by about 4000 BC (map 1).

There has been much debate about whether the spread of agriculture was due to the expansion of colonizing populations from the southeast or to the adoption of the new way of life by existing foragers. Current evidence from archaeology and the analysis of the DNA of modern populations suggests that there was a colonizing element, probably associated with the expansion through the Balkans and the loess lands of central Europe, but that in most of Europe the dominant process was the adoption of agriculture and its material attributes by existing populations, perhaps in part because of the prestige of the new way of life.

Meanwhile, beginning in the Balkans, copper-working spread after c. 4500 BC and by 2500 BC it had become common to alloy the copper with tin to produce bronze. The need for these two raw materials stimulated the development of extensive trade networks, which also conveyed other materials, such as amber from the Baltic. Amber is found as far afield as Mycenae in southern Greece, where graves filled with sumptuous funerary offerings of gold and jewellery appeared from 1600 BC.

Mycenae was not the earliest European state: that honour belongs to the island of Crete where from about 2000 BC 'Minoan' culture, based on palaces decorated with colourful frescoes and equipped with sanitary and drainage systems, developed. Bureaucracy and trade flourished, and a script known as Linear A developed around 1600 BC. Two centuries later, however, the Mycenaeans (named after the fortress of Mycenae in the eastern Peloponnese) took control of Crete and became the principal military and economic power in the

Aegean (see map 2). They adapted the Minoan culture, including its script which they modified (to a form known as Linear B, an early version of Greek) and used to administer their own lands. Mycenaean Greece was divided among a number of independent leaders, each of whom ruled a small kingdom, in much the same way as Greece in the Classical period was divided into city-states (see page 32). The legend of the Trojan War, recorded centuries later in Homer's *Iliad*, is thought to recall a Mycenaean campaign of c. 1250 BC against the city of Troy, strategically situated at the entrance to the Dardanelles, and controlling access to the trade of the Black Sea. But this success, if indeed it occurred, must have been the final fling of the Mycenean warlords because by 1200 BC their palaces lay in ruins, overthrown perhaps by rebellion or by outside attack, and a 'Dark Age' which left very few records ensued all over Greece for the next four centuries.

Snake handler from Knossos
This faience statuette, dating from c.1700 BC, possibly represents a household goddess. Little is known about Minoan divinities, but most appear to be female.

1 The spread of agricultural settlement

⇨ main routes of agrarian expansion

dates of agricultural settlement
(based on tree-ring corrected radiocarbon dating)

	by 7000 BC
	7000–6000 BC
	6000–5000 BC
	5000–3000 BC
	3000–2000 BC

bowl cultures early farming groups

● Hembury site of excavated farming village

SPAIN modern state names

2 Trade and exchange in the Bronze Age Aegean

products of the Aegean and Cyclades:
- ▼ spondylus shells (Aegean)
- ⌐ obsidian (Melos)
- ⬟ emery (Naxos)
- ▣ silver (Cyclades)
- ⚔ swords and daggers

products of Crete:
- ⬈ timber
- ● woven wool textiles
- ⚒ daggers (before 1600 BC)
- ⬇ stone lamps and vases
- ⬆ fine pottery (before 1500 BC)
- ▼ metal vases (before 1500 BC)

products of the Greek mainland:
- ⬆ fine pottery (after 1600 BC)
- ▼ metal vases (after 1600 BC)

- ▨ Mycenaean world (1300 BC)
- —— trade routes
- ⟶ imports to the Aegean

amber from the Baltic

TRANSYLVANIA

gold

Po

Sava

Balkans

Adriatic Sea

Corsica

ITALY

Sardinia

copper ingots

tin from the West

Sicily

Peloponnese

Pylos

Malta

Melos

Mediterranean Sea

Euboea

Chios

Troy

Thebes

Mycenae

Naxos

Aegean Sea

Miletus

Cyclades

Thera

Rhodes

Knossos

Crete

HITTITES

Anatolia

Hattushash (Bogazköy)

seal stones

CILICIA

Tarsus

Alalakh (Atchana)

copper

Cyprus

Ugarit (Ras Shamra)

cylinder seals

Byblos

Sidon

Tyre

Jerusalem

ostrich eggs
amethyst
ivory, gold, scarab seals
stone and faience
vases and ornaments

EGYPT

tin

lapis lazuli from Afghanistan

glass beads

ivory

cylinder seals

Tigris

Euphrates

ARABIA

Ballynagilly

IRELAND

cultures

BRITAIN

North Sea

Scandinavia

hunters

Hembury

Windmill Hill

Exloo

Köln-Lindenthal

bowl

North European Plain

funnel

Zwenkau

rim

Elbe

pottery

Oder

cultures

Baltic Sea

Atlantic Ocean

Brittany

Loire

FRANCE

Cuiry-lès-Chaudardes

Danubian linear incised

Bylany

St Michel-du-Touch

Pyrenees

A l p s

Schussenried

Rhine

pottery

HUNGARY

Carpathian Mountains

Samborzec

ware

cultures

Arène-Candide

Apennine Mountains

Molino Casarotto

Ripabianca

Dinaric Alps

Hódmezővásárhely

Balkan painted

Vistula

Corsica

Sardinia

Coppa Nevigata

Balkans

Starčevo

and impressed

Carpathian Mountains

Dniester

Pripet

pastoralists

Mediterranean Sea

Sicily

Stentinello

Pindus Mountains

Vardar

ware cultures

Danube

Balkan Mountains

Karanovo

Varna

Black Sea

hunters and pastoralists

early

Argissa

Aegean

Anatolia

painted

ware

Crete

Knossos

Hacilar

70°

10°

20°

60°

20°

30°

50°

20°

40°

30°

The Greek world

The Acropolis (below). Acting as the defensive strong point for Athens since the Mycenaean period, the acropolis was also an important religious sanctuary. Its most famous temple was the Parthenon, begun in 447 BC.

The Greek heartland is an area of islands and plains divided by mountains. After the collapse of the Mycenaean palace system, the *polis* or city-state emerged and soon became the dominant form of political organization in the Mediterranean world.

The 8th century BC was a period of great transformations in Greece. It saw the appearance of the first monumental public buildings, changes in burial practices and new artistic styles. At the same time, literacy re-emerged, with a new alphabet. Though contact with the wider world had not totally disappeared in previous centuries, it now increased dramatically, above all on the island of Euboea, perhaps as the result of Phoenician exploration and settlement.

From the middle of the century, following in the wake of the Phoenicians, groups of Greeks created settlements around the Mediterranean, first in Italy and Sicily, but by the middle of the 6th century also in north Africa and, to the east, along the Black Sea coast. These included many cities that have remained famous to the present, such as Marseilles and Naples (see map 1). In the central Mediterranean, the Greeks came into conflict with the Carthaginians, who for many centuries disputed control of Sicily with them.

In Asia Minor, however, the Greeks came up against the Persian empire, which first sought to annex the city-states of the Aegean coast and in 490 and 480-479 BC invaded Greece itself. The Persians met with defeat and the next 50 years marked the great age of Greek culture: the tragic drama of Aeschylus, Sophocles and Euripedes; the comedy of Aristophanes; the histories of Herodotus and Thucydides; the splendour of the Parthenon; the sculptures of Phidias. Athens also built up a formidable fleet and used it to create an Aegean empire which the cities of the Peloponnese, led by Sparta, saw as a threat. In 431 BC, Sparta declared war on

3 The campaigns of Alexander
→ Alexander, 334–23 BC → Nearchus, 325–24 BC

2 The Peloponnesian War, 431–404 BC

Legend:
- Athens and members of the Delian League
- ally of Athens
- Sparta and allies
- neutral states
- allies of Athens in Magna Graecia
- allies of Sparta in Magna Graecia
- Athenian campaigns
- Spartan campaigns
- ✕ Athenian victory
- ✕ Spartan victory

Athens. The Peloponnesian war lasted 27 years and, despite victories on both sides, Athens fatally overstrained her resources with a disastrous expedition against Syracuse in Sicily (415-13 BC) and was finally defeated in 404 BC. Her empire fragmented (map 2).

The 4th century saw more jockeying for power, as Persia sought to intervene in Greek affairs, until the well-trained Macedonian army of King Philip II (359-336 BC) first subdued the city-states and then united them under his leadership for an attack on Persia. Philip's remarkable son Alexander (336-323 BC) invaded Asia Minor with an army of 35,000 men, both Greeks and Macedonians, in 334 BC; moved on to annex Egypt (332 BC) and the Persian empire (331 BC); and campaigned successfully in India and Central Asia (map 3). Alexander's death in 323 BC and the ensuing struggles between his leading generals created three major powers: Macedon, Egypt, and the Seleucid kingdom of western Asia.

Although politically the empire of Alexander the Great proved ephemeral, in other respects its consequences endured. Alexander and his successors founded some 70 cities, not merely as military strongholds but as cultural centres, and thus Greek culture and language spread throughout the entire region, as far as the borders of India.

1 Greek colonization in the Mediterranean world, 750–550 BC

Legend:
- Greek heartland in 750 BC
- Greek parent community
- Greek oracular shrine
- Phoenician or Punic settlement
- Etruscan city
- 8th-century Greek colony
- 7th-century Greek colony
- 6th-century Greek colony
- Philistine city

World religions

Before the 1st millennium BC, polytheism was the dominant form of religious belief throughout Eurasia, with individual communities worshipping their own gods. As the empires of the ancient world emerged, a number of major religions, each characterized by a single doctrine and claims to universality, largely replaced these myriad cults, although elsewhere innumerable other creeds survived without making the transition to world religions.

All the great world religions originated in Asia, and three of them – Judaism, Christianity and Islam – developed in the same small region. Moreover, several were either established or radically reformulated at much the same time: the outstanding prophets and reformers of Hinduism, Buddhism, Judaism, Confucianism and Taoism all lived in the 6th century BC. Their appearance perhaps reflected a need in the rising empires for more universal creeds than local deities could provide, and their diffusion – particularly the spread of the great missionary religions, Buddhism and Christianity – played an important role in linking the different areas. The new religions also spread the values of those advanced cultures to people living beyond the frontiers.

All the world religions shared, to some degree, a belief in a single spiritual reality. Hinduism, the oldest of them, although it reveres

1 The diffusion of religions

- → dispersion of Jews to AD 500
- → spread of Christianity
- area converted to Christianity by AD 600
- → spread of Buddhism
- --- first area of Buddhist missionary activity
- ·-·- area of rise of Mahayana Buddhism
- ● Buddhist sites
- area of Hinduism
- area of Daoism and Confucianism
- area of Shintoism
- area of Zoroastrianism
- → spread of Mithraism
- ● Mithraic sites

A reclining Buddha from Polonnaruwa in Sri Lanka. The importance of Buddism grew after it was adopted by Mauryan emperor Ashoka and it spread throughout India. Missionary activity then brought Buddhist ideas to many places in south and east Asia. Buddhism reached Sri Lanka in the late third century BC.

numerous gods, emphasises the 'right way to live'; Buddhism, although it does not centre upon a god, instead stresses deliverance from suffering through the annihilation of desire. Originally a reformist movement within Hinduism, in its conservative, or Theravada form, Buddhism soon spread throughout India and on to Sri Lanka, Burma, Thailand and South-East Asia. It was the first and perhaps the greatest of all missionary religions, spreading to China by the 1st or 2nd century AD, Korea in the 4th century, and Japan in the 6th century.

Judaism spread mainly because of the persecution of the Jews by more formidable neighbours, beginning with their forcible removal to Babylon (586-538 BC). This led to a change in the emphasis of the faith from temple observance and ritual to morality and righteous living. Rebellion against Roman rule (64 BC) led to the destruction of the temple in Jerusalem (AD 70), and Jewish groups migrated until Judaism, too, became a worldwide religion. It was also associated with the origins of two other major creeds: Christianity (page 44) and Islam (page 50).

In East Asia, the 6th century saw the rise of the ethical system of Confucius (551-479 BC) and the mystical religion of the Tao, or 'the Way', associated with the shadowy figure of Lao-tzu. Zoroastrianism, the other great religion of the period, originated in Persia and saw life as a battleground between the forces of good and evil. It spread widely through the Roman world in the form of Mithraism, with shrines as far afield as northern Britain. Mithraism was ultimately suppressed in favour of Christianity while most Zoroastrian areas came under the control of Islam.

Most of the world religions spread along the trade routes, diffused by soldiers, administrators, merchants and ordinary travellers as well as by missionaries; and most tended to prosper under strong governments that brought peace. The development of larger, more centralized states and empires and the rise of these religions and codes thus went hand in hand, the new religions either becoming associated with or adopted by the great empires of the ancient world: Zoroastrianism with the Persian empire of Cyrus and Darius the Great; Buddhism with Ashoka's Indian empire; Confucianism and Taoism with China under the Chou. The world religions also provided the bonds that eventually linked areas of the world previously separate.

264 BC–AD 565
Rome

Rome, a city-state governed by aristocratic families leading an army of peasant soldiers, came to control an empire that stretched from the Atlantic to the Euphrates and from the English Channel to the Sahara. But military success brought social disorder; rivalries between warlords led to civil war; and republican institutions became an autocracy.

In the 6th century BC Rome was just a small fortress-town in central Italy commanding both the lowest crossing point on the river Tiber and a salt route between the mountains and the sea. By exploiting quarrels with its neighbours, the Roman Republic emerged as the dominant power first in central Italy and then in the whole peninsula. By 264 BC Rome controlled the whole of Italy and challenged the other major power in the western Mediterranean: Carthage. After three savage wars Rome defeated Carthage to acquire Sicily (241 BC), Spain (206 BC) and North Africa (146 BC). At the same time, conflict with the Hellenistic kingdoms further east resulted in the conquest of Macedon, Greece and Western Anatolia. In this way, almost by accident, Rome became an imperial power with far-flung possessions.

Administration of these provinces overstrained the Roman constitution, which had not been designed to manage an overseas empire, and the Republic finally collapsed in a series of civil wars. The last of these brought to power Octavian, who established himself as *Princeps* ('first citizen'), accepted the title Augustus (in 27 BC), reshaped the constitution, and extended and strengthened the frontiers (map 1).

While maintaining undivided power in his own hands, Augustus allowed the Senate – the traditional government of Rome – to take a share in running the empire, with responsibility for several provinces. Thus, in theory, the Republican forms endured, and administration remained in civilian not military hands. Under his successors, Roman rule expanded further still, but the Senate lost most of its power. Nevertheless, strong central control

ensured peace for over two centuries and population expanded, trade flourished and cities grew. In the mid-3rd century AD, however, Germanic invasions in the west and Persian victories in the east brought the empire temporarily to its knees. A series of strong emperors between AD 268 and AD 284 restored a semblance of orderly government to the empire, but Diocletian (AD 284-305) realized that a single ruler could no longer hold the whole edifice together. He divided power between himself and a joint Augustus,

An equestrian statue of the emperor Marcus Aurelius (161-80). Preoccupied for much of his reigns with wars against the Parthians and the Germans (who in 170 invaded Italy), Marcus Aurelius maintained, but did not expand the Roman frontiers. He was the author of the *Meditations*, espousing stoicism as his philosophy in the face of adversity.

with two deputies (Caesars), and split the empire into four prefectures and twelve dioceses (map 2). By now the military had triumphed over the civilian, and a new basis had to be found for imperial authority. Under the influence of eastern ideas, the *Princeps* became *Dominus* (lord), an absolute ruler, at the head of a vast bureaucracy. Gradually the centre of Roman power shifted eastwards: Diocletian's successor Constantine (305-37) established a new capital at Byzantium (330), which he renamed Constantinople.

Although theoretically governed by joint rulers, the empire gradually broke into eastern and western halves, and when the western provinces crumbled before a new wave of Germanic invaders in the early 5th century, little help arrived from the east. Rome itself was sacked in 410 and 455, and the Ostrogoths created their own kingdom in Italy in 493. Justinian (AD 527-565) briefly recovered some of the western provinces but failed to reunite the empire.

Nevertheless, the Byzantine (East Roman) empire survived for another millennium, and many Roman traditions continued in the West. The Latin tongue, although developing into the derivative 'Romance' languages, long remained the language of churchmen and scientists; Roman Law forms the basis of most modern Western legal systems; many feats of Roman engineering genius survive to this day; and the Roman church lives on as a direct link with the past.

2 The Roman empire, AD 305–565

- - - frontier of the Roman empire, AD 305
— boundary of dioceses under Diocletian
///// territory reconquered by Justinian, 533–54

Praetorian prefectures, c. 405:
- Praefectus Praetorio Galliarum
- Praefectus Praetorio Illyrici, Italiae, Africae
- Praefectus Praetorio per Illyricum
- Praefectus Praetorio per Orientem

1 The Roman empire, 31 BC–c. AD 250

- under administration of the Senate
- imperial provinces
- public provinces
- provinces added after AD 14, with date
- - - - - later subdivisions of provinces, with dates

China: the first empires

From the 16th to the 11th century BC China's first historical dynasty, the Shang, presided over a confederation of clans in the Yellow River valley. Around 1027 BC the Chou replaced them and extended their authority over the Yangtze valley as well, investing their supporters with fiefs to create a feudal hierarchy sustained by the services, food and clothes produced by peasant communities. Then in 771 BC western invaders sacked the Chou capital, and the feudatories seized the opportunity to break away. Over 100 belligerent political units sprang up. In the 5th century BC, however, bronze technology gave way to iron, animal power and irrigation transformed agriculture, increasing both food production and population, while warfare reduced the number of states. By 300 BC seven states still competed for hegemony; by 221 BC only one of them remained – Ch'in.

The Ch'in organized their subjects into groups which bore collective responsibility to maintain public order, and to provide manpower both for construction works (above all roads, canals and fortifications) and for the army (which was composed primarily of infantry). The defeated nobles suffered demotion and, instead of performing labour services to their lord, the peasants now paid taxes to the conqueror. A savage penal code, administered by a professional bureaucracy, enforced the new system.

In 221 BC Prince Cheng of Ch'in, took the title Shih Huang-ti (meaning 'first emperor'); ordered the construction of a national network of roads and canals, centered on his new capital at Hsieng-yang; rebuilt and strengthened the Great Wall; introduced a uniform coinage whose distinctive shape (circular with a square hole in the centre) remained standard until 1911; and took steps to standardize the written language throughout the empire. Small wonder that his dynasty gave 'China' its name.

The burdens imposed by the autocratic first emperor provoked civil war shortly after his death in 206 BC; but before long a new dynasty, the Han, reunited China. At first they worked through feudal principalities allocated to their family and supporters, but by 100 BC the fiefs had again come under strong central control. The Han also extended the Great Wall far to the north-west, undertook several military expeditions against the nomad Hsiung-nu in the north, invaded northern Vietnam and Korea, and for a brief period after 59 BC controlled the Tarim basin. They also eliminated the Min-Yüeh kingdoms of the south-east coast. A lively export trade, mainly in silk, began to Parthia and to the Roman empire.

Terracotta warriors from Sian (Xian). Discovered in 1974, close to the mausoleum of the first Ch'in emperor, thousands of terracotta warriors have since been excavated. Each figure was individually produced, and the varying uniforms, badges, weaponry and styles of armour provide information on the organization of the Ch'in army. By around 250 BC the Ch'in state was as large as all the other Chinese states put together. By 221 BC all the remaining states were absorbed by the Ch'in creating, for the first time, a unified China under Shih Huang-ti (the 'first emperor'). Although Ch'in rule collapsed in 206 BC, the Han dynasty inherited their unified kingdom.

HSIUNGNU TRIBES

residence of the
Hsiungnu King

western extension to wall
built by Han emperors
117–100 BC

Karashanr
(Yen-ch'i)   田 Turfan
Wu-lei   (Kao-ch'ang)
      Chiao-ho

Lo-lan
Lop Nor   Yü-men Kuan   田 Chuyen
      Yang Kuan   Gobi Desert
      Yang Kuan
I-hsün   Chang-yeh
      Tun-huang   Chiu
      CHIANG   -ch'uan
      TRIBES   Wu-wei
Tarim Basin

Li Ling's expedition
99 BC
Ho Ch'u-ping and Wei Ch'ing
119 BC
Li Kuang-li expedition 92 BC
Wei Ch'ing's expedition 128 BC

Great Wall rebuilt and strengthened
by Ch'in emperors 220–210 BC

put under Chinese
administration 109–106 BC

KOREA

Yellow
Sea

brought under Chinese
administration 117–115 BC

Yellow River
Yellow River   Mount Yi
Ch'ang-an   • Lo-yang
  • Sian

CH'IN EMPIRE
(221–207 BC)

1 The expansion of Han China

China, 207 BC

territory added under Former Han

maximum extent of Former Han empire

territory of Chinese protectorate of
Western Regions, c. 59 BC

journey of Chang Chien, envoy of
Han emperor, 138–126 BC

trade routes

田 administrative centre under Later Han
from AD 126

centre of Later Han protectorate,
AD 73–126

territory added under Later Han

new route opened by General
Pan Chao for Later Han

expeditions against Hsiungnu
(Huns)

Yangtze

(first explorations from 136 BC)
expeditions against Tien:
109 BC kingdom suppressed

86 BC expeditions to far
82 BC southwest

MIN-YÜEH
defeated 100 BC

KINGDOM OF NAN-YÜEH
(206–113 BC)

under Chinese
administration
after 111 BC

South
China
Sea

VIETNAM

A census in AD 2 revealed
some 57 million people in the
empire. Great cities abounded, the
largest – Ch'ang-an, the capital – housing
250,000 people. The heart of the empire
remained the Yellow River plain, where population
densities in some areas approached 150 per square
mile (see map 2). Shortly afterwards, however, court
families and great feudatories increased their influence, while agrarian unrest mounted. Real power
lay in the hands of the regional commanders and
warlords and the last Han emperor abdicated in
220. The Han empire fragmented into three regional
states and a century later the Hsiung-nu burst
through the Great Wall and overran northern China
(see page 40). China was to remain politically fragmented until AD 589.

Yellow River

2 The population of China, AD 2

very dense settlement,
approx. 150 per sq. mile

heavily settled,
approx. 100 per sq. mile

lightly settled,
approx. 30 per sq. mile

AD 300-600
The transformation of the ancient world

By the 3rd century AD, a continuous web of large states stretched across the southern half of the continents of Europe and Asia. In the West, Rome controlled the whole Mediterranean world and much of Europe; in China, the Han ruled a state that equalled the Roman empire in population and extended from the Pacific to the Takla Makan desert in central Asia; in between lay the Persian empire. The co-existence of these great states brought to vast areas of the Old World internal peace and centralised government, conditions that made possible commercial and cultural interchange on an unprecedented scale.

But this 'imperial zone' formed only a narrow corridor, flanked to the north by the domain of nomadic tribes, expert horsemen who possessed in war a speed and striking power that their sedentary neighbours could rarely match. In the 4th and 5th centuries AD, numerous nomad groups launched devastating attacks against all the major civilizations. A confederation known as the Hsiung-nu from Mongolia broke through the Great Wall of China in AD 304 and within a decade reached the Yellow River, sacking the ancient Han capital Ch'ang-an (AD 316). A succession of invaders from the steppes dominated northern China for the next three centuries.

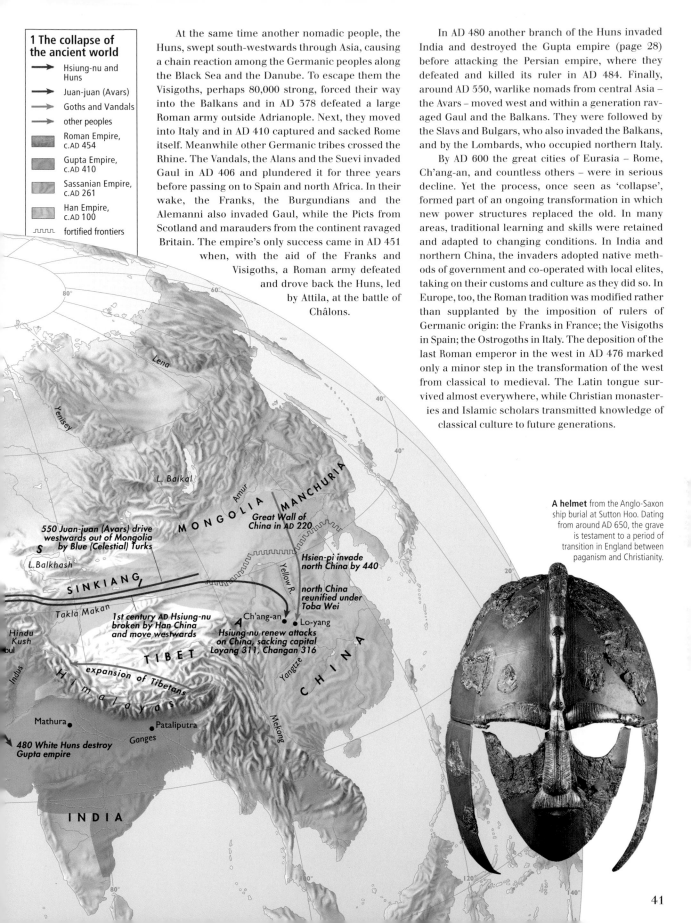

1 The collapse of the ancient world

→ Hsiung-nu and Huns

→ Juan-juan (Avars)

→ Goths and Vandals

→ other peoples

▢ Roman Empire, c.AD 454

▢ Gupta Empire, c.AD 410

▢ Sassanian Empire, c.AD 261

▢ Han Empire, c.AD 100

ᴖᴖᴖᴖ fortified frontiers

At the same time another nomadic people, the Huns, swept south-westwards through Asia, causing a chain reaction among the Germanic peoples along the Black Sea and the Danube. To escape them the Visigoths, perhaps 80,000 strong, forced their way into the Balkans and in AD 378 defeated a large Roman army outside Adrianople. Next, they moved into Italy and in AD 410 captured and sacked Rome itself. Meanwhile other Germanic tribes crossed the Rhine. The Vandals, the Alans and the Suevi invaded Gaul in AD 406 and plundered it for three years before passing on to Spain and north Africa. In their wake, the Franks, the Burgundians and the Alemanni also invaded Gaul, while the Picts from Scotland and marauders from the continent ravaged Britain. The empire's only success came in AD 451 when, with the aid of the Franks and Visigoths, a Roman army defeated and drove back the Huns, led by Attila, at the battle of Châlons.

In AD 480 another branch of the Huns invaded India and destroyed the Gupta empire (page 28) before attacking the Persian empire, where they defeated and killed its ruler in AD 484. Finally, around AD 550, warlike nomads from central Asia – the Avars – moved west and within a generation ravaged Gaul and the Balkans. They were followed by the Slavs and Bulgars, who also invaded the Balkans, and by the Lombards, who occupied northern Italy.

By AD 600 the great cities of Eurasia – Rome, Ch'ang-an, and countless others – were in serious decline. Yet the process, once seen as 'collapse', formed part of an ongoing transformation in which new power structures replaced the old. In many areas, traditional learning and skills were retained and adapted to changing conditions. In India and northern China, the invaders adopted native methods of government and co-operated with local elites, taking on their customs and culture as they did so. In Europe, too, the Roman tradition was modified rather than supplanted by the imposition of rulers of Germanic origin: the Franks in France; the Visigoths in Spain; the Ostrogoths in Italy. The deposition of the last Roman emperor in the west in AD 476 marked only a minor step in the transformation of the west from classical to medieval. The Latin tongue survived almost everywhere, while Christian monasteries and Islamic scholars transmitted knowledge of classical culture to future generations.

A helmet from the Anglo-Saxon ship burial at Sutton Hoo. Dating from around AD 650, the grave is testament to a period of transition in England between paganism and Christianity.

550 Juan-juan (Avars) drive westwards out of Mongolia by Blue (Celestial) Turks

Great Wall of China in AD 220

Hsien-pi invade north China by 440

north China reunified under Toba Wei

1st century AD Hsiung-nu broken by Han China and move westwards

Hsiung-nu renew attacks on China, sacking capital Loyang 311, Changan 316

expansion of Tibetans

480 White Huns destroy Gupta empire

MONGOLIA   MANCHURIA

SINKIANG

Takla Makan

TIBET

Himalayas

CHINA

INDIA

Lena

Yenisey

L. Baikal

Amur

Yellow R.

Ch'ang-an   Lo-yang

Yangtze

Mekong

L. Balkhash

Hindu Kush

Indus

Mathura   Pataliputra

Ganges

TWO

The World Fragmented

After AD 500 the narrow chain of empires extending from Rome to China crumbled under attacks from nomads from the Asian steppes. Contacts between China and the West, between north Africa and Italy and between Byzantium and western Europe dwindled as each region fell back on its own resources and had to fend for itself.

In Eurasia, two phenomena dominated: the expansion of Islam after 632; and the emergence of the Mongol empire after 1206. Meanwhile, the Maya, Aztec and Inca civilizations appeared in America, the empires of Sri Vijaya and Majapahit grew in southeast Asia, and the empires of Ghana, Mali and Songhay developed in Africa. Europe, by comparison, remained backward until, in the second half of the 15th century, a series of path-breaking voyages of exploration laid the foundations for overseas expansion. Even then, however, Europe's achievements remained overshadowed and threatened by the expanding power of the Ottoman Turks for another century.

Death strangling a plague victim,
from the 14th-century Stiny Codex (Prague University)

The spread of Christianity

Christianity began as a Jewish splinter movement in Roman Palestine. Its founder, Jesus of Nazareth, claimed to be the Messiah, or Saviour, sent to prepare the Jews for 'the kingdom of God' but, after an initial, short-lived success, he was executed as a revolutionary (AD 29). Jewish orthodoxy rejected his message, but his followers turned instead to the conversion of non-Jews and by AD 200, despite repression and persecution, communities of Christians (as the followers of Jesus came to be called) flourished in several cities of the Roman empire (especially Antioch and Edessa). In AD 313 the Emperor Constantine granted the new faith toleration and in AD 325 at Nicaea presided over the first ecumenical council, representing the whole church, which defined beliefs for all Christians. A full ecclesiastical organization developed, with a hierarchy of bishops and a framework of patriarchates, provinces and dioceses throughout the empire (map 1).

The council of Chalcedon (451) attempted to enforce orthodoxy on the Christian world, but instead alienated the Monophysite (or Coptic) Christians of Egypt, Syria and Armenia, and the Nestorians who, expelled from Edessa, took refuge in Persia. Meanwhile the disintegration of the Roman empire in the West (page 36) undermined the position of the church. But salvation came from the periphery. The Coptic church of Egypt, with a strong monastic tradition, sent missionaries down the Nile from the 4th century, converting the peoples of Nubia and Ethiopia; while from the 7th century, the Nestorians of Persia expanded south into Arabia and east to China. In the west, the impetus for revival came from the monastic missionary church of Ireland, which evangelized first its Celtic neighbours in Britain and Brittany, and then in the 7th and 8th centuries the pagan tribes of continental Europe (map 2).

As the Muslim onslaught devastated the Christian Mediterranean (page 50), both Rome and Constantinople launched missions northwards among the Slavs. Russia opted for Orthodox Christianity, and in 988 the Russian prince Vladimir was baptized, while Poland (966) and Hungary (1001) chose Catholic Christianity. Although rivalry between the two patriarchates resulted after 1054 in schism, the popes increased their authority by sponsoring Christian counter-offensives in Iberia, the Baltic and West Asia: the crusades (page 48). The attempt to restore Christianity to Palestine proved a costly failure, but the crusades made great advances elsewhere. Meanwhile, within Europe, monks and (from the 13th century) friars joined the expanding network of parish clergy in Christianizing the countryside and combating heresy. In 1387 Lithuania, the last remaining pagan state in Europe, converted to Catholicism, just as persecution by Timur and other rulers (page 60) extinguished the faith in Asia, the continent of its birth.

1 The early Christian churches

- main areas of Christian growth, to AD 300
- areas largely Christian by AD 600
- • important Christian communities of the 1st century
- • other important Christian centres, by AD 600
- ☥ the five patriarchates
- + important bishops with dates of episcopate
- ◆ other important figures, with dates

Map labels: Iona • Columba (c.521–97); Whithorn • Ninian (c.400); Armagh + Patrick (c.450); York; Lincoln; St. David's; St Albans; London; Canterbury + Augustine (597–604/9); Cologne; Trier; Paris + Denys (c. 250); Dol; BRITTANY; Tours + Martin (370–97); Poitiers + Hilary (350–67); Autun; Lyons + Irenaeus (177–200); Bordeaux; Vienna; Milan + Ambrose (374–97); Aquileia; Ravenna; Salona; Ariminum; Léon; Arles; Lefins; Marseilles; • John Cassian (c. 360–435); Rome ☥; • Justin (d. c. 162); • Novatian (c. 250); + Leo (440–61); + Gregory (590–604); Nola; Pompeii; Braga + Martin (570–9); Saragossa; Ávila; Toledo; Mérida; Cagliari; • Tertullian (c. 170–220); Cordova + Ossius (d. 357/8); + Isidore (d. 636); Seville; Elvira; Hippo Regius + Augustine (396–430); + Cyprian (249–58); • Donatus (d. c. 355); Carthage; Thagaste; Caesarea; Sicca Veneria; Mileviso; Leptis Magn

2 Christianity in medieval Europe

- Roman-rite Christians, c. 1400
- Byzantine-rite Christians, c. 1400
- Monophysite Christians
- Islam
- — extent of Catholic (Frankish) Christianity (c. 700)
- --- maximum extent of crusader states in the east in the 12th century
- ● important bishoprics
- (743) date of foundation of a bishopric or of conversion of a region to Christianity

Trondheim (1029)
FINLAND (13th cent.)
Bergen (1070)
Turku (1220)
Uppsala (1164)
Novgorod (1135)
Aarhus (948)
Riga (1198)
Moscow (1326)
Polotsk (1113)
Armagh
York
Lund (c. 950)
Smolensk (1128)
North Sea
Bremen (788)
Hamburg (834)
PRUSSIA (14th cent.)
LITHUANIA (1387)
Canterbury
Gniezno (1000)
Magdeburg (958)
POLAND (10th cent.)
Kiev (988)
Rouen
Mainz (743)
Prague (973)
MORAVIA (9th cent.)
Cracow (1004)
Paris
Rheims
Regensburg (739)
HUNGARY (10th cent.)
Tours
Salzburg (798)
Gran (1001)
Lyons
SERBIA (c. 870)
Kherson
Santiago de Compostela (c. 840)
Avignon
Black Sea
Lisbon (1147)
Saragossa (1118)
Rome
BULGARIA (c. 870)
Constantinople
Toledo (1085)
Valencia (1238)
Ochrida (c. 870)
GRANADA (1492)
Salonica
ICELAND (1000)
Antioch
Mediterranean Sea
Acre
Jerusalem
Alexandria

Sirmium
Singidunum
Black Sea
ARMENIA
Artashat
Sinope
Neocaesarea
PERSIA
Serdica
+John Chrysostom (398–404)
+Nestorius (428–31)
Sebastea
Constantinople
Gangra
Philippi
Nicomedia
Ancyra
Caesarea
Melitene
+Basil (370–7/9)
Amida
Nisibis
Thessalonica
Nicaea
Asia Minor
Cappadociae
Samosata
Edessa
Beroea
Troas
Cyzicus
Nyssa
Nazianzus
+Ephrem (306–73)
Pergamum
Iconium
Cyrrhus
Dura-Europos
Thyatira
Philadelphia
Sardes
Antioch
Tarsus
Antioch
Gondeshapur
Smyrna
Hierapolis
Lystra
+Ignatius (d. c. 112)
Athens
Ephesus 431
Laodicea
Derbe
Palmyra
Seleucia-Ctesiphon
Corinth
Patmos
Myra
Laodicea
SYRIA
Salamis
Damascus
Mediterranean Sea
Tyre
Pella
+Cyril (c. 350–86)
Caesarea
+Eusebius (d. c. 339)
Jerusalem
Diospolis-Lydda
Gaza
Bethlehem
Pelusium
Ptolemais
Cyrene
Alexandria
Thmuis
EGYPT
+Origen (c.185–254)
♦Arius (d. 336)
+Athanasius (328–73)
+Cyril (412–44)
Oxyrhynchus
Red Sea
Lycopolis
Chenoboskion

A stone slab of the Apostles Peter and Paul from the sepulchre of the child Amellus dating from after 313 (below). Following the conversion of Constantine, Christian art became more public and explicit representations of Christ and the saints were common. Portraits of Peter and Paul from Rome proudly allude to the connection of the two leading apostles with the city and its powerful bishops. In this example, they are depicted as Roman gentlemen of high social status, as the purple stripe of their togas attests.

PETRVS   PAVLVS

China

TIMELINE

581-617
China reunified under the
Sui dynasty

618-907
The T'ang dynasty

960
Coup d'état of General
Chao K'unag-yin, who
becomes first Sung emperor

963-79
Sung reunite China

1126-7
Tatar Chin conquer northern
China

1211-34
Mongols conquer northern
China

1235-79
Mongols conquer southern
China

After the barbarian invasions of the 4th and 5th centuries (page 38) the Sui dynasty (581-617) reunified China. They consolidated their empire through standardized institutions, a state-supported broad-based Buddhism, and the construction of a canal system linking the Yangtze with the Yellow River and the Lo-yang region. The T'ang dynasty (618-907) continued the process, creating a uniform administrative organization of prefectures, in which officials recruited through an examination system replaced the traditional aristocracy. The T'ang also extended their control to the Tarim basin and northern Korea: in the 660s, the Chinese empire reached its greatest extent and 88 Asiatic peoples recognised Chinese overlordship, adopting its culture, its written language and its political institutions (map 1).

In 751, however, at the Talas River, an Arab army defeated the Chinese, while a major rebellion rocked T'ang power in 755-62, causing many of the new conquests to be abandoned. Within the empire, power began to pass to the provinces until in 907, following a wave of peasant uprisings, China split into ten separate regional states. Although the Sung dynasty reunified the country between 960 and 979, they failed to regain the new territories. Nevertheless, Chinese economic growth continued. A massive movement of population into the fertile Yangtze valley and southern China produced large agricultural surpluses which stimulated trade and economic development. Between 750 and 1100, the population of the empire doubled; trade reached new heights; and a great concentration of industries arose around the capital, K'ai-feng, centre of the canal system and of the eastern road network.

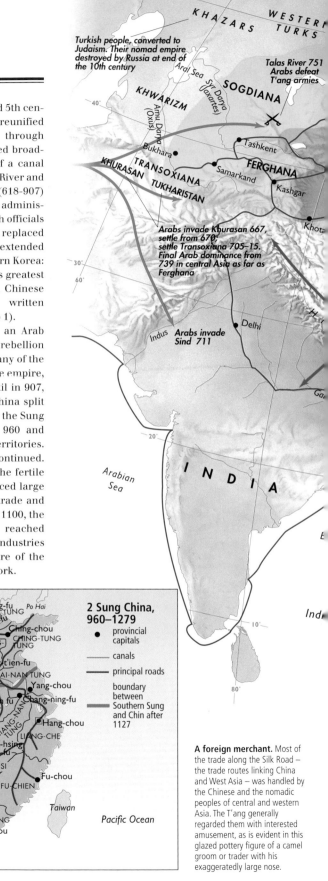

A foreign merchant. Most of the trade along the Silk Road – the trade routes linking China and West Asia – was handled by the Chinese and the nomadic peoples of central and western Asia. The T'ang generally regarded them with interested amusement, as is evident in this glazed pottery figure of a camel groom or trader with his exaggeratedly large nose.

powerful unified Turkish kingdom in 6th century, split into Eastern and Western groups c.585. Eastern Turks conquered by T'ang 630, but re-emerge from 681 and 699-715 are re-united with Western Turks. In 715 Western Turks break away: Eastern Turks finally destroyed 744

SHIH-WEI

KIRGHIZ

AMUR

MALGAL

powerful kingdom on the T'ang model set up by remnants of Korean ruling clan of Koguryo. Independent from 710. Destroyed by Khitan 934

URKESTAN

KHITAN (LIAO)
proto-Mongol people, raid T'ang border from 695, sometimes vassals of Turks. Set up own empire (Liao) in Manchuria in early 10th century

TURKS
to 744

DZUNGARIA

UIGHURS
Uighurs replace Turks in the steppe 745-840; more stable, less anti-Chinese than Turks. Destroyed by Kirghiz

Gobi   Desert

PO HAI
(PARHAE)

still occupied by Emishi aboriginal peoples

Turfan

Kucha
Hami

arim Basin

NINGSIA

under T'ang
control 645-763

Tun-huang

Yellow River

Po Hai

T'ang occupation
668-676

SILLA

Sea of Japan

KANSU

T'ANG

to Tibet 763-843

EMPIRE

Ch'ang-an
Lo-yang

Yang-chou

JAPAN

Kyoto   Nara

independent politically; increasing Chinese cultural influence from 6th century. In 7th century a strong centralized kingdom developed, based on T'ang institutions

unified kingdom c.600.
Expansion after 650;
under Chinese cultural
influence until c.750 then
Indian influence.
Central control collapsed
c.840

TIBET

OF

Ch'eng-tu

Yangtze

Ning-po

NEPAL

alayas

Brahmaputra

CHINA

before 660 there were three states in Korea: Koguryo, Paekche and Silla. The T'ang destroyed Paekche in 660, Koguryo in 668 and occupied N. Korea. Strong resistance led to Chinese withdrawal in 676, leaving all Korea under Silla, a powerful, centralized state on T'ang lines

NAN-CHAO
kingdom formed by
federation of tribal groups
organized on T'ang model

850-70

Canton

1 The Chinese world, 7th–8th centuries

under permanent T'ang civil administration

area of temporary occupation during 7th century

under T'ang military control

zone of Chinese cultural dominance

trade routes ———   ⟵ Tibetan expansion

canals ———   ⟵ advance of Islam

c.800

ANNAM

Chiao-chou

South
China Sea

PYU

Pagan

Sukhothai

Bengal

Indianized Buddhist kingdom
invasion by Nan-chao in 8th
and 9th centuries

Mekong

KHMER

Hue

CHAMPA

kingdom under strong
Indian/Hindu influence

kingdom centred
on Hue. Strong
Indian influence

northern heartland of China. Population continued to increase rapidly; trade and industry boomed; and the new capital, Hang-chou, became the world's largest city. This was also a period of great cultural achievement. The visual arts, literature, philosophy, science and technology all reached new heights; education became more widespread, aided by the dissemination of printing, which had been invented in T'ang times and now became commonplace. Merchants formed guilds and partnerships, setting up a complex commercial organization with banks, credit systems and paper money. The government was run by a mandarinate of career bureaucrats.

In 1126-7 the Chin, a powerful nomadic state north-east of the Great Wall, invaded and conquered all of northern China, with terrible devastation. The Sung now controlled only the centre and the south, but stood constantly on the defensive, maintaining huge armies and paying vast subsidies to their aggressive neighbours (map 2). Even after the Chin invasion, however, the Sung state remained immensely prosperous, since its southern territories proved far more productive than the old

But their days were numbered. Between 1211 and 1234 the Mongols (page 60) had overrun the Chin empire, causing widespread devastation, and in the 1270s the forces of Kublai Khan – 'the most powerful man since Adam' according to a European visitor – annexed the entire Sung empire. For the first time, all of China lay under foreign rule.

610–1453
The Byzantine world

TIMELINE

628
Heraclius defeats Persians at Nineveh

674-8 & 717-18
Muslim sieges of Constantinople

976-1025
Reign of Basil II, the Bulgar slayer

1054
Schism between Orthodox and Catholic churches

1071
Seljuq Turks defeat Byzantines at Manzikert

1096-9
The First Crusade

1204
Constantinople sacked by Fourth Crusade; Latin empire established

1261
Greek empire re-established

1453
Fall of Constantinople

Almost from its inception, the Roman empire's centre of gravity moved to the east, first pulled by the lure of economic wealth in Egypt and western Asia; then pushed by the loss of the western provinces to Germanic invaders (page 36) and by the pressure of Sassanid Persia on its eastern frontier. Except during the reign of Justinian (page 37), the west was neglected and the Roman empire became an eastern, Greek-speaking state – normally known, from the reign of Heraclius (610-641), as Byzantium.

Heraclius ended the long contest with Persia victoriously, capturing Nineveh in 628, but almost at once Byzantium faced two even more redoubtable foes: Islam (page 50) and the Slavs. However, after the failure of two long Arab sieges of Byzantium (674-8 and 717-18), the empire launched a succession of vigorous counter-offensives. Basil II (976-1025) even managed to advance the imperial frontiers close to their earlier limits: the Arabs retreated into Palestine; the Russians met defeat at Silistra on the Danube; the Bulgars, who had advanced to within 60 miles of Constantinople, became imperial subjects; plans were laid to recover the former Byzantine territories in Italy. However, the constant campaigns imposed heavy financial strains, as well as profound and debilitating social change, and in spite of further phases of recovery, the frontiers steadily shrank (map 1).

The crucial development was the emergence, in the 11th century, of the Seljuk Turks (page 50), whose crushing victory over Byzantine forces at Manzikert in 1071 induced Emperor Alexius I (1081-1118) to call on the west for help, thus initiating the sequence of events that led to the First Crusade (1096-9). It proved

a disastrous move since the Franks were less concerned to aid Byzantium than to set up their own principalities in Palestine and Asia Minor; the Normans, already in control of Sicily and Byzantine Italy, coveted lands in Greece; and the Italian cities, led by Venice, strove to increase their share of Mediterranean trade. After a century of mounting tension, the soldiers of the Fourth Crusade in 1204 conquered and pillaged Constantinople, partitioned the Byzantine empire, and established Latin states all over the Balkans (map 2).

The Latin Empire proved short-lived – its Greek-speaking subjects resented it and a new dynasty, the Palaeologi, restored the Greek empire in 1261 – but the new Byzantine state was only a shadow of its former self and when, shortly afterwards, the Ottoman Turks established themselves first in Asia Minor and then advanced into Byzantium's European territories, its fate was sealed. The capital of the east Roman empire fell in 1453 (page 70).

Nevertheless, the history of Byzantium includes both greatness and lasting achievements. For centuries it transmitted Roman culture back to areas from which earlier invasions had largely effaced it. It also passed on its culture and its religion to the Balkan peoples and to Russia. 'Two Romes have fallen', a Russian monk wrote shortly after 1453, 'but the third is still standing and a fourth shall never be.' He referred to Moscow (page 56), now emerged as the heir to the Byzantine inheritance.

The emperor Constantine IV Pogonatus and his brothers hand privileges to the Ravenna church of Sant'Apollinare in Classe and to archbishop Mauro. During his reign Constantinople withstood a four year siege by Arab armies (674–8), although much of the Balkans was overrun by Slav tribes and the Bulgars.

1 Byzantine greatness and decline

Imperial frontiers
- c. 628
- c. 1030
- c. 1143
- 1328

special areas:
- Exarchate of Ravenna to Lombards, 751
- Exarchate of Africa to Arabs from 670
- Catapanate of Italy to Normans from 1071

temporary reconquests:
- Africa, 685–710
- Syria, 975–6
- Sicily, 1038–43
- Ani, 1054
- Edessa, 1052
- Rum, c. 1118

general territorial losses:
- to Arabs, 636–641
- to Arabs after 641
- to Seljuk Turks from 1065
- Sultanate of Rum from 1071

Vera
Bonc
Genoa
Florer
Corsica
Sardinia
Caralis
Valentia
Balearic Islands
Carthago Nova
Carthage
AFRICA

2 The West attacks Byzantium

- ┈┈▶ the Norman attack, 1084–5
- ━━▶ the Norman attack, 1185
- ━▶ routes of the First Crusade, 1096–9
- ━▶ route of the Fourth Crusade 1204
- ┈┈▶ the Norman attack, 1147
- ━━ imperial frontier in 1180
- territory lost to other powers, 1180–1214
- despotate of Epirus (est. 1204)
- imperial territory in 1214
- Latin Empire in 1214
- Venetian territory in 1214
- other Greek states

The rise and expansion of Islam ranks as perhaps the most significant development in world history between the fall of Rome and the European invasion of the Americas. Within a remarkably short time, a new world religion created a dynamic civilization which now embraces one-seventh of the global population: 600 million Muslims, spread from Morocco to Indonesia, and from Siberia to Zanzibar. 'Islam', which means 'submission to the will of God', was conveyed to humankind through the Koran, a volume of prescriptions on behaviour as well as belief, revealed by God to Mohammed his prophet, who was born in the religious and commercial centre of Mecca about 570. As Mohammed's followers grew in number, they aroused the hostility of the merchants of Mecca and in 622 the group withdrew to the neighbouring town of Medina (the *hijra*). But Mohammed returned to Mecca in triumph in 630, transforming it into the focal point for the new faith of Islam, and when he died in 632 his authority extended over the Hejaz and much of central and southern Arabia.

For the next century Islam expanded rapidly: Arab armies defeated Latin Christian, Byzantine, Persian, Indian and Chinese armies to spread the new faith from the Himalayas in the east to the Atlantic in the west (map 1). In 711 they crossed over the Straits of Gibraltar and conquered Spain. Until 656 political control over the empire remained with Mohammed's relatives, but then a split occurred, with some Muslims following Ali, the Prophet's cousin and son-in-law (the Shi'ites), and others – the majority – accepting the rule of the Umayyad dynasty from Mecca who claimed to represent the Sunna or traditions of the Prophet. The Umayyads ruled from Damascus in Syria between 661 and 750, followed by the rival Abbasid dynasty, who created a new capital at Baghdad in Mesopotamia and opened government to non-Arab Muslims (known as *mawali*).

Gradually, the Muslim world lost its political unity and split into a number of local dynastic entities, some Sunnite and others Shi'ite (map 2). In 1055, however, the centre of the Islamic world was strengthened when the Seljuk Turks established themselves in Baghdad and shortly thereafter drove the Christians from most of Anatolia (page 48). Despite invasions from the west in the 12th century (the Crusades: page 49) and from the east in the 13th (the Mongols: page 60), Islam retained its hold over West Asia, while missionaries and merchants carried the faith eastwards to Malaysia, Indonesia and the Philippines, and southwards both to the sub-Saharan states and the cities of the Swahili coast of Africa (page 58). For a millennium after the birth of Mohammed, Islam remained the western hemisphere's leading and most extensive civilization.

2 The Muslim world, 786–1260

- Abbasid caliphate at greatest extent during rule of Haroun al-Rashid, 786–809
- areas recognizing Abbasid sovereignty, c. 1090
- disputed between Seljuks and Byzantine empire, c. 1070–c. 1180
- Zaidi Imams
- Almohads, c. 1160
- → lines of nomadic advance

The mosque at Córdoba with its ornate exterior decoration bears witness to the great wealth of Islamic Spain. The mosque was built by 'Abd ar Rahman I, a member of the ruling Umayyad family in Syria, who escaped their overthrow by the Abbasids to found a new Umayyad dynasty in Spain. Seizing power in 755, he made Córdoba his capital and resisted all attempts by the Abbasids to unseat him.

Map 2 labels

EMPIRE
Aral Sea
Jaxartes
Urgench
KHWARIZM
SELJUK TURKS
QARAKHANIDS
Kasghar
Baku
Bukhara • Samarkand
Oxus
TRANSOXANIA
ardil
Merv
Caspian Sea
AZERBAIJAN
Balkh
SELJUK TURKS
Rai
Nishapur • Tus
KHURASAN Herat
AFGHANISTAN
Hamadan
ermanshah
Isfahan
Kabul
Ghazni
KASHMIR
Yazd
Zaranj
GHAZNAVIDS Lahore
SEISTAN
Kandahar
PUNJAB
Basra
Multan
Shiraz
Siraf
Ormuz
Indus
INDIA
75°
BAHRAIN
Persian Gulf
Tiz
SIND
Daybul
60°
Muscat
OMAN
ARABIA

1 The spread of Islam

- growth under Mohammed
- growth under Abu Bakr, (632–4)
- growth under Omar, (634–44)
- growth under Othman (644–56) and Ali (656–61)
- expansion of Umayyad Caliphate, (661–750)
- expansion under the early Abbasids, (750–850)
- → routes of advance
- **638** date of Muslim conquest

Map 1 labels

na
YEMEN
zz
Aden
45°
KHAZAR EMPIRE
Aral Sea
TRANSOXANIA
Talas River 751
FERGHANA
Don
Caspian Sea
Oxus
Bukhara 710
Samarkand 710
Dnieper
Tiflis
Derbent
Merv ✕ 651
Balkh 651
Hindu Kush
PUNJAB
Black Sea
Constantinople besieged 673–78
ARMENIA
AZERBAIJAN
Ardabil
Nishapur 651
Herat
Kabul 664
Erzurum
Tabriz
Rai
GURGAN
KHURASAN
PERSIA
717–18
Mosul 641
Tigris
Nihavand 642
Isfahan
Multan 712
EMPIRE
MESOPOTAMIA
Jalula
Sus
SEISTAN
Antioch Edessa
Euphrates
Persepolis (Istakhr) 648
Indus
Tarsus
Kerbela 680
Baghdad
FARS
KIRMAN
SIND
Cyprus 649
Kufa
Basra 656
MAKRAN
SYRIA
Damascus 635
Yarmuk 636
Al Qadisiyya 637
Persian Gulf
60°
des 654
Fihl
Ramla
Jerusalem 638 ✕
BAHRAIN
Gulf
OMAN
Muscat
te 25
Alexandria 643
Heliopolis 640
PALESTINE
Ajnadain 634
YAMAMA
20°
RENAICA
Tabuk
Hiji
Fustat (Cairo) 670
EGYPT 640
Nile
HEJAZ
Medina
ARABIA
Badr 624
Mecca
flight from Mecca, 622
HADHRAMAUT
Red Sea
NUBIANS
Najran
YEMEN
Dongola
KINGDOM OF AKSUM
Aden
30°
40°
50°

51

Franks and Anglo-Saxons

Within a century of the Germanic invasions, settled kingdoms had grown up in western Europe, but not in Britain, where invaders from the continent met with resistance. During the 7th century, however, seven separate important kingdoms – which are traditionally known as the Heptarchy – emerged in England. Geographical obstacles seem to have prevented the states in the south-east (Sussex, Kent, Essex, East Anglia) from expanding, and leadership at first passed to Northumbria, whose progress benefitted from its early conversion to Christianity. Mercia led the opposition, sometimes in alliance with the 'Britons' on the periphery, and by the time of Offa (757-96) its pre-eminence was unquestionable: it controlled the four southeastern kingdoms, and even Wessex recognized Mercian overlordship.

On the continent, the Franks (whose original power base lay in what is now northern France, the Low Countries and the Rhineland) converted to Christianity under Clovis (481-511) and began to expand south and east. From their new capital at Paris, Clovis and his sons and grandsons defeated the Visigoths, conquered Burgundy and Provence, and extended their overlordship in Germany as far as the middle Danube.

Most of the new lands served to maintain the loyalty of the Frankish warriors, however, and when the conquests ceased in the mid-7th century the kings had to reward their followers and endow the Church by granting away their own estates and

revenues. In doing so they diminished their resources and, in time, power passed to the families which had benefitted from royal favour. Eventually Pippin of Herstal, from a leading Austrasian family, achieved prominence, and at Tertry (687) defeated his chief rivals.

Pippin and his son Charles Martel (from whom the dynasty took the name 'Carolingian') restored Frankish fortunes and inaugurated a second surge of territorial expansion (map 2). Charles Martel (714-41) defeated the Arabs at Tours in 732, halting their rapid incursion into western Europe, while his son Pippin the Short (d. 768) expelled them from southern France. In 751, with the sanction and support of the pope, Pippin made himself king of the Franks. His son Charles the Great or Charlemagne (768-814) conquered Lombardy (774) and established Frankish rule in much of Italy. He won great victories over the Frisians (784-5), Bavarians (788) and Saxons (finally subdued in 804); and created a march, or boundary province, across the Pyrenees

An image of Charlemagne from his tomb at Aachen. The tomb was endowed by Frederick Barbarossa in the 12th century. The masterpiece of gold enamels and gems shows that, for the later emperor, Charlemagne was a saint and a personal patron, able to confer political legitimacy.

between 795 and 812. In 800 the pope in Rome crowned him emperor of the west .

However, Frankish custom called for the royal domain to be partitioned. Charlemagne's father had divided it between his two sons – Charlemagne only inherited the whole when his brother died in 771 – and the new emperor likewise planned in 806 to partition his possessions among his three sons, a scheme frustrated only by the early death of two of them. This made it possible for the survivor, Louis the Pious (814-40), to inherit the whole empire. After his death, however, the treaty of Verdun (843) created three kingdoms: one in the east, one in the west, and a 'middle kingdom' which ran from the North Sea to Italy.

The Carolingians ruled through direct agents, rather than through Gallo-Roman bishops and counts as their predecessors had done; and throughout the 8th century these men generally remained loyal. After Charlemagne's death, however, their descendants tended to identify with the particular interests of their own localities, at the expense of the whole. Frankish hegemony in western Europe was thus disrupted by fragmentation just as it came under attack from the Vikings and Magyars.

1 Anglo-Saxon England, c. AD 800

Mercia and subordinate kingdoms under Offa (757–96)

allied with Mercia

British kingdoms

2 The empire of Charlemagne

Frankish realm 714

added to Frankish empire by 814

Frankish dependencies (with date of formation)

Frankish royal residences

archbishoprics

important monasteries

GASCONY 769 province with date of acquisition

Three separate groups of invaders in the 9th century shattered the relative stability achieved by Charlemagne in western Europe and by Offa of Mercia in England (page 52). The Saracens occupied the islands of the western Mediterranean and raided Italy and France; the Magyars of Hungary devastated northern Italy and Germany; the Vikings from Scandinavia not only plundered settlements around the European coast as far as the Mediterranean, but also created trade routes through Russia to Byzantium (page 56) and settled substantial parts of Britain, Ireland, northern France, Iceland and even Greenland.

The invasions disrupted royal authority and caused political fragmentation. In the Carolingian empire, the Frankish kings virtually capitulated to the Vikings, leaving defence to the local magnates who swiftly created their own power bases. In England, although determined resistance by Alfred the Great of Wessex (871-99) held the Danes at bay,

a second wave of Scandinavian invasions a century later proved irresistible. However in the eastern half of the Frankish empire, Otto I's defeat of the Magyars at the Lechfeld (955) proved a turning point, and Germany became the first country in Europe to recover from the invasions. This achievement assured its predominance in Europe for almost three centuries.

German rulers rarely sought to assert control over the west Frankish lands but, as heirs to the Carolingians, they claimed the imperial title and the right to rule over Italy and the lands of the former "middle kingdom" (page 53). In 962 Otto's coronation as emperor sealed the connection between Germany and Italy, and in 1034 his successors annexed Burgundy. However the emperors became increasingly dependent upon the wealth of Italy, and this embroiled Frederick I of Hohenstaufen (1152-90) with both the papacy and the populous fortified cities of the Lombard plain,

1 Viking, Magyar and Saracen invasions
→ Saracen attacks
→ Magyar attacks
→ Viking routes
● Viking bases
✹ main Viking raids (with dates)

areas affected by Saracen raiders (with dates)

areas most affected by Magyar raiders (with dates)

areas of Viking settlement:
Danish
Norwegian
Swedish

A carved wooden head from the Oseberg cart (c. 800) depicts a fearsome Viking warrior. Viking success was in large part achieved not through superior organization or tactical skill, but depended on their greater mobility. They were able to launch lightning attacks on undefended coastal settlements and penetrate far inland in shallow boats or on horseback.

which all saw Imperial power in Italy as a threat to their independence. The conquest of Sicily by Frederick's son Henry VI in 1194 made the Hohenstaufen the richest rulers in Europe; but the prospect of total encirclement once more alarmed the papacy and the Lombard towns, leading to a long and costly struggle with Henry's son Frederick II (1212-50). After his death, the Imperial position in Italy steadily deteriorated, and the last Hohenstaufen prince met defeat and death at the battle of Tagliacozzo in 1268.

Meanwhile, in Germany, the princes took advantage of their rulers' preoccupation with Italy both to consolidate their power and, on the eastern frontier, to direct a major expansion. The Slavs were driven out or enslaved, in favour of German settlers who, by 1250, had increased the German kingdom by about one-third and shifted its centre of gravity from the Rhine to the Elbe. The empire might no longer have been the strongest or richest polity in Europe, but it remained the largest.

2 The German empire to 1250

- eastward spread of German peasant settlement, 12th century
- German settlement, 1200–1250
- • city with over 10,000 inhabitants
- ⊙ member of Lombard Leagues of 1167 and 1226
- ◑ member of 1167 League only
- ◐ member of 1226 League only
- main royal routes
- → German invasions, 1190–94
- ⇢ Henry VI's Genoese and Pisan fleet, 1194
- ⌂ main Hohenstaufen palaces and castles
- ▲ monasteries

The first Russian state: Kievan Russia

Three factors shaped the early history of Russia: the eastward movement of Slav settlers; the impact of the Vikings (who were known to the Slavs as Varyagi or Varangians) from the north; and, most important of all, the division of the region into forests (in the north and centre) and treeless steppe (in the south). Before the arrival of the Vikings in the 9th century, the Slavs had begun to settle the central river basins, clearing the forests and living by agriculture, hunting, trapping and the fur trade, while nomadic tribes from Asia, such as the Pechenegs, occupied the grasslands of the south. At first the Slavs resisted the Varangians, but in 862 they called in 'Rurik the Viking' to protect them from Pecheneg raiders.

Since most of the rivers of Russia follow a north-south axis, great potential existed for trade between the Baltic and the Black Sea, and the Vikings sought to dominate and exploit these waterways and the territories adjoining them (map 2). Rurik therefore occupied Novgorod, and his followers soon pushed south to Smolensk and then down the Dnieper to Kiev (882). The principal trade route established by the Vikings ran from the Gulf of Finland up the river Neva, through Lake Ladoga to the river Volkhov, thence by portages to the Dnieper and on across the Black Sea to Byzantium.

Grand Prince Svyatoslav (962-72) campaigned to the south and east, greatly extending the frontiers of the Kievan state, which forged strong links with Byzantium, its chief trading partner; and from Byzantium it received the Christian faith during the reign of Vladimir Svyatoslav (980-1015). At the same time Kiev retained numerous connections with the West: one of Vladimir's granddaughters married the king of France, another the king of Hungary and a

A scene from Novgorod's victory over Suzdal in 1169. Novgorod was the capital of the Rus until Oleg moved his capital to Kiev in 882. In 1019 Iaroslav I granted Novgorod a charter of self-government, and thereafter the town elected its own prince. Grown rich on the trade in furs, Novgorod became pre-eminent in northern Russia. During the 12th century it came into conflict with the growing power of Vladimir-Suzdal to the south. However Novgorod defeated Vladimir-Suzdal in 1169 and 1216. It avoided the Mongol destruction and defeated the Germans and Swedes in 1240–2. A struggle for supremacy with Moscow in the 14th and 15th centuries saw the eclipse of Novgorod.

third the king of Norway. Half a century later, however, dynastic conflict and administrative inefficiency brought weakness and a new wave of Asiatic nomads, the Polovtsy, broke through the defences built by Svyatoslav and Vladimir. In 1093 they sacked Kiev itself.

A great northward exodus ensued to safer regions between the Oka and the Volga, where many new towns were founded (such as Vladimir, Suzdal, Rostov and Tver) and several new states developed – notably Vladimir-Suzdal, which included the fast growing commercial centre of Moscow (first mentioned in 1147), and Novgorod, which built up a fur-trading empire that reached to the Arctic and the Urals. Meanwhile, further south, Novgorod-Seversk, Vladimir-Volynsk and Galich broke away from Kievan rule (map 1).

Mongol invaders struck the final blow to the old order (page 60). In 1237-8, moving along the frozen rivers, they struck north and sacked the wealthy towns of Vladimir-Suzdal; in 1239-40 they advanced through southern Russia, systematically destroying settlements, including Kiev. Meanwhile Novgorod, although it escaped the Mongol onslaught as the onset of spring thawed the frozen rivers, faced repeated attacks by both Swedes and Germans in the Baltic region until Prince Alexander decisively defeated the former in 1240 on the river Neva (thus earning the title 'Nevsky') and the latter in 1242 on the ice of Lake Peipus. Despite these successes, however, even Novgorod had to recognize Mongol overlordship, exercised by the Golden Horde on the lower Volga, while the Lithuanian state expanded into the old Kievan heartland.

The Mongol invasion had other lasting economic, social and political effects. The destruction of so many towns decimated both trade and industry, while the elimination of the urban middle class smoothed the path of an autocracy which imitated its overlords in ruthless terror and extortion. The fall of Kiev destroyed the cultural centre of medieval Russia, with its rich Byzantine-based literature and art, while the Mongol forces, controlling the grasslands around the Caspian and the Black Sea, prevented almost all contact with Byzantium. Russia therefore inevitably developed a distinctive culture, society and political system of its own.

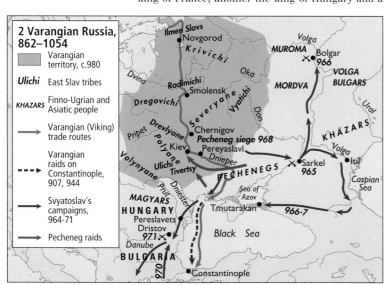

2 Varangian Russia, 862–1054

Varangian territory, c.980

Ulichi East Slav tribes

KHAZARS Finno-Ugrian and Asiatic people

→ Varangian (Viking) trade routes

---▶ Varangian raids on Constantinople, 907, 944

→ Svyatoslav's campaigns, 964-71

→ Pecheneg raids

Arctic Ocean

1 Kievan Russia, 964–1242

——— Kievan Russia, 1054	➔ campaigns of Svyatoslav, 964–71
Yatvagi tribes of the East Slavs	- - - waterway trade routes
MARI other peoples	∿∿∿ defensive works built against nomads
➔ movements of steppe nomads in the 11th century	♛ Russian principalities, c.1200

White Sea

Pechora

Pinega
Mezen
SAMOYED
Northern Dvina
Onega
YUGRA
PERM
Vychegda

KARELA
L. Onega
CHUD
Sukhona
VYATKA TERRITORY
L. Ladoga
Beloozero
Kama
Gulf of Finland
Storoyn
Neva Ladoga
Volkhov
Ves
Baltic Sea
Vod
ESTS
Ilmen
Galich
MARI

Gulf of Riga
L. Peipus
Yuriev
Slavs
Novgorod
L. Ilmen
Yaroslavl
Kostroma
KURS
Riga
Pskov
Izborsk
Lovat
Torzhok
Rostov
Merya
Nizhniy Novgorod
LIVONIAN ORDER
Kukeynovs
Tver
Pereyaslavl
VLADIMIR
-SUZDAL
ZHMUD
Gertsike
Polochanye
Toropets
Dmitrov
Suzdal
Kyazma
Polotsk
K
Moscow
Vladimir
Bolgar
966
Bilyar
TEUTONIC ORDER
Vitebsk
SMOLENSK
i
Mostvai
Murom
VOLGA BULGARIA
LITVA
Orsha
Smolensk
Golyad
e
Muroma
Suvar
POLOTSK
Kopys
v
Koselsk
Oka
Kolomna
Gorodno
Minsk
i
Ryazan
Meshchera
Yatvagi
Nesvizh
Klechesk
CHERNIGOV
c
Vyatichi
MORDVA
Berestye
Drogochin
TUROV
Radimichi
h
Bryansk
Novosil
MUROM
Volynyane
Pinsk
-PINSK
Rechitsa
Karachev
Desna
-RYAZAN
VLADIMIR-
Turov
1024
Listem
NOVGOROD-
Ural
Kholm
Vruchy
SEVERSK
VOLYNSK
Drevlyane
Lyubech
Novgorod-Severskiy
Vladimir
Korosten
Kursk
POLOVTSY
Cherven
Chernigov
Rylsk
(in 1054)
Belz
1036
KIEV
Gorodets
Severyane
eremyshl
Terebovl
Kiev
Pereyaslavl
966
GALICH
Galich
Polyane
PEREYASLAV
Kamenets
Rodiya
Ros
Donets
Kolomyya
Pereyaslavl
Don
POLOVTSY
Poltava
TORKI
Volga
Khorvaty
Tiversty
PECHENEGS
Donets
965
Peresechen
Prut
P
O
L
O
V
T
S
Y
SAKSINY
NGARIAN
Belgorod
Bug
965
Sarkel
KINGDOM
Dniester
Dnieper
KHAZARS
Carpathian Mts
Oleshe
Itil
Pereslavets
Sea of Azov
Dorostol
971
Sugdeya
Tmutarakan
Caspian Sea
970
Khersones (Korsun)
966-7
Kuma
BULGARIA
Black Sea
KASOGI
Tuban
YASI

Trade and empire in Africa

By the end of the first millennium AD great changes had taken place in Africa. The rise of a culture based on iron-working (page 26) led to the appearance of extensive states and empires based on trade. In the south, Zimbabwe, with its monumental stone buildings, exported gold and copper via the port of Sofala; in the west, the Kongo state carried on an important trade. Further north, Arab traders developed the trans-Saharan trade routes and so assisted the growth of major sub-Saharan states. Although Ghana rose to prominence before the Islamic era, its successors, Mali and Songhay, owed much of their wealth and culture – described in glowing terms by Arab travellers – to the impact of Islam. So did the Kanem-Bornu empire around Lake Chad and the Hausa city-states. In the east Arab merchant colonies also spread down the Swahili coast as far as Kilwa and Sofala, bringing this part of Africa into an Indian Ocean trading complex. The staple exports in all cases were gold, ivory and slaves (map 1).

The arrival of the Portuguese in the 15th century at first made little impact on Africa. Their immediate object was to share directly in the gold trade, previously dominated by Muslim middlemen; the slave trade remained a secondary interest. However, with the development of labour-intensive sugar-plantations in the Americas (page 86), the slave trade attracted others. By the 18th century, nine European states maintained almost 50 fortified trading posts on the west coast, from Arguim to Lagos, to handle this burgeoning commerce, while the Portuguese continued to export slaves further south from Angola and Mozambique. Of some 15 million Africans shipped abroad by Europeans between 1450 and 1870, almost 90 per cent went to South America and the Caribbean, most of them during the 18th century. Muslim traders exported perhaps as many more again northward across the Sahara and from the Swahili coast. The effects on Africa of this appalling trade in human beings are impossible to quantify, not least because the loss of population was not evenly divided. Some states, such as Kongo and Lunda, suffered disproportionately, while others seem to have profited. Thus, after the destruction of the powerful Songhay empire by Moroccan troops in 1591, the forest states of Asante, Dahomey and Benin, having direct access to the Atlantic and thus to European slave-traders, increased in importance and political power (map 2).

1 The emergence of states, 1000–1500

Islamic states or influence, 1000
Christian states, 1000
other states, 1000
new states by 1300
limit of Islamized areas, 1500
Christian Ethiopia, 1500
new states by 1500
IFAT states that disappeared by 1500
major gold producing region
■ Muslim settlement
gold   \ bananas
M musk   rice
slaves   cattle
C copper
salt
millet
ivory

Apart from the Portuguese in Angola and Mozambique, and the fortified posts along the west coast, only the Dutch attempted to create a European colony in Africa before 1800: in the far south, around Cape Town. In the north-east, Islam continued to spread, but the Christian kingdom of Ethiopia still held its own. In the north, the Ottoman empire (page 70) maintained only nominal suzerainty over the states from Morocco to Egypt. In 1800, almost all of Africa thus remained independent of foreign control: a world unto itself, the 'dark continent'. However, precisely because of its autonomy, it would lack the ability to compete with the technological dynamism of the West in the 19th century (page 110).

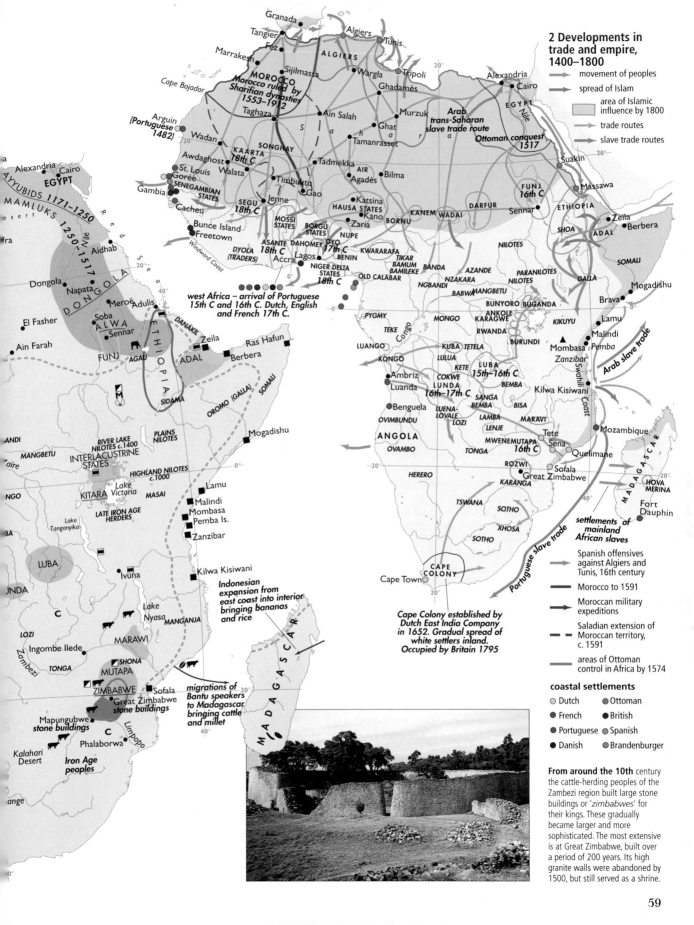

2 Developments in trade and empire, 1400–1800

→ movement of peoples
→ spread of Islam
▨ area of Islamic influence by 1800
→ trade routes
→ slave trade routes

Granada
Tangier
Algiers
Tunis
Marrakesh **Fez** **Sijilmassa** **ALGIERS**
Cape Bojador **MOROCCO** **Wargla** **Tripoli** **Alexandria** **Cairo**
Morocco ruled by Sharifian dynasties 1553–1912 **Ghadamès** **EGYPT**
Arguin (Portuguese 1482) **Ain Salah** **Murzuk** **Ottoman conquest 1517**
Wadan **Taghaza** **Ghat** **Arab trans-Saharan slave trade route**
SONGHAY **Tamanrasset**
Awdaghost **KAARTA 18th C** **Walata** **Tadmekka** **AIR** **Suakin**
St. Louis **Timbuktu** **Agades** **Bilma** **FUNJ 16th C** **Massawa**
Gorée **SENEGAMBIAN STATES** **Gao** **DARFUR** **ETHIOPIA** **Zeila**
Gambia **Cacheu** **SEGU 18th C** **Jenne** **HAUSA STATES** **Sennar** **SHOA** **ADAL** **Berbera**
Bunce Island **MOSSI STATES** **Kano** **BORNU** **KANEM WADAI** **NILOTES** **SOMALI**
Freetown **BORGU STATES** **Zaria** **GALLA** **Mogadishu**
ASANTE 18th C **DAHOMEY** **OYO 17th C** **NUPE** **KWARARAFA** **PARANILOTES** **Brava**
DYOLA (TRADERS) **Accra** **Lagos** **BENIN** **TIKAR BAMUM BAMILEKE** **BANDA** **NZAKARA** **NILOTES** **Lamu**
NIGER DELTA STATES 18th C **OLD CALABAR** **NGBANDI** **MANGBETU** **KIKUYU** **Malindi**
west Africa – arrival of Portuguese 15th C and 16th C. Dutch, English and French 17th C. **BABWA** **BUNYORO BUGANDA** **Mombasa** **Pemba**
PYGMY **MONGO** **ANKOLE KARAGWE** **Zanzibar**
TEKE **RWANDA BURUNDI** **Kilwa Kisiwani**
LUANGO **KUBA TETELA** **LUBA 15th–16th C**
KONGO **LULUA KETE** **BEMBA**
Ambriz **COKWE** **SANGA BEMBA** **BISA**
Luanda **LUNDA 16th–17th C** **LUENA-LOVALE LOZI** **MARAVI**
Benguela **OVIMBUNDU** **LAMBA LENJE** **Mozambique**
ANGOLA **MWENEMUTAPA 16th C** **Tete Sena**
OVAMBO **TONGA** **Quelimane**
HERERO **ROZWI** **Sofala**
Great Zimbabwe **KARANGA**
TSWANA **SOTHO**
CAPE COLONY **XHOSA** **SOTHO**
Cape Town

Cape Colony established by Dutch East India Company in 1652. Gradual spread of white settlers inland. Occupied by Britain 1795

Alexandria **Cairo**
EGYPT
AYYUBIDS 1171–1250
MAMLUKS 1250–1517
Aidhab
Dongola **DONGOLA**
Napata
El Fasher **Meroë** **Adulis**
Soba **ALWA** **Zeila**
Ain Farah **Sennar** **Berbera** **Ras Hafun**
FUNJ **AGAU** **ADAL**
ETHIOPIA
SIDAMA **SOMALI**
OROMO (GALLA)
ANDI **Mogadishu**
MANGBETU **RIVER LAKE NILOTES c.1400** **PLAINS NILOTES**
aire **INTERLACUSTRINE STATES** **HIGHLAND NILOTES c.1000**
NGO **KITARA** **Lake Victoria** **MASAI** **Lamu**
Lake Tanganyika **LATE IRON AGE HERDERS** **Malindi**
BA **Mombasa**
Pemba Is.
LUBA **Zanzibar**
JNDA
Ivuna **Kilwa Kisiwani**
LOZI **Lake Nyasa**
Zambezi **MANGANJA** **Indonesian expansion from east coast into interior bringing bananas and rice**
Ingombe Ilede **MARAWI**
TONGA **SHONA**
MUTAPA
ZIMBABWE **Sofala**
Great Zimbabwe stone buildings **migrations of Bantu speakers to Madagascar bringing cattle and millet**
Mapungubwe stone buildings **C**
Phalaborwa **Limpopo**
Kalahari Desert **Iron Age peoples**
ange

MADAGASCAR
HOVA MERINA
Fort Dauphin

settlements of mainland African slaves

→ Spanish offensives against Algiers and Tunis, 16th century
━ Morocco to 1591
➤ Moroccan military expeditions
┅ Saladian extension of Moroccan territory, c. 1591
→ areas of Ottoman control in Africa by 1574

coastal settlements
- ○ Dutch
- ● French
- ● Portuguese
- ● Danish
- ● Ottoman
- ● British
- ○ Spanish
- ● Brandenburger

From around the 10th century the cattle-herding peoples of the Zambezi region built large stone buildings or *'zimbabwes'* for their kings. These gradually became larger and more sophisticated. The most extensive is at Great Zimbabwe, built over a period of 200 years. Its high granite walls were abandoned by 1500, but still served as a shrine.

1206–1696
The Mongol empire

The Mongols, a nomadic people from the grasslands of Central Asia, staged a sudden and devastating irruption into world history in the first half of the 13th century (map 1). Theirs was not the first empire of the steppe, however. In the 7th century AD, in the wake of the upheavals that destroyed the ancient world (page 40), a confederation of Turkish tribes had managed to dominate the plains of Asia from the Great Wall of China to the Black Sea; but by 750 their rule had collapsed and the area disintegrated into feud and faction. Thus it remained for four centuries, when a charismatic leader, Temujin (1167-1227), gained recognition as supreme ruler and in 1206 took the title Genghis Khan, 'prince of all that lies between the Oceans'. Under his leadership the Mongols first invaded the Chin empire in north China and then turned against the Islamic states to the west. By the time of Genghis's death, his empire stretched from the Pacific Ocean to the Caspian Sea. His successors continued the tide of destructive conquests: Kievan Russia (1237-40); the Abbasid Caliphate (1256-60); Sung China (1271-9). Europe and Japan were also threatened: one Mongol army reached the gates of Vienna while another defeated a German-Polish army at Liegnitz in 1241; two amphibious expeditions unsuccessfully attacked Japan in 1274 and 1281.

However the vast empire lacked coherence and stability, and the Mongols failed to develop appropriate institutions. On hearing of the death of Genghis's successor Ogedei in 1241, the victorious commander of the Mongol forces in Europe withdrew eastwards with his army, in order to take part in choosing a successor. They never returned. Likewise in 1260, on

Mongol brutality in war did not end with Genghis Khan. In this late-16th century Mughal miniature (right), the troops of Tamerlane are shown demolishing the fort of Mikrit in the Hindu Kush, and using the defenders' heads to erect a tower of skulls.

2 The conquests of Tamerlane, c. 1360–1405

1 The Mongol empire

———	the Mongol empire by 1259
→→→	campaigns under Genghis Khan
➡➡➡	campaigns of his successors
⊪⊪⊪	Mongol incursions and limited Mongol control
OIROTS	Mongol tribes around 1220
———	empire of Kublai Khan, 1260–94
CUMANS	other peoples

unsuccessful expedition to Java 1292–3

hearing of the death of Ogedei's successor, the victorious commander of the Mongol forces in the Near East decided to return to the Mongol heartland, leaving only a skeleton force behind him. This soon became known in Cairo, and the Sultan of Egypt marched to the defence of Islam, still reeling from the sack of Baghdad, the capital of the Caliphs, two years before. At Ain Jalut on 3 September 1260 the Mongols suffered a defeat and withdrew to Persia.

The Mongol empire now fragmented. The title of Great Khan went to Kublai who, although never forgetting that he was the grandson of Genghis, spent most of his long reign (1260–94) seeking to reunify China and conquer Japan. The other Mongol states – the Golden Horde in the west; the Il-Khans in Persia; the Chagatai empire in the traditional Mongol heartland – went their own way.

Despite the widespread destruction of the Mongol onslaught, their temporary unification of Eurasia permitted the exchange of goods and ideas between the far east and the far west on an unprecedented scale.

For over a century the 'Silk Road' of ancient times revived: silver and gold from Europe and the Near East reached China while Chinese silks and porcelain circulated in Europe. But the Black Death (see page 66) and the rise of Timur, or Tamerlane, (1336-1405) changed all that, for he destroyed the Chagatai khanate, dislocated the Golden Horde, defeated the Ottoman empire at the battle of Ankara in 1402 (page 70), and initiated a policy of religious intolerance. However Timur died in 1405 before he had created the institutions and traditions required to ensure the survival of his vast empire (map 2). Instead, Mongol power in the west steadily lost ground to Russia (see page 84), and crumbled in China with the rise of the Ming dynasty (see page 94). Mongolia itself came under Chinese dominion in 1696.

The Muslim empires of India and Persia

Delhi, founded in the 8th century by a Rajput chief, remained the focus of north Indian politics and also the centre of Muslim culture from the 13th to the 19th century. It served as the capital of the six Muslim dynasties, all of Turkish or Afghan extraction, who sought (unsuccessfully) to extend their rule into the Deccan between 1206 and 1526; and, after the defeat of the last of the Sultans of Delhi at Panipat (1526) by Babur – a descendant of Timur (page 60) – it became the headquarters of his descendants, the Mughals.

Babur's grandson, Akbar (1556-1605), extended the frontiers of the empire to Bengal in the east, to Gujerat and the river Godavari in the south, and to Kashmir in the north. New territories were added under Akbar's grandson, Shahjahan (1627-56) and his son Aurangzeb (1656-1707), who annexed Bijapur and Golconda in the south, and Orissa in the east. However, these achievements depended absolutely upon the acquiescence of the 150 million or so Hindu peasant farmers and petty landlords who paid the taxes that supported the Mughals' 4 million warriors, and the court grandees who commanded them. It was a delicate balance, for if the peasants and landlords were overtaxed, they would revolt; and if the grandees were not rewarded with office and wealth they would desert the court. Around 1700 the Hindu Marathas began to ravage southern regions, while some Rajput states and the Sikhs rebelled. All this reduced tax yields, and after the death of Aurangzeb several frontier provinces split off from the empire (page 96).

Meanwhile, to the West, after 1500 the leader of a fanatical sect of Shi'a Muslims, Ismail Safavi, re-unified Persia – which had been in a state of chaos since Timur's invasions – and proclaimed himself Shah. However the Sunnite Ottomans under Selim I (page 70) invaded in 1514, defeated Ismail at the battle of Chaldiran and captured Tabriz, thus initiating a duel between the two powers that lasted for over a century. The conflict centred around the key cities of Mesopotamia, and Baghdad, Tiflis, Derbend and Basra changed hands repeatedly; but its intensity stemmed from the religious division within Islam between Sunnite and Shi'ite (page 50), which excited the same passions as the split between Protestant

and Catholic Christians at the same time. Eventually Shah Abbas (1587-1629), with assistance from both Russia and the Christian West, managed to regain most of the lost territories; but the Turks recaptured much of Mesopotamia in the 1630s.

Both empires boasted a rich civilization. Akbar and Abbas each built luxurious new capital cities – at Fatehpur Sikri and Isfahan respectively – and attracted to their courts local and foreign writers, artists and craftsmen. Shahjahan built the magnificent Taj Mahal outside Delhi. Nevertheless, two developments threatened these achievements. On the one hand, as in all autocracies, government authority could suddenly collapse under a weak ruler. Thus in 1739 Nadir Shah, who had usurped the Persian throne three years previously, invaded India and sacked Delhi, leaving the Mughal empire fatally weakened; but in 1747 Nadir was assassinated and Persia too suffered a period of anarchy. On the other

Aral Sea

Urgench

Khiva

Syr Darya

Tashkent

Khokand

UZBEK KHANATE

KHANATE OF KASHGAR

Kashgar

Bukhara

Amu Darya

Samarkand

Merv

Balkh

Much of the early part of Akbar's reign was spent in the conquest of the Hindu Rajputs, who were to become important allies of the Mughals. In this typically sumptuous miniature of 1569, Surjan Hara, ruler of the fort of Ranthanbhur, submits to Akbar, offering him the keys to the fort and many gifts.

Meshed

Nishapur
*1588–9
Safavid conquests*

Herat *1506, 1588–9*

Kabul
Mughal conquest 1504

Attock

Khyber Pass
Peshawar

KASHMIR

SIKHS

LAHORE

Lahore

T I B E T

P E R S I A

Kandahar

Hindu Kush

Indus

Multan

Kerman

Multan

MULTAN

*Panipat
1526*

Samana

Delhi

SATAMIS

DELHI
Mughal conquest 1504

Himalayas

Agra

Fatehpur Sikri

Biana
Gwalior

JATS
OUDH

Lucknow

Bandar
Abbas
1551

Ormuz
*(Portuguese
1515–1622)*

BALUCHISTAN

**(TATTA)
SIND**

AJMER

Ajmer
Hindaun

Ganges

Allahabad

Benares

(RAJPUTANA)

RAJPUTS

Jodhpur

ALLAHABAD

Brahmaputra

Patna

KUTCH

Rajmahal

BIHAR

Kasimbazar

Dacca

*Gulf of
Arabia*

Muscat *1551*

Sarkhej

Ahmadabad

Cambay

Baroda

MALWA

Narmada

I N D I A

Plassey

BENGAL

GUJERAT

Diu *1538
(Portuguese)*

Broach

KHANDESH

Surat

Asirgarh

Nagpur

Pipli

Assaye

D e c c a n

BERAR

Bay of
Bengal

Daulatabad

Ahmadnagar

Poona
Janjira

AHMADNAGAR

MARATHAS

Dabhoi

Satara

Golconda

Hyderabad

Godavari

Vizagapatam

ORISSA

Rajapur

Kolhapur

Bijapur

GOLCONDA

Krishna

Nizampatam
(Petapoli)

Vengurla

Goa
(Portuguese 1509)

BIJAPUR

Vijayanagar

Nellore

Chandragiri

Madras
Saint Thomé

Bhatkal

Mangalore

MYSORE

Calicut

Mysore

Tanjore

Madurai

Quilon

Kayal
Tuticorin

Ceylon

1 The Safavid and Mughal empires

extent of Mughal empire

   at Akbar's death, 1605

   under Shahjahan, 1627–56

   under Aurangzeb, c. 1700

extent of Safavid empire

——— at the death of Abbas the Great, 1629

Ottoman conquests from Safavids

   conquests of Suleiman I, 1520–66

●   conquest of town with date

   from 1566–1639

hand, the armed forces of various European states established themselves around the fringes of the empires. In the north, the Russians in the 1550s advanced to the mouth of the Volga (page 84), gaining access to the Caspian. In the south, the Portuguese created fortified bases around the Indian Ocean in the early 16th century, followed after 1600 by the Dutch, English and French. Although the number of Europeans in each enclave remained relatively small, they served corporate entities – the East India Companies – that never died. Whenever Mughal or Safavid control faltered, the Europeans stood poised to take advantage (page 96).

South East Asia

Situated at one of the world's main cross-roads, civilization developed early in South-East Asia: traces of 'Java man' date from the middle Pleistocene and remains of *homo sapiens* from c. 40,000 BC; rice cultivation in South China began about 6000 BC and bronze working in Thailand and Vietnam in 1500 BC or earlier (pages 12 and 18). Early trade routes linked India with ports along the coasts of Burma, Thailand, Cambodia and Vietnam; Hindu-Buddhist influences from India reached the area around the 2nd or 3rd century AD; and by the 5th century Buddhist images and votive tablets appeared, along with Sanskrit inscriptions. These influences never obliterated the unique character of South-East Asian civilization; instead, the next thousand years saw their assimilation to produce distinctive societies in the area. The culture of Java and southern Sumatra likewise became Indianized, but these areas also developed commercial and political links with China, which welcomed tribute missions from a growing number of states. From the 8th century temple complexes, each combining Hindu and Buddhist influences, evolved in four main areas: central Java (notably at Borobudur and Prambanan, from the 8th to 10th centuries), Cambodia (especially at Angkor, from the 9th to 13th centuries), Burma (Pagan, from the 11th to 13th centuries) and, associated with the Hindu-Buddhist

kingdom of Champa, along the coast of central Vietnam. Meanwhile Palembang (a centre of Sanskrit culture from perhaps as early as the 7th century) emerged as the capital of the maritime empire of Srivijaya, which for centuries controlled international trade passing through the straits of Malacca and Sunda, and across the Isthmus of Kra (map 1).

The great temple-states fell into decline after the 12th century. In Java, the area of Prambanan was superseded in importance by eastern Java, where three states developed in succession: Kediri (12th century), Singhasari (13th century) and finally Majapahit (late 13th-early 16th century). On the mainland, first Mongols and then Shans sacked Pagan in the 13th century, while Angkor fell to Thai attacks after 1369. Sukothai, the first of the lowland Thai cities, was itself in decline by the late 14th century. New political centres replaced the old temple cities: in Burma, Toungoo (1347), Ava (1364), and Pegu (1369), capital of a new Mon kingdom in the south; in Thailand, Chieng Mai (1296) and Ayutthaya (1350); in Cambodia, Phnom Penh and other cities along the Mekong; in Laos, Luang Prabang (1353). All were Theravada Buddhist in the Sinhalese tradition, with stupas rather than temples. Meanwhile, in Vietnam, after the failure of Chinese attempts at reconquest (despite invasions in 1075-7 and 1285-8) a

2 Cultural divisions southeast Asia, 1500

distribution of major religions:

- Theravada Buddhism
- Mahayana Buddhism mixed with Confucianism and Taoism
- Hindu-Buddhism
- Islamic states
- places sending tribute to China between 1370 and 1440

Halin
Ava
Pagan
Beikthano
KINGDOM OF PAGAN
11th–16th centuries
Sri Ksetra
Toungoo
PYU KINGDOM
Pegu
Thaton
Chieng Mai
Luang Prabang
LAO KINGDOMS
VIETNAM
from 1471
KINGDOM OF SUKHOTHAI
Sukhothai
Si Thep
Phimai
MON KINGDOMS
8th–17th centuries
U-Thong
Nakhon Pathom
Ku Bua
Ayutthaya
Tonle Sap
(Great Lake)
Angkor Preah Khan
Mi Son
Dong Duong
Tra Kieu
Vijaya
CHAMPA PRINCIPALITIES
4th–15th centuries
Po Nagar (Nha Trang)
KHMER KINGDOM
7th–15th centuries
KINGDOM OF AYUTTHAYA
Phnom Penh
Angkor Borei
Mekong
Po Klaung Gerai
Chaiya
Oc Eo
Takuapa
Ko Kho Khao
Ligor
Aceh
Straits of Malacca
Malacca
Sumatra
South China Sea
Manila
Philippines
JOLO SULTANATE
from 14th century
Celebes Sea
Borneo
Ternate
Tidore
SULTANATES OF TERNATE AND TIDORE
from 14th century
SRI VIJAYA
7th–13th centuries
Sri Vijaya
Celebes
Java Sea
MAJAPAHIT EMPIRE
14th–16th centuries
Straits of Sunda
Dieng Plateau
Borobudur
Prambanan
SALENDRA KINGDOM
8th–10th centuries
Trowulan
Singhasari
Kediri
Java

new kingdom, called Dai Viet, emerged and gradually absorbed Champa (annexing its capital, Vijaya, in 1471). Further south, Srivijaya declined and a powerful new Muslim state developed after 1400 at Malacca, commanding the narrow straits through which most east-west trade passed. By that time the east Javanese empire of Majapahit was in decline, and the west Javanese kingdom of Pajajaran also collapsed before Muslim pressure from the northern coastal ports in the early 16th century.

Islam had began to influence northern Sumatra just before 1300; now it spread further, often under Malaccan influence, to the north Javanese trading ports, the Spice Islands, Borneo and, in the 16th century, the Philippines (map 2). When the Spaniards arrived, Mindanao had already been converted and the spread of Islam in Luzon was only halted by the Spaniards' capture of the Muslim fort at Manila in 1571 and their determined promotion of Christianity (page 80).

Meanwhile, in Vietnam, Confucian scholarship strengthened, despite the failure of another attempt at reconquest under the Ming; and all over South-East Asia the series of voyages made by the Muslim admiral Cheng Ho in the early 15th century revived and reinforced China's system of tributary relationships (page 74). From the 1430s, however, China abandoned its interest in the wider world and South-East Asia began to assume its modern pattern of cultures and polities which even the arrival of the Europeans, starting with the Portuguese capture of Malacca in 1511 (page 80) influenced little until the 19th century.

Prambanan was built in the mid-9th century and was the largest and most ambitious temple complex ever constructed in central Java. There are three main temples dedicated to the gods of the Trimurti: Shiva in the centre; Vishnu on the north side; and Brahma on the south.

The 14th century brought to an end the rise and consolidation of national monarchies in western Europe (page 54). Though growth in population and productivity was steady until the later 13th century, both began to decline thereafter. Part of the problem lay in a sudden climatic deterioration which terminated the agricultural boom that had prevailed since 1150: crop yields fell and marginal areas brought into cultivation were abandoned. In 1315-17 Europe experienced the first of many famines; and the weakening of human powers of resistance through inadequate nourishment may have accelerated the spread of the 'Black Death', or bubonic plague, which killed perhaps 20 million Europeans between 1346 and 1353, wiping out in some areas as much as a third of the population within two years (map 1).

However, the impact of the plague was not even. Some areas escaped altogether, and Eastern Europe seems to have suffered relatively little: Bohemia under Charles IV (1333-78), Poland under Casimir III (1339-70) and Hungary under Louis the Great (1342-82) all made rapid strides – aided in part by skillful exploitation of their natural resources, such as the silver mines of Kutna Hora in Bohemia. Above all, in the wake of the Mongol invasions (page 60) Lithuania expanded into the former heartland of Kievan Russia and united in 1386 with Poland to form the largest state in Eastern Europe (map 2).

1 Famine, plague and popular unrest

— main sea-trade routes

| wine | important commodities

extent of the spread of the Black Death

1346	end 1349
1347	1350
mid-1348	c. 1351
end 1348	c. 1353
mid-1349	little or no plague mortality

social unrest

areas of disturbance during Peasants' Revolt in England, 1381

● centre of urban revolt

▭ rural uprisings

⊗ defeat of lower orders in battle

religious unrest

▭ spread of Lollardy in England to death of Richard II, 1399

▥ area of Hussite influence

■ Hussite centre

2 Eastern Europe, 1278–1389

growth of Lithuania, 1300-1377:

| to 1300 |
| under Gedymin, 1316–41 |
| under Olgierd, 1345–77 |
| under Jagiello and Witold from 1377 |
| — Poland-Lithuania after union of 1386 |
| Habsburg lands |
| Bohemian lands |

Unlike famine, plague affected every social class, and the psychological impact was profound. Until the mid-17th century, scarcely a decade passed without a recurrent outbreak. The disease, spread by infected fleas carried by rats, was particularly virulent, and few who caught it ever recovered. This illustration *(left)* from the Stiny Codex shows death strangling a plague victim.

But elsewhere the setback proved more serious. All the western states had overextended themselves financially, and the economic and demographic crisis exacerbated by the Black Death – combined with the tensions caused by the fragmentation of Italy and Germany after the end of Hohenstaufen rule in 1250 (page 55) or the Hundred Years' War between England and France – produced a series of popular uprisings in both cities and the countryside: the Jacquerie (1358) in France; the Peasants' Revolt (1381) in England; urban insurrections in Spain, Italy and the Low Countries. Few rebellions achieved their aims, but they all weakened state power even further.

China and Japan

Hami

The Mongol invasion of China caused immense destruction. During the conquest of the north (1211-34: page 60) much of the land went out of cultivation, many cities and industries perished, and countless people died or became slaves. The conquest of the south (1271-9) brought similar hardships, and Mongol rule proved harsh. Popular resentment erupted in a wave of popular uprisings after 1335, exacerbated by disastrous floods in coastal regions in the 1350s. One of the rebel leaders, Chu Yüan-chang, gradually overcame his rivals and in 1368 established a new dynasty, the Ming.

The Ming rebuilt irrigation and drainage works in great numbers, reforested on a grand scale, and moved vast numbers of people to repopulate the devastated north. New crops were introduced and the canal system extended to transport produce: by 1421 the 'Grand Canal' stretched from Hang-chou to just south of Peking and carried some 200,000 tons of grain northwards every year. Thanks to these measures, the Chinese population rose from some 60 million in 1393 (40 per cent fewer than a century before) to about 130 million by 1580. The great cities of the Yangtze delta became major industrial centres, particularly for textiles, while the southern ports fitted out the enormous fleets sent by Chu's son, the Yung-lo emperor (1402-24), to the South China Sea and the Indian Ocean (page 74).

The Ming entrusted control over the vast population to a gentry class of degree-holders, who had passed through the examination system and shared the values of the bureaucracy without actually holding office. But the system discouraged innovation and was overcentralized, with all major decisions dependent upon the emperor; and few of Yung-lo's successors possessed the dedication necessary for such heavy responsibilities. Nevertheless, the early Ming engaged in an aggressive foreign policy. They restored Korea to vassal status in 1392, occupied Annam from 1407 to 1427, and invaded Mongolia (map 1). However, after a northern campaign in 1449 resulted in the capture of the emperor, the Ming reverted to a defensive strategy, strengthening the Great Wall until it ran for almost 2,500 miles, and increasing the garrisons in the north and north-west. China remained relatively stable for another century, but in the 1430s the government banned all overseas trade by sea, except under close supervision. Not surprisingly, by 1500 smuggling had become commonplace in the south-eastern provinces and by 1550 heavily-armed bands of smugglers and pirates infested the seas around China and terrorized the coastal regions from their bases in Japan.

Central authority in Japan had collapsed in the 1330s and the country became plagued by local and provincial wars – almost continuously in the century after 1467. By about 1560, some nine leading families had formed alliances that covered most of the country, and competed openly for supreme power (map 2). In 1568 Nobunaga, leader of the Oda clan, captured Kyoto, the imperial capital, and by the time he was assassinated in 1582 by a jealous rival he had forced almost all the other lords to accept his orders. Within a decade, his ablest general Toyotomi Hideyoshi had completely reunified Japan, reorganizing the tax system and redistributing land to provide sufficient funds for his ambitious policies – including the invasion of Korea in the 1590s. After his death in 1598 another of Nobunaga's generals, Tokugawa Ieyasu, assumed power and in 1603 established the dynasty of shoguns who ruled Japan until the 19th century (page 88).

The Tokugawa put an end to the pirate problem, thus easing the pressure on the Chinese coast; but at just this time a new threat arose in the north-east, where the Manchu gradually expanded their power into the areas immediately to the north of the Great Wall and (in 1637) into Korea. Ming authority now

Sha-cho

Li-chiang

Ta-li
T'eng-yüeh
Meng-hua

B U R M A

Y U N N A N

Mekong

A N [V I

S I A M

2 Civil War in Japan, 1467–1590

spheres of influence of the most powerful Daimyo clans

boundaries of Daimyo domains

Uesugi

Takeda

Hojo

Oda

Sea of Japan

Kyoto
Nara

Imagawa

Mori

Sogabe

Otomo

Shimazu

Pacific Ocean

1 Ming China

- **——** major post roads
- **——** minor roads
- **⌐⌐⌐** Great Wall
- **——** Grand Canal
- **⊡** national capital
- **⊙** provincial capitals
- **☐** the nine frontier defence areas
- **○** prefectures and regional military commissioners
- **⚑** guard units
- **➜** attacks by pirates based in Japan before 1600
- Japanese invasions of Korea in 1590s

expeditions of Yung-lo against the Mongols:
- **——** 1st 1410
- **- - -** 2nd 1414
- **-·-·-** 3rd 1422
- **·····** 4th 1424

The 'Willow Palisade' surrounding area of Chinese settlement in Liao-tung.

Ming counter-attacks to defend Korea, 1592, 1597–8

Japanese invasions of Korea under Toyotomi Hideyoshi, 1592, 1597–8

Chu Yüan-chang (1328–98), founder of the Ming dynasty. In 1368 he proclaimed himself the founder of a new imperial dynasty, taking the title Hung-wu, meaning 'mightily martial'.

collapsed. After 1627 a wave of rebellions broke out in the wake of repeated crop failures in the north-west, and much of central and northern China soon came under rebel sway. In 1644, one of the rebel leaders captured Peking and the last Ming emperor committed suicide. Almost immediately the Manchus intervened, seized Peking, and began the conquest of China (page 94).

The Ottoman empire

The overthrow of the Abbasid Caliphate by the Mongols in 1256-60 (page 60) left the Muslim world in disarray for half a century. One of the centres of recovery lay in north-west Anatolia where, around 1300, a Turkish leader named Osman founded a state which became the core of the future Ottoman empire (map 1). The damage to the structure of the Byzantine empire caused by the Fourth Crusade in 1204 (page 48) facilitated the Ottomans' rapid advance in the 14th century. By 1354 the Turks had crossed the Dardanelles to Gallipoli, and their victories at Kosovo (1389) and Nicopolis (1396) left them masters of the Balkans. The invasion of Timur (page 61) and his destruction of the Turkish army at Ankara (1402) gave the hard-pressed Byzantine empire some respite, but the renewal of expansion under Murad II (1413-51) and Mohammed II (1451-81) sealed its fate. In 1453 Constantinople fell, and Mohammed went on to extend control over Moldavia, the Crimea and Trebizond, thereby turning the Black Sea into an Ottoman lake.

Selim I (1512-20) defeated the new Safavid rulers of Persia (page 62) and conquered the Mamlukes, and his son Suleiman the Magnificent (1520-66) annexed much of Hungary and besieged Vienna (1529), making the Ottoman empire one of the world's largest powers. It now extended over one million square miles, with some 14 million inhabitants; and its capital, Istanbul, had become the largest city in Europe with 500,000 inhabitants. Suleiman's son, Selim II managed to add Cyprus (1570-1) and Tunis (1574), although his fleet of galleys met with defeat at the hands of a Christian coalition at Lepanto (1571). However the wars of his successors against Persia (1578-90 and 1607-39) and against the Austrian Habsburgs (1593-1606) resulted in the loss of the Caucasus to the former and of annual tribute for Hungary from the latter.

The end of expansion, coupled with rapid price inflation (from 1584), a rising population and a static economy provoked a spate of popular and military uprisings between 1596 and 1610 in the Anatolian heartland of the empire (map 2). Nevertheless, Mesopotamia was regained from Persia in the 1630s and Crete conquered from the Venetians in the 1660s; and in 1683 a great army laid siege once more to Vienna. But it failed, and a Christian counter-attack drove the Turks out of Hungary by 1699 – although the Turks still remained a formidable power, controlling the entire Arab world east of Libya and most of the Balkans until the 19th century.

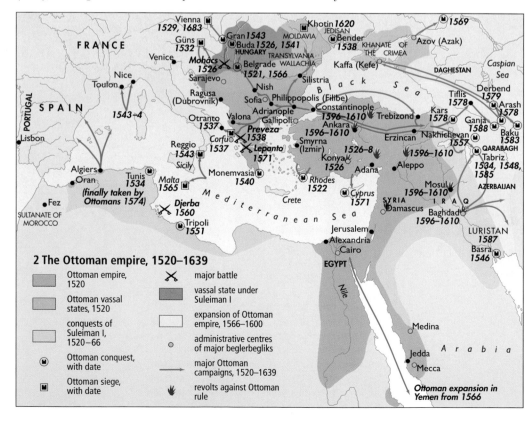

2 The Ottoman empire, 1520–1639

- Ottoman empire, 1520
- Ottoman vassal states, 1520
- conquests of Suleiman I, 1520–66
- ◉ Ottoman conquest, with date
- ▣ Ottoman siege, with date
- ✕ major battle
- vassal state under Suleiman I
- expansion of Ottoman empire, 1566–1600
- ○ administrative centres of major beglerbegliks
- → major Ottoman campaigns, 1520–1639
- ♦ revolts against Ottoman rule

Ottoman expansion in Yemen from 1566

1 The rise of the Ottoman empire, 1301–1520

- probable extent of Ottoman state, c. 1300
- conquests of Osman, c. 1300–26
- conquests of Orkhan, 1326–62
- conquests of Murad I, 1362–89
- **TEKE 1390** absorbed Emirates with date of first absorption
- conquests of Bayezid, 1389–1402
- ✕ major battles
- *1398* dates of Ottoman control
- Venetian territories, 1510
- ◉ successive centres of Ottoman state, with dates of conquest
- reduced frontiers of Ottoman state after Tamerlane's invasion and civil war of 1403–13
- ● Emirates restored by Tamerlane, 1402
- 1427 final reincorporation into Ottoman empire
- boundary of Ottoman state at the accession of Mehmed II, 1451
- vassal states, 1512
- Ottoman empire, 1512
- western frontiers of Safavid state, c. 1512 including tributary states
- Ottoman sphere of influence, c. 1520

The fall of Constantinople, in 1453, came as no surprise to observers in the east. Sultan Mehmet II had managed to close the Bosphorus by building castles at its narrowest point; the city was now cut off from western naval assistance and from its traditional sources of food and supply. When the final siege began, on 6 April, there were only some 7000 Christian defenders facing and Ottoman army of more than 80,000. On 29 May a final assault took the city within a few hours.

Precolumbian America

Two major civilizations confronted the Spaniards when they arrived on the American mainland in the early 16th century: the Aztec Empire in Mexico, with a subject population of perhaps 12 million, and the Inca empire in Peru, ruling some 6 million. The rest of the continent remained sparsely inhabited – perhaps 1 million people lived north of the Rio Grande with another million in the rest of South America – divided among more than a thousand small tribal societies with distinct languages. Few regions, particularly in the north, had reached the stage of settled agriculture, despite some contacts in the north-east with Europeans around the year 1000 (map 1).

The Aztec and Inca Empires differed markedly in character, and no evidence exists of any contact between them. Like the Toltecs, who between 968 and about 1170 controlled much of the valley of Mexico from their capital at Tula, the Aztecs came from the north. In 1325 they arrived in the valley and settled on a group of islands in the swampy margins of Lake Texcoco, where they built their capital,

Tenochtitlán (site of Mexico City). Serving at first as mercenary warriors for neighbouring towns, by 1428 they had overthrown them all and, led by a priest-king and an hereditary warrior aristocracy, embarked upon an ambitious programme of conquest. When the Spaniards arrived in 1519, the Aztecs controlled the greater part of Mexico and had entered Maya territory in Yucatán (map 2).

The Inca formed one of the numerous tribes of Quechua stock inhabiting the central Andes, but until the accession of Pachacuti Inca in 1438 they played only a minor role. Within 45 years, however, Pachacuti's conquests extended Inca control from Lake Titicaca to Huánaco in the north, while his son Topa pushed north into Ecuador and south to Chile, and from the Pacific coast to the Upper Amazon. This created an empire 200 miles wide and 2500 miles long, held together by an impressive system of highways, post-stations and relay runners (map 3).

The Incas created a genuine imperial system, with an hereditary dynasty of absolute, 'divine' Incas, a Quechua aristocracy, and a highly trained bureaucracy. All land was state-owned, with a complex system of irrigation. The ordinary Inca subject spent 9 months working for the state, but in return received protection from

2 The Aztec empire to 1519

- Post-Classic Maya area
- area of Aztec domination, 1519
- → Post-Classic trading routes

famine (through state-owned food stores) and support during sickness and old age. The Aztec Empire, on the other hand, exercised harsh military dominion over vassal peoples who enjoyed political autonomy provided they paid heavy tribute to Tenochtitlán in food, textiles and other goods – increasingly in humans for ritual sacrifice to the Aztec gods (up to 50,000 a year by 1510). These demands help to explain why so many people in the valley of Mexico welcomed the Spaniards, just as a recent succession dispute provided allies for the European invaders in Peru. Although both the Aztec and Inca polities expanded faster than any 15th-century state in Latin Christendom, neither empire proved as stable as it seemed. Mexico fell to a force spearheaded by under 2,000 Europeans in 1519-22, Peru to a band of less than 200 in 1531-3 (see page 86).

An Aztec or Mixtec sacrificial knife. The Aztecs believed that the continuation of human society required that the sun and earth be nourished with human blood and hearts. War was necessary to provide the sacrificial victims, whose hearts were removed with knives such as this. It is 12 inches long with an inlaid handle in the form of a warrior costumed as an eagle, or *quauhtli*, which was also a name for the sun.

1 North America to AD 1000

- Hopewell core territory, 300 BC – AD 550
- principal areas of Hopewell influence
- ▲ Adena site, 1000 BC – AD 550
- ▲ Hopewell site, 100 BC – AD 550
- ▲ Mississippian site from AD 800
- △ other sites
- ▲ Viking colony

Gull Lake
Ruby
Tiburon Hills
first Pueblos built c. 700
Mesa Verde *cliff houses*
Chaco Canyon
Snaketown
Swarts
Casas Grandes
Sierra de San Francisco *gatherer-hunters' rock art from 2300 BC to AD 1450*
Aztalan
ILLINOIS HOPEWELL
OHIO HOPEWELL
Mound City
Cahokia
Ohio
Appalachian Mts
Howlett Hill
Atlantic Ocean
L'anse aux Meadows
Etowah
Spiro
MARKSVILLE GROUP
Marksville
Moundville
Macon
Kolomoki
SWIFT CREEK / SANTA ROSA GROUP
Crystal River
Missouri
Mississippi
Rio Grande
Rocky Mts
Gulf of Mexico
Pacific Ocean

site of the last centralized government of Yucatán destroyed in 1441

Mayapán
Chichén Itzá
Champotón
Yucatán Peninsula
Tulum
late Post-Classic fortified town
Cozumel *island trading centre*
Ichpaatun *late Post-Classic fortified town*
Santa Rita *murals in Mixtec style*
ACALAN
Lamanai
Tipu
Tayasal
lakeside town; last centre of Maya resistance to Spain
Maya centres occupied continuously until mid-17th century
Gulf of Honduras
Wild Cane Cay island trading centre

3 The Inca empire, 1438–1525

The growth of the Inca empire:

- under Pachacuti, 1438–63
- added under Pachacuti and Topa Inca, 1463–71
- added under Topa Inca, 1471–93
- territory under Huayna Capac, 1493–1525
- imperial roads

Quito
Cuenca
Japurá
Amazon
Marañón
Ucayali
Purus
Mamore
CHIMU
Chan Chan
Cajamarca
Huánuco
Bombón
Pachacamac
Machu Picchu
Incahuási
Ollantaytambo
Vilcashuamán
Cuzco
Limatambo
Lake Titicaca
Tiahuanaco
Cochabamba
Pacific Ocean
Andes Mountains
Salado
Maule

The world circa 1492

The central feature of world history since the 1490s has been the expansion of Europe and the spread of European civilization throughout the globe. Until then, the world had, on the whole, pressed in on Europe; thereafter the roles became reversed. In the 16th century, however, Europe continued to stand on the periphery of the civilized world, eclipsed by Ming China (the most powerful and advanced state of the period, with over 100 million inhabitants – equal to the whole of Europe) and by the rising Ottoman, Safavid and Mughal empires of the Middle East. Meanwhile Islam won converts in central and South-East Asia, and among the peoples of sub-Saharan Africa.

The total area occupied by the major civilizations, roughly co-terminous with the area of plough cultivation, nevertheless remained relatively small. Almost 80 per cent of the world's surface was inhabited either by food gatherers or herdsmen (as in Australia and most of Siberia, North America and much of Africa) or by hand cultivators (especially in South-East Asia, West Africa and Central and South America). But plough cultivators proved far more productive, and the relatively small area that had been brought under the plough probably supported between two-thirds and three-quarters of the global population (map 1).

Until the 1490s, worldwide racial segregation prevailed. Although Christians and Muslims from all over Eurasia made pilgrimages to their Holy Places in the Middle East, they seldom settled; and although merchants travelled widely across and around Asia, their numbers remained few. In the early 15th century a succession of Chinese voyages, commanded by the Muslim admiral Cheng Ho, secured tribute and extended recognition of the new Ming dynasty; but they led to no lasting interchange of population.

Until the 1490s, therefore, the Negroids remained concentrated in sub-Saharan Africa and a few Pacific islands; the Mongoloids in Asia and the Americas; the Caucasoids in Europe, North Africa, the Middle East and India; and the Australoids in Australia (map 2). By 1800, however, the pattern had fundamentally altered as the result of six inter-continental migrations: from Europe and Africa to the Americas; from northern Europe to Africa and (later) Australasia; from Russia into Siberia; from China to South-East Asia; and from India to Africa, South-East Asia and the Caribbean. By far the greatest change occurred in the Americas, where the native population declined dramatically in the

1 The economies of the world, c. AD 1500

non-agricultural economies

  generalized gathering, hunting and fishing

  specialized hunting

agricultural economies

  root crops dominant

  grain crops dominant

  nomadic pastoralism

    ▴ dromedary   ▫ horse/reindeer   ○ cattle

  limit of plough cultivation

  Cheng-ho's voyages, 1405–33

century following the first contact with the Europeans – in some cases by 90 per cent – to be replaced by Europeans, Africans, and in some parts of Latin America by a mixed race of mestizos (map 2).

Nevertheless, the tempo of change must not be exaggerated. Although in America the Aztec and Inca empires collapsed suddenly in 1521 and 1533 respectively (page 72), elsewhere the political impact of Europe remained limited until the 18th century. China and Japan survived intact, and India kept the Europeans at arm's length for 250 years following the arrival of Vasco da Gama in 1498. There, as in Africa and South-East Asia, the European presence long remained confined largely to trading stations and fortresses along the coast.

A pepper harvest in Malabar. Pepper accounted for over 70 per cent by volume of the world spice trade in the 16th century. The most valuable variety, *piper nigrum*, shown here, was native to India and hard to transplant successfully. Demand from Europe and China spread it to selective parts of the East, but Portuguese efforts to introduce it in Africa and America in the 17th century met with little success.

2 The Diffusion of races

Mongoloid	Caucasoid	Australoid	Negroid

before 1492

after 1492

NORTHERN EUROPEANS
SOUTHERN EUROPEANS
AFRICAN SLAVES
NORTHERN EUROPEANS
INDIANS
INDIANS
INDIANS
RUSSIANS
INDIANS
CHINESE

The cultural influence of Europe was even more negligible: Christianity made little headway, except when imposed by the conquerors (as in the Americas and the Philippines), until it received the backing of western technology in the 19th century.

The comparative fragility of the Aztec and Inca civilizations in the Americas, and of the African kingdoms immediately south of the Sahara, despite their outstanding achievements, may be partially explained, first, by their geographical isolation and relative lack of external stimulus and, second, by their dependence on hand cultivation. After 1492, when all the continents came into direct contact with each other for the first time, many of these non-Eurasian civilizations proved unable to offer more than a feeble resistance to outside aggression. To be sure not until the 19th century, with the opening of the Suez Canal and the construction of the transcontinental railways in North America, Siberia and Africa, did areas that had previously been separate finally blend into a single world economy; but the first stages of global integration were completed in the three centuries following 1492.

THREE

The Rise of the West

Before 1500, civilization had been essentially land-centred, and contacts by sea relatively unimportant; thereafter direct sea contact linked the continents. This resulted not only in the growth of a global system of regions which hitherto had developed in isolation, but in a challenge to the traditional land-centred balance between the civilizations of Eurasia.

Nonetheless, the impact of European expansion should not be exaggerated. To many Europeans, the Ottoman, Mughal and Chinese empires exemplified civilized living. Industrialization put Europe ahead; but the fruits of that process – some of them poisonous – were only garnered in the 19th century. Until then, for all its thrusting novelty, Europe remained closer to its agrarian past than to its industrial future.

Between 1815 and 1914 Europe expanded and inaugurated the process of transformation throughout the world which dethroned agricultural society as it had existed for thousands of years, replacing it with an urban, industrialized, technocratic society.

Marble bust of Louis XIV
by Bernini, 1665

1480–1630
European exploration

In 1480 European shipping remained largely confined to the North Atlantic, the Baltic and the Mediterranean, while the West African coast had been explored cursorily, and only very recently by Europeans; Indian, Persian, and Arab vessels plied the northern Indian Ocean; Chinese and Indonesian junks sailed in the western Pacific, but rarely went beyond Japan, the Philippines and the Indonesian archipelago; and local craft navigated the Caribbean and the coasts of Peru and Ecuador. No shipping used the southern Indian Ocean, the South Atlantic, or the main basin of the Pacific. In the course of the next 150 years, however, European navigators opened all the seas, except in the regions of circumpolar ice and the South Pacific, to European ships. Initially, in the 15th century, two series of voyages sought a sea passage to southern Asia in the hope of initiating direct trade in spices. One series, mounted from Portugal, sailing by a south-eastern route and employing local navigators in the East, eventually reached their declared destinations: the entrance to the Indian Ocean (1488), Malabar (1498), Malacca (1509), and the Moluccas (1512-13). The other series, mounted from Spain and sailing west or south-west, proved less successful in its immediate purpose but more fruitful in incidental discovery: the Spaniards hit upon the West Indies (1492) and the Spanish Main (1498). Eventually they too reached South-East Asia (1521), but by a route too long and arduous for commercial use – for to reach the Pacific they had to circumnavigate an immense land-mass which, although it was initially thought to be a peninsula of Asia, by the 1520s had been recognized as a new world. They immediately began to settle the area (page 72). Taken together, the Spanish and Portuguese discoveries proved that all the oceans of the world, at least in the southern hemisphere, were connected.

For most of the 16th century, by the use and threat of force, the Iberian powers managed to prevent other Europeans from using the connecting passages, except for occasional raids. The third great series of voyages, therefore, mostly by English, French and Dutch navigators, searched for alternative routes to Asia in the northern hemisphere, in the west, northwest, and northeast. Although unsuccessful in their primary purpose, they revealed another continental land-mass with a continuous coast extending from the Caribbean to the Arctic, and opened the way for the European exploration and settlement of eastern North America (page 86).

VOYAGES INTENDED FOR SOUTH ASIA BY SOUTH-EAST ROUTE:

1/Dias 1487–8 (outward) discovered open waters of Cape Agulhas; entered Indian Ocean; reached Great Fish River.

2/Vasco da Gama 1497–8 (outward) made best use of Atlantic winds on way to Cape of Good Hope; reached India, guided by local pilot.

3/Cabral 1500 (outward) second Portuguese voyage to India; landed in Brazil, probably accidentally.

4/First Portuguese voyage to Malacca, 1509.

5/Abreu 1512–3 visited Moluccas.

6/First Portuguese visits to Macao, 1516.

VOYAGES INTENDED FOR CHINA AND SOUTH ASIA BY WEST OR SOUTHWEST ROUTE:

7/Da Mota, Zeimoto and Peixoto 1542–3 Portuguese reach Japan.

8/Columbus 1492–3 (outward and homeward) visited Bahama group, explored north coasts of Cuba and Hispaniola; found best return route.

9/Columbus 1493–4 (outward) explored south coast of Cuba; reported it as peninsula of mainland China.

10/Columbus 1498 (outward) explored Trinidad and Venezuela; recognized coast as mainland.

11/Columbus 1502–4 explored coast of Honduras, Nicaragua and the Isthmus.

12/Ojeda and Vespucci 1499–1500 (outward) reached Guiana coast, failed to round Cape São Roque, followed coast west to Cape de la Vela.

13/Coelho and Vespucci 1501 (outward) followed coast south from Cape São Agostinho to 35°S.

14/Solís 1515 entered River Plate estuary and investigated north bank.

15/Magellan and Elcano 1519-22 discovered Strait of Magellan, crossed Pacific, reached Moluccas via Philippines; first circumnavigation.

16/Saavedra 1527 discovered route from Mexico across Pacific to Moluccas.

17/Urdaneta 1565 found feasible return route Philippines to Mexico in 42°N. using west winds.

18/Schouten and Le Maire 1616 discovered route into Pacific via Le Maire Strait and Cape Horn.

VOYAGES INTENDED FOR ASIA BY NORTHWEST AND NORTHEAST ROUTE:

19/Cabot 1497 (outward) encountered Newfoundland, first sighted by Norsemen 11th C.

20/Corte-Real 1500 visited Greenland.

21/Verazzano 1524 traced east coast of North America from (probably) 34°N. to 47°N.; revealed continental character of North America.

22/Cartier 1534 and 1535 explored Strait of Belle Isle and St Lawrence as far as Montreal.

23/Willoughby and Chancellor 1553 rounded North Cape and reached Archangel.

24/Frobisher 1576 reached Frobisher Bay in Baffin Island, which he took for a 'strait'.

25/Davis 1587 explored west coast of Greenland to the edge of the ice in 72° N.

26/Barents 1596–7 discovered Bear Island and Spitsbergen; wintered in Novaya Zemlya.

27/Hudson 1610 sailed through Hudson Strait to the south extremity of Hudson Bay.

28/Button 1612 explored west coast of Hudson Bay, concluded Bay landlocked on the west.

29/Baffin and Bylot 1616 explored whole coast of Baffin Bay; concluded no navigable northwest. passage existed in that area.

1 Major European voyages of discovery, 1480–1630

→ voyages intended for Southern Asia by southeast route

→ voyages intended for China and south Asia by west or southwest route

→ voyages intended for Asia by northwest and northeast routes

⇨ approximate prevailing winds (shown for the first quarter of the year)

⇨ alternating monsoons

A 17th-century Spanish painting of Columbus's fleet *(below)*. Under the sponsorship of the Spanish monarchs Ferdinand and Isabella, Columbus made his first voyage across the Atlantic in 1492. Making landfall on Haiti, Columbus believed he had found a westward route to Asia. He made three further voyages to the Americas.

European overseas expansion

TIMELINE

1480
Portuguese found and fortify Elmina

1507
Portuguese occupy Mozambique

1510
Portuguese capture Goa

1511
Portuguese capture and occupy Malacca

1515
Portuguese occupy Ormuz

1557
Portuguese established at Macao

1600
English East India Company incorporated

1602
Dutch East India Company incorporated

1619
Dutch East India Company established at Batavia

1652
Dutch settlement at Cape of Good Hope

By 1492, Portugal already possessed several archipelagos in the Atlantic and the Gulf of Guinea, some fortresses in Morocco, and a few trading stations in West Africa (above all the castle at Elmina). In the next half century she established some 50 forts and trading posts around the shores of the Indian Ocean, as well as coastal enclaves in Angola and Brazil. Strategically, the most important bases were Mozambique (1507), a port of call for fleets sailing to India; Goa (1510), headquarters of Portuguese Asia; Malacca (1511), a major market on the strait connecting the Indian Ocean with the South China Sea; and Ormuz (1515), a key entrepôt of the international spice trade. East of Malacca the position of the Portuguese was far more precarious and their activities remained purely commercial. A few bases, some fortified, grew up in the Moluccas; a clandestine settlement developed at Macao on the Chinese mainland after 1557; and from 1580 Jesuit missionaries held a lease on the Japanese port-city of Nagasaki (map 1).

In Africa and Asia the Portuguese generally sought to control trade rather than production; and though they could not eliminate the commerce of others in the Indian Ocean, they forced many ships to use harbours under their control, and extorted tolls or duties from the rest. The Spaniards in the Americas, by contrast, embarked on a deliberate policy of conquest and colonization: from the 1490s in the Caribbean islands; from the 1520s in Mexico; from the 1530s in Peru; and from the 1570s in the Philippines.

Few dared to challenge the Iberian monopoly – apparently enhanced by the union of Portugal and Spain in 1580 – before the 17th century. However, the

2 Commercial expansion to the East, c. 1600–1700

- places under Dutch control
- places under English control
- places under French control
- places under Portuguese control
- areas under Portuguese control

trade routes
→ Dutch
→ English
→ French
→ Portuguese

Manila to Acapulco with silk

→ principal Portuguese trade routes
→ principal Spanish trade routes

■ areas under effective Portuguese control
■ areas under effective Spanish control

• Portuguese-controlled towns
• Spanish-controlled towns

■ seat of Audiencia (Spanish admintraive division)

MEXICO

Manila galleons with silk

Manila galleons with silver

Tenochtitlan
Veracruz
Charcas
Havana
San Agostín
Santo Domingo
Havana to Seville via Azores
North Atlantic Ocean
Seville to Nombre de Dios via Canary Is.
Seville to Veracruz via Canary Is.
Azores
Lisbon
Seville
approximate position of Tordesillas demarcation line
BRAZIL
Olinda
Pernambuco
Recife
Bahia
Elmina to W. Indies with slaves
Elmina to Bahia with slaves
Cape Verde Islands
Canary Islands
Elmina
Guato
Gulf of Guinea
São Tomé
Luanda to Bahia with slaves
Bahia to Luanda with tobacco and sugar
South Atlantic Ocean
Luanda
ANGOLA

AFRICA

Alexandria
Cairo
Red Sea
Bab el Mandeb
Aden
Arabian Sea
Malindi
Mombasa
Pemba
Zanzibar
Kilwa
Mozambique
Sofala
Madagascar
Réunion
Indian Ocean

Lisbon to Goa (alternative route, second half of year)

ASIA

Sea of Japan
JAPAN
Nagasaki
CHINA
Canton
Macao
South China Sea
Luzon
Philippines
Manila
Cebu
Ternate
Moluccas
Amboina
Spice Islands
Timor
Java
Borneo
Celebes
Malay Archipelago
Sumatra
Malacca

Ormuz
Diu
Hooghly
INDIA
Goa
Calicut
Cochin
Ceylon
Laccadive Islands
Colombo
Maldives

foundation of East India Companies by the Dutch, the English and (later) the French brought the Portuguese under increasing attack. Dutch forces first established independent bases in the East (above all at Batavia, the heavily fortified headquarters of the Dutch East India Company) and then between 1640 and 1660 wrested Malacca, Ceylon, most South Indian ports and the lucrative Japan trade from the Portuguese. In 1652 they also created a useful south African base on the route to the East at Cape Town. The English and French also established modest settlements in India, and developed a promising trade with China. Even the Spaniards undermined the Portuguese, exporting Chinese goods after 1572 through their colony in the Philippines (map 2). Elsewhere in Asia, however, Europeans during this period traded in competition with local merchants on terms laid down by local rulers, and their efforts constituted but a fraction of Asia's total commerce.

The murder of Atahuallpa
(right) in November 1532 set the seal on Spain's conquest of the Inca empire. Although there were perhaps only 180 Europeans in Peru, most of them young men in their twenties, their brutal murder of the 'divine Inca' broke the resistance of the Peruvian peoples. This vigorous illustration of the deed comes from the *Royal Commentaries* published between 1609 and 1616 by Garcilaso de la Vega, the son of a conquistador and an Inca princess

CONQVISTA
CORTALELACAVESAA
ATAGVALPA INGA VMATACVCHV

The expansion of France

In 1415 English troops invaded France and by 1429 had established suzerainty over almost half the kingdom. In the 1440s, however, with the aid of a powerful artillery train, Charles VII (1422-61) began a rapid reconquest which by 1453 had expelled the English from all but the port-city of Calais, and doubled the size of the royal domain. His successors annexed Burgundy (1477), Brittany (1491) and Bourbon (1527) by force, and inherited Anjou and Provence (1481). Several other semi-independent fiefs came to the crown at the accession of Louis XII (1498), Francis I (1515) and Henry IV (1589) (map 1).

After Henry's death in 1610, continuing religious division, costly foreign wars and aristocratic faction, culminating in the Fronde revolt (1648-53), brought France to the brink of dissolution again. However Henry's grandson Louis XIV (1643-1715) restored order and made France the dominant state of Europe. During the relatively peaceful years between 1659 and 1672 the king and his ministers struggled to develop the French economy (agriculture, manufacture and trade), to extend overseas possessions, and to expand the army and navy. They also developed commercial harbours and sponsored public works, such as the Languedoc Canal connecting the Atlantic and the Mediterranean. The richness of resources available to the French, including a population of perhaps 20 million (the largest of any 17th-century European state), undoubtedly played a part in these achievements; but so did the ceaseless efforts, directives, and resources emanating from the Court (map 2).

Despite France's gains at the peaces of Westphalia (1648) and the Pyrenees (1659), Louis still feared Habsburg encirclement (page 92). He sought both to secure territories that might plug the gaps in his frontier (in wars fought in 1667-8 and 1672-8 which brought the acquisition of territory from the Spanish Netherlands and of Franche-Comté), and to erect an 'iron frontier' of state-of-the-art fortresses, thickest on the ground in the north and east, to create a defence in depth that would prevent any enemy forces from penetrating to the heart of the realm as the English and the Habsburgs had done in the past. Perhaps his success in this endeavour made him too bold, for in 1700 he accepted the will of the childless Spanish Habsburg Carlos II which bequeathed to Louis's grandson Philip the entire Spanish empire – Spain, Spanish America, the South Netherlands and half of Italy – even though he knew this sudden concentration of territory in the hands of the Bourbon dynasty would provoke a general European war. After some initial French victories (1702-3), followed by a string of searing defeats (1704-9), the 'iron frontier' showed its worth and forced France's exhausted enemies to conclude the compromise peaces of Utrecht (1713) and Rastatt (1714), by which Philip retained Spain and Spanish

1 The reunification of France 1440–1589

- lands recognizing English suzerainty, 1429
- frontier of France, 1492
- Royal domain, c. 1475
- lands annexed from Burgundy, 1477
- lands of René of Anjou, annexed 1481
- lands of Duke of Brittany, annexed 1491
- lands brought to the crown by Louis XII, 1498
- lands brought to the crown by Francis I, 1515
- lands of Duke of Bourbon, annexed 1527
- lands brought to the crown by Henry IV, 1589
- other fiefs annexed, with date
- fiefs still independent at the end of the 16th century

Calais *1558*

ARTOIS *(lost 1493)*

ST POL *1477*

PICARDY

NORMANDY

BRITTANY

ALENÇON *1525*
PERCHE *1483*

VALOIS

RETHEL

Verdun
1552 Metz

CHAMPAGNE

BAR *1552*
Toul *1552*

MAINE

ORLÉANAIS

NEMOURS *1503*

VENDÔME

BLOIS

ANJOU

TOURAINE

POITOU

BERRY

NEVERS

BURGUNDY

LA MARCHE

BOURBON

CHAROLAIS
Habsburg possession from 1493

ANGOULÊME

FOREZ

LIMOGES

PÉRIGORD

AUVERGNE

DAUPHINÉ

ALBRET

GUYENNE

ROUERGUE

GASCONY

ARMAGNAC

BÉARN

BIGORRE

ASTARAC

COMMINGES

LANGUEDOC

COMTAT VENAISSIN
papal state

PROVENCE

In the vast palace of Versailles, seen in the background behind Jean-Baptiste Tuby's bronze sculpture of Apollo rising from the waters *(right)*, Louis XIV directed the fortunes of France. The complex served as the king's court, the centre of his government and a source of inspiration – and envy – to monarchs throughout Europe.

America, while Savoy, Britain and the Austrian Habsburgs partitioned the rest (map 3).

Louis had thus secured the integrity of France's frontiers, and ended for ever the threat of Habsburg encirclement; but the ruinous cost of his wars created a legacy of financial disorder and internal discontent which served to hamstring his successors. Although Louis XV (1715-74) managed to incorporate Lorraine in 1766, and his successor Louis XVI (1774-93) assisted the successful rebellion of the American colonies against Great Britain (page 104), both monarchs sacrificed (as Louis XIV had done) France's overseas possessions and accumulated such monstrous public debts that, in 1789, the government summoned a representative assembly, the States-General, to solve the financial crisis. In doing so, it unleashed revolution (page 116).

2 Administrative units and defensive fortifications

— frontier of France 1713–14

— administrative units of Louis XIV's reign, the *généralités* (generalities)

⊙ seat of *intendants*, Louis XIV's royal commissioners

⊕ *parlement* (law courts)

ALSACE *pays d'état*

defence:

■ fortifications (the so-called *barrière* or *frontière de fer*)

▣ fortifications built by Vauban but ceded during the reign of Louis XIV

⊷ galley port

⊞ naval port

economic:

‡ commercial harbours

major manufactures:

▤ brandy   ▮ pottery
◇ cloth   ✒ printing
□ glass   ⊟ salt
⊟ iron   ◉ silk
⊝ madder   ◗ soap
  dye
⬠ paper   ▼ tapestry
              and carpets
              ▼ wine

3 The War of the Spanish Succession, 1701–14

✕ Allied victory

✕ Bourbon (French) victory

✕ inconclusive

principal territorial changes

to Spanish House of Bourbon

to Great Britain

to Austria

to Savoy

to France

to Prussia

Russian expansion in Europe and Asia

After the Mongol invasion of the 13th century (page 60), the lands which had formed part of Kievan Russia fragmented. Lithuania expanded in the west, while the east and south became subject to Mongol overlords, in whose service the principality of Muscovy rose to prominence. Ivan III (1462-1505) opened another phase of expansion: in 1478 he annexed the city republic of Novgorod and in 1480 proclaimed independence from the Mongols. In 1510 his son Vassily (1505-33) overran the republic of Pskov, bringing Muscovite control close to the Baltic; and his grandson Ivan IV (1533-84) conquered the Tatar states of Kazan (1552) and Astrakhan (1556), gaining control of the Volga down to the Caspian Sea (map 1). In addition, from the 1580s, the lucrative fur trade lured enterprising Russians deep into Siberia. Crossing the Urals, they followed the River Ob until they came within portage of the Yenisey, where they built and fortified Turukhansk (1607); thence they reached the Lena river system, where they built Yakutsk (1632), and finally the Pacific, where they built Okhotsk (1649) – some 6,000 miles (9,700km) east of Moscow (map 2).

However Ivan IV failed to realise his principal territorial ambition, the acquisition of Livonia and direct access to the Baltic, while his attempt to break the power of the traditional nobility by creating a 'private domain' (the *oprichnina*) around Moscow resulted in massive depopulation. Muscovy was also still not entirely safe from the Crimean Tatars, who sacked Moscow in 1571. Then succession disputes following the extinction of the old Muscovite ruling house (the 'Time of Troubles', 1598-1613) caused the loss of much territory to Poland and Sweden.

Recovery came only in the mid-17th century, when a successful war with Poland (1654-67) brought substantial gains, including Smolensk and the Ukraine. Meanwhile the settlement of Siberia continued: 23,000 Russians lived there by 1622, 105,000 by 1662 and 230,000 by 1709. However the Amur Basin, acquired in the 1650s, had to be ceded to China in 1689 (albeit in return for useful trading concessions: map 2) and attempts to force access to the Black Sea failed. Instead, Peter I ('the Great', 1682-1725) concentrated on achieving a 'window on the west', wresting Estonia and Livonia from Sweden in 1721, acquiring the ancient port of Riga and founding the new one of St Petersburg (1703). Peter's successors reverted to his policy of expansion on the Black Sea. Catherine II ('the Great', 1762-96) annexed the Tatar khanate of the Crimea. She also acquired large parts of Poland – although the cost of her campaigns, on top of the oppressive social system which required serfs to spend almost all their time labouring on their lords' lands, provoked a major peasant uprising under Emelyan Pugachev (1773-5). The period 1772 to 1815 saw the Russian land frontier expand 600 miles (970 km) at the expense of Poland. Finally, despite a French invasion which reached Moscow in 1812, the Congress of Vienna in 1815 confirmed Russia's acquisition of Finland, Poland, Bessarabia and Transcaucasia (page 116).

The population ruled from Moscow had grown, both by territorial acquisition and by natural increase, from some 10 million in 1600, to over 15 million in 1725 and to almost 43 million in 1812, and the empire – the largest in the world – now stretched over 11 of the world's 24 time-zones.

2 Russian expansion in Siberia, 1581–1800

- Russian territory in 1581
- territory added 1581–98
- territory added 1598–1618
- territory added 1618–89
- territory added in 1650s; returned to China 1689
- territory added 1689–1725
- territory added 1725–62
- territory added 1762–1800
- •Bratsk forts and trading posts
  1630 (with date of foundation)

1 From Muscovy to Russia, 1462–1815

— boundary of all Russian territories in 1462

— Lithuania, 1462

1783 date of foundation of new town

KALMYKS native peoples

the expansion of Muscovy:

- Moscow territory at end of 13th century
- *1478* date of acquisition by Muscovy
- acquisitions to 1462
- acquisitions under Ivan III, 1462–1505
- acquisitions during 16th century
- acquisitions during 17th century
- acquisitions during 18th century
- acquisitions, 1801–15
- territory ceded to Sweden 1617 and Poland-Lithuania, 1618
- acquired from Poland-Lithuania, 1634
- acquired from Poland-Lithuania, 1667

Russian woodcut showing a procession of merchants carrying furs at the court of the Holy Roman Emperor c. 1570. In the early 17th century the demand for luxury furs fuelled expansion eastwards into Siberia to tap its seemingly inexhaustible supply.

ceded temporarily by Persia, 1723–32

The Americas

The daring conquest of Mexico by Hernán Cortés in 1519-21 and of Peru by Francisco Pizarro in 1531-3 (page 73) laid the foundations of a huge Spanish colonial empire in the Americas. By 1535, when the crown established viceregal government in Mexico and Lima became the capital of Peru, all the major centres of indigenous population in the former Aztec and Inca empires lay in Spanish hands: an area four times the size, and containing eight times the population, of the country from which the conquerors had come. Although the frontiers of colonial settlement continued to advance – with new viceroyalties in New Granada (1739) and Rio de la Plata (1776) and new military governments in Texas (1718) and California (1767) – none of these later, sparsely inhabited conquests compared with Mexico and Peru in wealth and importance. Potosí in Peru and Zacatecas in Mexico became the largest producers of silver in the world, and by 1560 silver formed America's principal export to Europe.

Elsewhere on the continent colonization proved slower. The Portuguese only settled the Atlantic coast of south America after 1549 for fear that the French might do so. By 1600, although coastal Brazil had become studded with profitable sugar plantations and mills, worked by slaves from Africa, the Brazilian interior remained the domain of native Indian tribes until the 1690s, when the discovery of enormous gold deposits in the interior provoked a new wave of colonization. In the northwest, Russian explorers and traders pressed on; but by 1819 only 19 settlements existed between the Aleutian islands and California (map 1).

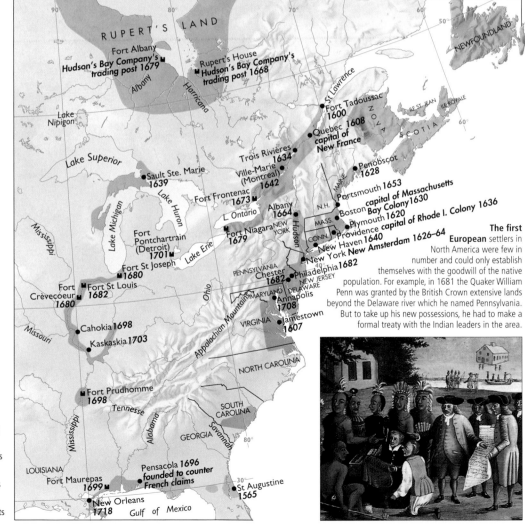

The first European settlers in North America were few in number and could only establish themselves with the goodwill of the native population. For example, in 1681 the Quaker William Penn was granted by the British Crown extensive lands beyond the Delaware river which he named Pennsylvania. But to take up his new possessions, he had to make a formal treaty with the Indian leaders in the area.

2 European settlement in North America

- early English settlements and claims
- early French settlements and claims
- early Spanish settlements

The Atlantic seaboard of north America, with its harsher climate and poor soil, also at first attracted few Europeans (who came mostly for fish and furs). Settlement only began with the foundation of Acadia (Nova Scotia) by the French in 1604, of Virginia (1607) and Massachusetts Bay (1620) by the English, and of New Amsterdam (later New York) by the Dutch (1624). Gradually, however, the Europeans pressed inland: the French advanced down the St Lawrence and (after 1682) the Mississippi, creating a chain of fortified posts all the way to the Gulf of Mexico and founding New Orleans in 1718; the English spread out around the rich fur-hunting grounds of Hudson Bay. Wars between the European states now regularly involved the Americas, with England gaining first the Dutch colonies along the Hudson (1664) and then French Canada (1763). By 1700, perhaps 250,000 Europeans lived in North America, but by 1820 that number had soared to 9 million (compared with just over 3 million in Spanish America).

The Spaniards in America relied from the first on Indian labour, both in ranching and mining, and readily intermarried; hence an extensive mestizo population developed, especially in Mexico and Peru. The British, however, who wanted land for farms and plantations, expelled or exterminated the native population: by 1820, only 600,000 lived in the English speaking areas (compared with 7.5 million in Spanish America). Instead, in Virginia, and then later in the Carolinas, where tobacco was introduced as a cash-crop, African slaves were imported to work on the plantations (like those of the sugar producers of Brazil and the Caribbean islands). By 1820, almost 2 million Africans lived in north America (compared with 800,000 in Spanish America).

Throughout the period, each mother country maintained a tight grip on its colonies. The colonists tolerated this as long as they felt insecure – whether from the threat of native uprisings or through the series of wars between the mother countries. Britain's resounding victory over France in 1763, however, brought total security to her American colonies, whose elites soon came to resent the continuing tax demands of the government in London. In 1776 they demanded their independence (page 98) and the colonies of Latin America followed suit after 1808. (page 112).

1 Colonial America

- British-claimed territory to 1763
- French-claimed territory to 1763
- Spanish territory, 1650
- ceded by France to Britain, 1763
- ceded by France to Spain, 1763
- additional Spanish territory by 1775
- Portuguese territory, 1650
- Portuguese territory, 1775
- Dutch territory, 1630
- Dutch territory, 1775
- Russian territory, c. 1775
- Jesuit missions, with date of foundation
- The United States from 1783

colonization routes
- Spanish
- Portuguese
- British
- Russian
- French
- major exports
- viceroyalty borders, 1800 (with date of foundation)

South-east Asia and Japan

In 1603 the Japanese emperor conferred the title of Shogun (military leader) on Tokugawa Ieyasu, who had established control over the state re-unified in the 1590s (page 68). The Tokugawa dynasty exercised power until 1868, giving Japan a prolonged period of political stability. A complex system of government emerged in which the shoguns in Edo (modern Tokyo) dominated or regulated the 250 or so fiefs of the feudal lords, organized society in a hierarchy of classes, and enacted a comprehensive legal code. From 1612 they banned the Christian missionaries (active in many areas since the mid-16th century) and persecuted their adherents. They also forbade all Japanese to travel abroad; limited foreign contacts to the Dutch (who maintained a trading post at Nagasaki), the Chinese and the Koreans; and until 1853 successfully repulsed various attempts by the Russians, British, French and Americans to open trade (map 1). Yet despite this isolation, Tokugawa Japan prospered: trade and cities grew rapidly; the population rose from 20 to 30 million; high literacy rates prevailed; industry and credit spread widely. By the mid-19th century, Japan was far better prepared than any other part of Asia to meet the challenge of Western expansion (page 122).

Initially, however, Western traders showed far more interest in the spices of South-East Asia. The disintegration of the empires of Srivijaya and Majapahit (page 64) left behind scores of petty states with little cohesion, opening the way to Portuguese acquisition of Malacca (1511) and footholds in the Moluccas (page 80). Their presence at first changed little: in Asia they aimed to dominate the spice trade

through a chain of fortified stations, linked by naval power, not to acquire territory. The arrival of the Dutch and then the English after 1595 (page 80) did not initially change this, for they too sought primarily to monopolize the spice trade, and even after the establishment of a fortress at Batavia (1619) the Dutch directed most of their territorial ambitions towards acquiring Portuguese and English bases, rather than to conquering native states. The only substantial European colony in the area remained the Philippines, where the Spanish authorities began to foster the cultivation of tobacco, sugar, hemp and other commercial products from the later 18th century (map 2).

The mainland monarchies of Southeast Asia – Arakan, Burma, Siam, Cambodia, Luang Prabang and Annam – had little direct involvement in European trade, and concentrated instead on extending their power at the expense of their neighbours. Over the period as a whole, Annam (Vietnam) and Siam expanded at the expense of Luang Prabang (Laos) and Cambodia. Burma almost disintegrated after the Mons rebelled in 1740, set up a king of their own at Pegu, and in 1752 captured the Burmese capital of Ava. However a charismatic leader, Alaungpaya (1735-60), defeated the Mons and established Rangoon as the southern port of a reunited Burma (1755), while his successors invaded Siam (1767) and conquered Arakan (1785).

Two factors complicated state-building in the area: the constant pressure of the hill peoples of the interior (like the Mons), always eager to assert their independence, and the steadily increasing interference of the Europeans. A group of Iberian adventurers temporarily seized power

Daimyo **and their retinues** enter Edo castle to participate in one of the many courtly ceremonials *(right)*. Edo, now Tokyo, was originally a fishing village, near which a castle was built in 1456. It rapidly became a powerful centre and in 1590 Tokugawa Ieyasu selected Edo for his residence, building an elaborate castle which remained the seat of the shogunate for 260 years, although it became the capital only in the 19th century.

1 Japan in isolation

— provincial borders
═ Five Highways
▬ extensions to the Five Highways
— secondary roads
— sea routes
● important castle towns

feudal territories:
major Tokugawa domains

→ American, Russian, British and other naval visits

CHOSHU (NAGATO) · Shimonoseki · Hagi · Fukuoka · Yamaguchi · HIZEN · Mitajiri · Tottori · Nagasaki · Saga · Kurume · Hiroshima · Kanazawa · Niigata · Miyako · SAGA · Kumamoto · Okayama · KAGA · Sendai · KYUSHU · SHIKOKU · Nishinomiya · Kyoto · Fukui · Aizu · SATSUMA · TOSA · Tokushima · Hyogo · Nakasendo · HONSHU · Kagoshima · Kochi · Sakai · Osaka · OWARI · Koshu-kaido · Nikko-kaido · Oshi-kaido · MITO · Wakayama · Gojo · Tsu · Nagoya · Mito · KII (KISHUI) · Tokaido · Yokohama · Edo (Tokyo) · Yokosuka · Uraga

HOKKAIDO · EZO · Hakodate · Sea of Japan · Kubota · Morioka

C H I N A

ASSAM

Naga Hills
Mogaung • Myitkyina
Imphal
MANIPUR   YUN-NAN
Tagaung • Bhamo
BURMA
Shwebo • Ava • Mandalay   SHAN
Chin Hills Amarapura STATES
Magwe
Myohaung KARENNI
An Pass STATE
Thayetmyo
Toungoo
Prome Lamphun
Pegu Lampang
Taungup Sawankhalok
Pass Sukhothai
Bassein Thaton SIAM
Rangoon Martaban
from 1755 Moulmein Lopi Buri
Syriam MONS Korat
to 1755 Bangkok Ayutthaya
Tavoy Sisophon Angkor
Thon-Buri
Mergui Chanthaburi Battambang
Mergui Phnom Penh
Archipelago Kampot
Andaman Is. Gulf of Siam Ha Tien

TONGKING
Hanoi • Bac Ninh Haiphong
Chiang Saen Thanh Hoa
Luang Hainan
Prabang
Chiang Rai Ha Tinh
Chiengmai Porte d'Annam
Vientiane Hue
Tourane French from 1787

Champassak
Stung Treng Binh Dinh
Qui Nhon
CAMBODIA Nha Trang
Kratie
Kompong Cham COCHIN
CHINA
Bien Hoa South China
Saigon
Chan Cho Lon Sea
Doc

Nakhon Si Thammarat
Phuket Trang Songkhla
Pattant

Penang
British from 1786
MALAYA
Malacca
Portuguese 1511–1641
Dutch 1641–1826
Singapore
British from 1819

to Japan
Canton
Macao
to Japan
FORMOSA
Spanish colonies in
north Taiwan, 1626–37;
Dutch in southwest
Taiwan, 1624–61 Pacific
Ocean
to Acapulco
20°
from Canton
to all
major
S.E. Asian
ports
Luzon
PHILIPPINES
Manila
from Acapulco

Balambangan
Sulu
Sea
Brunei Mindanao
Sulu Archipelago
SARAWAK
Borneo Manado
Pontianak Tidore
Halmahe
Moluccas
(Spice Islands)
Celebes Buru Ceram
Bandjarmasin Amboina
Banda Is.
Macassar Strait of Macasser
Banda Sea

to Madras
and Calcutta
Tiku
Fort de Kock
(Bukit Tinggi)
Padang
Painan
Sumatra
Djambi
Palembang
Bangka
Benkulen
Billiton
Sukadana
Bantam
Batavia
(Jakarta) MATARAM
Jogjakarta Surabaya
Indian
Ocean Lombok
110° Bali Sumbawa
Flores Timor
Sumba

Karimata Strait
Java Sea
Sunda Strait
10°

**2 The Europeans
in southeast Asia**
European possessions, 1826
British   Spanish
Dutch   Portuguese

trade routes:
developed by Dutch and
English East India Companies
developed by Arab and Gujerati traders
developed by the Dutch in the 17th cen
used by English shipping from 1786
used by the 'Manila Galleon'
local trade routes
⊙ principal trading centre

Vietnamese expansion
Vietnamese border, 1500
expansion to 1611
acquisitions from
Cambodia in early
18th century
Vietnamese expansion
in 19th century
kingdom of Luang
Prabang, 1707
area which broke away
under Vientiane in 1707
Burmese conquests
Siamese conquests

in Cambodia in the 1590s; the French briefly garrisoned some Siamese strongholds in the 1680s; both the French and English East India Companies intervened in Burma in the 1750s. Meanwhile, the Dutch began to extend their control over Java and the Spice Islands, and at the same time the British established their base at Penang (1786) and a free trade port at Singapore (1819) on the Malayan peninsula.

These acquisitions led to tension between the two colonial powers, which only abated after a treaty in 1824 obliged the British to withdraw from Sumatra

and the Dutch from Malacca. Secure in the east, the British now turned on Burma and, after a short war (1824-6), annexed Arakan, Assam and Tenasserim. The future Dutch and British colonial empires in Southeast Asia were taking shape, but their control remained loose and indirect. Only after the industrial revolution, and the expanding demand for raw materials at home, did the Europeans seriously impinge upon the lives and fortunes of the peoples of the region.

The Reformation and Catholic Reformation

Of the 250,000 or so works printed in Europe between 1447 and 1600, about 75 per cent concerned religion. The Reformation and the Catholic response would have been impossible without printing presses like this one *(below)*, from the cover of a book printed in Frankfurt in the early 17th century.

The shattering of the unity of Latin Christendom altered the course of European history. The fall of Constantinople (page 48) allowed the Roman church to ignore the Orthodox areas; and, except in Bohemia and Moravia, heresy scarcely existed in the West. Complacent, the Papacy failed to deploy its immense wealth adequately, producing widespread pluralism and absenteeism; this, coupled with the materialism of the hierarchy, discredited the Western church in the eyes of many Christians. Some, like Erasmus of Rotterdam (1466-1536) and Thomas More (1478-1535), hoped for spiritual renewal within the church; but in Saxony Martin Luther (1483-1546) criticized clerical abuse and in 1520 called upon the German nobility to reform the church. Meanwhile, inspired by Huldreych Zwingli (1484-1531), the magistrates of the Swiss canton of Zürich renounced allegiance to Rome.

These successful protests sparked others. By 1560, seven out of every ten inhabitants of the Holy Roman Empire no longer accepted papal authority, and Protestantism (as the dissident creeds became known) also prevailed in Scandinavia, the Baltic lands, and England. Further defections from Rome came through the teaching of John Calvin (1509-64) in Geneva. Calvinism made rapid progress in France, Poland, Hungary and Scotland (where it became the official creed after 1560).

In addition, a number of more radical sects sprang up, called 'Anabaptists' by their enemies because of their belief that only adult baptism was valid. They rejected ritual, spiritual and temporal authority, and many social conventions in favour of Biblical simplicity. Many combined evangelism with social protest, and participated both in the major rising of the German peasantry in 1524-5 and in the radical government of the city of Münster in 1534-5. Both movements were brutally repressed and Anabaptism, where it survived, became a secret, separate creed.

Eventually the Catholic church reformed itself. The Council of Trent (three sessions 1545-63) condemned abuses, defined doctrine, and created a more effective and educated clergy; at the same time new religious orders (most notably the Jesuits, incorporated in 1540) targeted key areas for reconversion. By 1650 the Protestants had been expelled from Bavaria (1579), Austria (1597) and Bohemia (1628), and the number of Protestant churches in Poland had declined from 560 in 1572 to 240 in 1650. Spain eradicated its small Protestant minorities, and in 1609 expelled its substantial Moorish population. In the Holy Roman Empire, however, the Protestants fought back, provoking the savage religious conflict known as the Thirty Years' War (page 92).

1 Religious divisions in 1570

Roman Catholic	Lutheran	Islam
Orthodox	Calvinist	Anglican
Greek Catholic (Uniate)	Anabaptist	Hussite

NORWAY (Danish)

SWEDEN

ICELAND ■1552

■1528

Bergen

Åbo

Helsingfors

Christiania ■1539

■1527

Stockholm

COTLAND ▲1560

sgow Edinburgh

Reval ■1524

ESTONIA

RUSSIA

Pskov

LIVONIA

0

North Sea

York

■1561 Riga ■1524

COURLAND

Dünaburg

Chester

Aarhus

ENGLAND

1 ▲1534

istol Oxford

London

Copenhagen Malmö

DENMARK

SLESVIG ■1542 ■1536

HOLSTEIN ■1542 ■1529

Lübeck

Königsberg ■1523

Vilna

LITHUANIA

Minsk

PRUSSIA ■1525

Emden ■1526 ■1542

Hamburg ■1531

Danzig

POMERANIA ■1534

Amsterdam

Bremen ■1525

■1548 1549

Stettin

Poznán

Warsaw

NETHERLANDS

2

Rhine

Münster

Brunswick Lüneburg ■1545

Hannover

BRANDENBURG ■1539

Berlin ■1525

Cologne

Brussels

Mons

HESSE ■1524

Magdeburg

Wittenberg ■1522

Leipzig

Dresden ■1525

Breslau ■1524

SILESIA

Oder

Cracow

Lwów

POLAND

NASSAU ■1528

DUCHY OF SAXONY ■1539

ELEC. OF SAXONY ■1525

Rouen

Rheims

Seine

Paris

Frankfurt ■1530

Prague

BOHEMIA ■1524

Elbe

2

Orléans

Loire

PALATINATE

Metz ▲1546 ▲1559

Nuremberg

■1528

MORAVIA

Brünn

Kassa

Dniester

FRANCE

Tours

FRANCHE-COMTÉ

Dijon

Strassburg WÜRTTEMBERG ■1534 ▲1524

Ulm ■1530

Munich

Danube

Vienna

Pozsony

HUNGARY

Eger

2

Debrecen

MOLDAVIA

Jassy

BASLE ▲1523 THURGAU ▲1524

Limoges

26

NEUCHÂTEL ▲1530

Zurich ▲1524 APPENZELL

▲1528 SANKT GALLEN ▲1524

Salzburg

AUSTRIA

Buda

Kolozsvár

VAUD Berne

SWISS CONFEDERATION ▲1524 GLARUS ▲1525

Graz

Szeged

TRANSYLVANIA

Brassó

Lyons

▲538 Geneva ▲1536

GRAUBÜNDEN

SAVOY

MONTFERRAT

Turin

Milan

MANTUA

Trieste

Zágráb

Pécs

Temesvár

Belgrade

Bucharest

WALLACHIA

Ruschuk

Toulouse

VENAISSIN ORANGE

Avignon

MILAN

Verona

Venice

VENETIAN

Danube

Marseille

Nizza

MONACO

REP. OF GENOA

Genoa

PARMA

FERRARA MODENA

Bologna

San Marino

1

Zara

Bosna Saray

Nish

Sofia

ANDORRA N

Barcelona

MASSA LUCCA

Florence

DUCHY OF URBINO

REPUBLIC

Spalato

Mostar

Üsküb

Philippopolis

OTTOMAN

TUSCANY

PAPAL

187

PONTECORVO

Perugia

STATO DEI PRESIDI

Rome

STATES

MONTENEGRO

REPUBLIC OF RAGUSA

Adrianople

DUCHY OF CASTRO

BENEVENTO

Naples

Bari

Salonica

SARDINIA

Taranto

NAPLES

EMPIRE

Cagliari

10

Janina

delegates sent to last session of Council of Trent, (1562–3)

date of change from Catholicism to Lutheranism

date of change to Calvinism, Zwinglianism or Anglicanism

Palermo

Messina

SICILY

Athens

20

SCOTLAND ▲1560

Baltic Sea

60

The Habsburg ascendancy in Europe

Charles V's election as Holy Roman Emperor in 1519 created a Habsburg hegemony in Europe. He already ruled lands in Austria, South Germany and the Netherlands, and the realms bequeathed by his maternal grandparents in Spain, Italy and North Africa. Each of these inheritances soon increased. In 1526 his brother Ferdinand succeeded to the crowns of Bohemia (which included Moravia, Silesia and Lusatia) and Hungary. In 1535 Charles himself acquired both Lombardy and Tunisia, and throughout his reign he added to his holdings in the Netherlands (map 1). Moreover, in America, his Castilian subjects toppled first the Aztec and then the Inca states (see page 80). Although the central European lands (and the Imperial title) passed to Ferdinand and his successors, Charles's son Philip II also ruled a formidable inheritance. He, too, managed to extend it – adding the Philippines by conquest after 1571, and Portugal with her overseas possessions by inheritance after 1580.

Such centralization did not prove popular, however. Apart from provoking the enmity of France, which felt encircled, Charles V faced rebellions from his subjects in Spain (1520-2) and Germany (1552-5), the former provoked by taxation,

Spain's attempts to suppress the Dutch Revolt provoked much hostile propaganda. Here *(below)* the devil crowns the duke of Alba, who led Spain's efforts 1567-1573, while a Cardinal wields bellows to fill his head with Catholic zeal. Alba holds allegorical figures of the Dutch provinces on a chain, while his agents execute Counts Egmont and Hornes, defenders of Dutch liberties. (The execution itself took place in Brussels on 5 June 1568).

the latter arising from religious dissent provoked by the Reformation (page 90). Philip II (1556-98) contended, in the Netherlands, with the longest-lasting revolt in modern European history (map 2). The various provinces inherited or acquired by Charles V became part of a single state only in 1548. Local customs, often guaranteed by charter against central government interference, nevertheless survived and Philip II's attempts to override them – both to raise taxes and to persecute heretics – provoked insurrection. A timely display of force stifled an uprising in 1566; but in 1572 the provinces of Holland and Zeeland sustained rebellion, helped by the threat of a French invasion which made difficult a concentration of Spanish forces, until the cost of opposing them compelled Philip to withdraw his troops in 1576-7. Although forces loyal to (and maintained by) Spain reconquered many areas in the 1580s, fighting went on with the northern rebels for more than 20 years. Only in 1609 did Spain finally conclude a 12-year truce with the largely Calvinist Dutch Republic.

The Netherlands' struggle resumed during Emperor Ferdinand II's war against his rebellious subjects in Bohemia and Austria (map 3). He routed them at the battle of White Mountain in 1620.

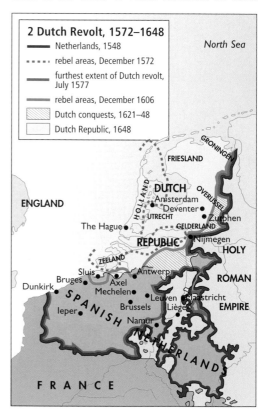

2 Dutch Revolt, 1572–1648
— Netherlands, 1548
---- rebel areas, December 1572
— furthest extent of Dutch revolt, July 1577
— rebel areas, December 1606
▨ Dutch conquests, 1621–48
☐ Dutch Republic, 1648

North Sea

GRONINGEN
FRIESLAND
DUTCH
ENGLAND
HOLLAND
OVERIJSSEL
Amsterdam
Deventer
UTRECHT
Zutphen
The Hague
GELDERLAND
REPUBLIC
Nijmegen
HOLY
ZEELAND
Sluis
Antwerp
ROMAN
Bruges
Axel
Dunkirk
Mechelen
Leuven
Maastricht
Brussels
Liège
EMPIRE
Ieper
Namur
SPANISH
NETHERLAND

FRANCE

Encouraged by this success, with Spanish and Papal support Ferdinand turned in 1621 against the German Protestant states, especially the Calvinists. Despite aid from Britain, Denmark and the Dutch, they lost and in 1629 Ferdinand issued an 'Edict of Restitution' by which he reclaimed Church lands acquired by Protestant rulers. Swedish military aid turned the tables against the emperor, and saved the German Protestants from collapse: an army led by King Gustavus Adolphus routed the Imperialists at Breitenfeld (1631) and drove them from much of Germany. Spain intervened to restore Habsburg fortunes but its victory at Nördlingen (1634) provoked France to declare war first on Spain (1635) and then on the emperor (1636). The war spread to almost the whole continent.

After many more years of largely unsuccessful campaigning, at the peace of Westphalia (1648) the emperor was abandoned virtually all his powers in Germany, agreed to toleration for Protestants and Catholics, and promised not to assist his Spanish cousins in their war against the Dutch rebels; by the peace of Münster (1648) Spain formally recognized the independence of the Dutch Republic (and their possession of all territories conquered since 1621); and by the peace of the Pyrenees (1659), Spain ceded all areas gained by France on the frontiers of both Spain and the Netherlands. The religious and political frontiers of central Europe which were agreed by these treaties lasted unchanged for 100 years. The Habsburg bid for European hegemony had failed.

3 The Thirty Years' War, 1618–48

→ route of Gustavus Adolphus, 1630–2
→ route of the Spanish army, 1634
✗ Imperial (Catholic) victory
✗ Imperial (Catholic) defeat
— Holy Roman Empire
— affected by Edict of Restitution, 1629

■ date region became Lutheran
▲ date region became Calvinist

the religious position in 1640:
Lutheran
Calvinist
Catholic
regained by Roman Catholics

1 The Habsburg empire in Europe

Aragonese inheritance of Charles V
added by Charles V, with date
Austrian inheritance of Charles V
added by Ferdinand I, with date
Castilian inheritance of Charles V
Burgundian inheritance of Charles V
added by Charles V with date
states favourable to Charles V
'The Spanish Road' connecting Habsburg dominions
ruled by Charles V as Holy Roman Emperor

1644–1911
China under the Ch'ing Dynasty

A new era in Chinese history opened in 1644 when the Ming dynasty, beset for a century by pirate raids, civil wars, and northern invaders (see page 68), fell to the forces of a Manchurian dynasty which ruled the country until 1911. The Manchu, or Ch'ing, rulers met with resistance in southern China for half a century, but quickly established a working relationship with the gentry who staffed the Chinese bureaucracy and, with its support, began a successful policy of territorial expansion which continued until the mid-18th century (map 1).

At the same time population trebled from about 100 million in 1650 to 300 million in 1800 and reached 420 million by 1850, while vast quantities of tea, silk, cotton, lacquer and porcelain were exported (mostly to Europe). But the financial strain of the

wars of expansion and the pressure of the growing population on land and food caused hardships that led to recurrent unrest and revolt, not only among the ethnic minorities who were harshly exploited by Chinese and Manchus alike, but also in the heartland itself, beginning with the 'White Lotus' rebellion, 1796-1805. China remained the world's largest and most populous state, but its economic difficulties and inadequate bureaucracy prevented effective resistance to the pressures of the Western powers who sought to open the Chinese market for the goods produced by their empires.

China's defeat in the Opium War (1839-42) resulted in the cession of Hong Kong to Britain and the opening of the first five Treaty Ports (their number steadily increased)

1 Chinese imperial expansion from c. 1620

Manchu expansion Phase 1: China

- Manchu homeland
- expansion before 1644
- expansion, 1644–59

1644 date of incorporation

tributary states:
- before 1644
- after 1644

- ⊗ seat of main Lamaistic patriarch
- ★ risings of non-Chinese people
- ● sectarian risings of Chinese
- ■ official centre of foreign commerce

Phase 2: New Territories

- *1724* New Territory with date of incorporation
- → military expeditions
- —— border of China under the Ch'ing dynasty, at its greatest extent

Map labels (main map)

RUSSIAN EMPIRE

TANNU TUVA
Russian protectorate 1912

Manchouli

Aigun · to Russia 1860
MARITIME PROVINCE

occupied by Russia 1897–1905;
Japanese influence after 1905

Harbin
Suifenho

Lake Balkhash

ILI PROTECTORATE

to Russia 1871–81

MONGOLIA
tributary territory;
autonomous 1912

Yellow River (Huang Ho)

Kalgan
Changchun
Mukden
Hunchun
Vladivostok

Peking
Newchwang
Antung
KOREA
to Japan 1910

Tientsin
Dairen
to Russia 1898
to Japan 1905

Taiyüan
Port Arthur

SINKIANG
tributary territory

Chefoo
Weihaiwei
to Britain 1898

Sea of Japan

CHINA

Tsinan
Tsingtao
to Germany 1898

TIBET
tributary territory;
autonomous 1912
under British influence

Ichang

Yangtze

Nanking
Chinkiang
Soochow · Wusung
Wuhu · Shanghai
Hangchow
Ningpo

British protectorate 1817

Chungking

Kiukiang

BRITISH INDIA

Yochow

NEPAL
SIKKIM
BHUTAN

ASSAM,
to Britain 1826

Changsha

Wenchow

Santuao
Foochow

to Japan 1872

Kunming

Tengyueh

Mengtze
Manhao

New Territories
to Britain 1898

Nanning
Lungchow

Canton
Macao
to Portugal 1557

Kowloon to Britain 1898
Hong Kong
to Britain 1842

Tamsui

Amoy
to Japan 1895

Taiwan
to Japan 1895

BURMA
to Britain 1886

TONGKING

Pakhoi
Haiphong
Kwangchowwan
to France 1898

LAOS
to France 1893

FRENCH INDO CHINA
1884

Kiungchow

Hainan

SIAM

JAPAN

Inset map (Manchuria)

Treaty of Nerchinsk, 1689: Russia recognizes Chinese border along the Argun and Amur rivers

Amur

MANCHURIA

1629–30 KHORCHIN

Mukden (capital, 1625–44)

1645 SHANTUNG

Eight Trigrams rising, 1813

1645 KIANGSU

...HWEI

...9–52
...NGSI

1645 CHEKIANG

1646 FUKIEN

1646 KIANGSU

KOREA
Manchu invasions, 1627, 1636–7 vassal status 1637

TAIWAN
Dutch, 1624–62; Ming loyalists, 1662–83; occupied by Ch'ing, 1683

rising of Heaven and Earth Society, 1787–8

Vietnamese pirate raids, 1800–9

Caption

In the Sino-Japanese war of 1894–5 the carefully modernized Western-style Japanese army disastrously routed the ill-led Chinese forces.

Legend

2 The dismemberment of the Ch'ing empire, 1842–1911

— boundary of Ch'ing empire in 1850
— states formerly tributary to China
— area affected by Taiping rebellion, 1850–64

colonial possessions:
spheres of influence:
Russian
British
Japanese
French
German

railways:
– – – Russian
– · – British
— · — Japanese
······ French
⊢–⊢ German
⊣–⊣ Chinese

Treaty ports and towns:
◐ 1842 Treaty of Nanking
⊗ 1858 Treaty of Tientsin
⊙ 1860 Peking Convention
◑ 1876 Chefoo Convention
▲ 1897 Sino-French Trade Convention
○ additional ports opened by 1911
● other towns and cities

in which foreigners enjoyed extra-territorial rights. More seriously, it served to weaken imperial authority and encouraged the Taiping rebellion (1850-64), the most serious of the many revolts that shook Manchu power. The Taiping and Nien uprisings alone left 25 million dead. These grave disorders also convinced the Western powers that Ch'ing China stood on the verge of collapse and encouraged them to secure a share: Russia gained the Amur basin, the

Maritime Province (1858-60) and, temporarily, the Ili valley in Turkestan (1871-81); France occupied Indo-China (1884-5); Britain took Burma (1886); Japan annexed Taiwan (1895) and Korea (1910) (map 2). These losses convinced many Chinese that radical changes were inevitable, and when in 1911 a small mutiny broke out among the Manchu army, disaffection spread rapidly throughout the whole country and the imperial government collapsed (page 130).

95

George V was crowned King Emperor of India at a durbar, or assembly of notables, in Delhi in 1911. In an effort to placate nationalist emotions, the annulment of the unpopular partition of Bengal was announced at the durbar.

2 India in 1857

- territory under British rule in 1805
- territory under British rule at close of Lord Dalhousie's administration, 1856
- - - main area affected by Indian Mutiny, 1857
- • main centres of rebellion

Map labels: PUNJAB, NW PROVINCES, BAHAWALPUR, Meerut, Bulandshahr, Delhi, Aligarh, Bareilly, Fatehgarh, Agra, RAJPUTANA, Mainpuri, OUDH, NEPAL, CHINA, AJMER, Gwalior, Lucknow, SIND, Jhansi, Kalpi, Cawnpore, ASSAM, Allahabad, BIHAR, KUTCH, GUJERAT, CENTRAL INDIA, BENGAL, BURMA, KATHIAWAR, AGENCY, NAGPUR, Calcutta, BERAR, ARAKAN, BOMBAY, Bombay, HYDERABAD, *Arabian Sea*, GOA *Portuguese*, MADRAS, MYSORE, COCHIN, TRAVANCORE, *Ceylon*

Shortly after Aurangzeb's death in 1707 (page 62), Mughal power declined. In the north, Oudh and Bengal became effectively independent, owing only nominal allegiance to Delhi; in the centre, the power of the Maratha confederacy increased; in the south the Muslim state of Mysore expanded rapidly. Meanwhile European influence in India continued to increase, with both the French and English East India Companies acquiring new territory in the southeast. Robert Clive's victory at Plassey in 1757 gave the English control over the lands and resources of Bengal, Orissa and Bihar, allowing the Company to maintain an army of over 100,000 men – most of them Indian soldiers (sepoys) trained to fight in European fashion – with which they not only destroyed France's Indian ambitions but also extended their control over the entire eastern coast of the subcontinent (map 1). Mysore went down to defeat in 1799, the Marathas in 1805, both delivering extensive new territories to British control, and most other major Indian rulers soon recognized British suzerainty.

Over the next half-century the conquest of Sind (1843) and the Punjab (1849), brought the dominions of the Company up to the country's natural frontier in the northwest, while a war with Nepal (1814-16) extended them to the Himalayas. To the east the

British clashed with the Burmese empire and in 1824-6 annexed Assam and Arakan (page 89). Within India, the 'Doctrine of Lapse' introduced by Governor-General Dalhousie (1847-56) resulted in the absorption of autonomous but dependent states, such as Oudh and several Maratha kingdoms, into the directly administered territories (map 2). Not surprisingly, this policy provoked disaffection which found violent outlet in 1857. Beginning as a mutiny of the Company's native soldiers, the revolt soon involved princes, landlords and peasants throughout northern India; but the loyalty of the Sikhs and the passivity of southern India enabled the British to restore control after 14 months of bitter fighting.

The mutiny proved a watershed in the history of British India. It thoroughly discredited the Company and in 1858 the London government assumed direct control. The subcontinent now acquired a pivotal position in Britain's Imperial system, leading to intervention in Afghanistan to block Russian expansion into central Asia (page 114), and in Burma to counter French influence in Southeast Asia. From East Africa to China, the Indian army regularly acted to advance British interests. Within India, the autonomy of the princes was henceforth respected and active steps were taken to develop the economy: the construction of first-class roads and a major rail network, together with the opening of the Suez Canal in 1869, made possible the exploitation of raw materials and the introduction of export crops, such as tea. Between 1869 and 1929 India's foreign trade increased sevenfold. However, although some modern industries developed under Indian entrepreneurs, most of the trade involved importing British manufactures and exporting raw materials; and in most areas neither the character of the economy nor traditional agriculture experienced any basic change (map 3). The

3 British India, 1931

- territory under British rule
- territories permanently administered by Government of India (mostly tribal)
- states and territories administered by local Indian rulers
- Portuguese enclave
- French enclave
- ▬ Hindu majority provinces
- ▬ Muslim majority provinces
- ▬ area of Buddhist predominance
- ▨ area of large Sikh population

manufacturing products

- ▶ cotton textiles
- ▭ woollens
- ♦ tea
- ❘ chemicals
- ◆ metals
- ▦ machinery and transport material
- ▨ tobacco
- ▥ sugar
- ◯ rice mills
- ■ iron and steel (large scale)
- ⚓ shipping
- ▨ mills (various grains)

Gross National Product increased only slowly, while from 1921 (thanks to sustained population growth) per capita income declined.

The rise of a new middle class, partly through industry but more through the recruitment of educated Indians into the colonial administration, coupled with overt British racism, awakened a new political consciousness. The Indian National Congress (established with official blessing in 1885) at first accepted British rule, but soon developed an extremist wing which questioned the foreigners' right to rule India. The decision to partition the province of Bengal in 1905 provoked mass agitation and terrorist attacks; and from 1919, under the leadership of Mohendas K. Gandhi (1869-1948), Congress fought actively for home rule and, after 1929, for independence. Profiting from the unrest caused by unemployment and the world economic depression, Gandhi launched a civil disobedience campaign (1930-4) that galvanized the Indian masses, and forced Britain to pass the Government of India Act (1935) which provided a framework for participation in central and provincial government.

By 1937 Congress controlled 11 of the 14 provincial administrations, but failed to represent adequately the interests of the large Muslim minority whose leaders in 1940 passed a resolution calling for an autonomous Islamic state in the subcontinent: Pakistan. In 1942 Gandhi launched a 'Quit India' campaign and in 1946-7, faced by massive disaffection, a naval mutiny, and strong pressure from the United States, the British drew up hasty plans for partition along sectarian lines. India and Pakistan became independent in 1947, Burma and Ceylon in 1948 (page 162).

1 The growth of British power to 1805

- territory ceded to Britain by 1805 with dates
- ✕ British victories with dates

The age of revolution

The later 18th century saw an unprecedented wave of uprisings throughout the western hemisphere (map 1). Many reflected a long-standing desire for independence, as in Corsica (1755, 1793), Haiti (1791), Sardinia (1793), Ireland (1798), Serbia (1804) and Spain (1808). Most, however, owed something to the Enlightenment, a European intellectual movement which emphasized certain fundamental rights of human beings and rejected traditional authority. Paradoxically, this could lead to rebellions by conservative elements against reforming rulers – such as the Austrian Netherlands (1787) and Hungary (1790) against the 'Enlightened' policies of Emperor Joseph II – or the resistance of colonial societies to the centralizing policies of the home government – as in North America after 1775 (page 104) and in South America after 1808 (page 112). More commonly opposition came from the middle classes: against a closed patriarchate in the Dutch Republic (1785-7); against the absolute monarchy and its aristocratic supporters in France.

In France, between 1789 and 1791 a representative assembly, summoned to solve a financial crisis, abolished feudalism, and created a constitutional monarchy and equality before the law. The king, however, refused to cooperate and was deposed in 1792, provoking Austrian, Prussian and (from 1793) British attempts to overthrow the Republic by force. They failed: instead, the revolutionary government in Paris purged its opponents at home and, by mobilizing unprecedented numbers of its citizens, conquered the Low Countries, Switzerland and Italy, imposing satellite republics.

In 1799 a successful general, Napoleon Bonaparte, took power as military dictator. He secured peace abroad (1802), and reorganized French local government, laws and education. But Britain declared war again in 1803 and, although her command of the seas (confirmed at Trafalgar, 1805) provided immunity from invasion, Napoleon defeated her continental allies – Austria, Prussia and Russia – in a brilliant series of battles (1805-7). Next, in order to create a continental blockade against British trade, Napoleon overran Spain (1808) and extended France's frontiers to Catalonia, the Baltic and Rome (1809-10). However Britain supported his opponents in the Iberian peninsula, expelling French forces by 1814. Meanwhile Russia's refusal to cooperate in the continental blockade led to a French invasion in 1812 which, although it reached Moscow, exhausted Napoleon's resources and led to his defeat and abdication in 1814 and again in 1815 (the 'Hundred Days').

Nevertheless, despite his failure, Napoleon's achievements inspired even his enemies: throughout the 19th century, Spanish, German and Italian reformers envisaged the state in essentially Napoleonic mode (page 116), while his administrative, legal and educational reforms in France survived the restoration of royal power.

1 Revolts and revolutions in Europe and America (*below and right*)

— borders, 1789

areas of nationalist revolt

areas of peasant revolt

areas of anti-colonial resistance

areas of revolt against royal authority

2 Napoleon and the reshaping of Europe

- (dark shading) French territories ruled from Paris, c. 1812
- (medium shading) states ruled by members of Napoleon's family, c. 1812
- (light shading) other dependent states, c. 1812
- ☒ French victory
- ☒ French defeat

- ☒ battles of the Italian campaign
- ☒ battles of the War of the Second Coalition
- ☒ battles of the War of the Third Coalition
- ☒ battles in the Austrian War, 1809
- ☒ battles in the Peninsular War
- ☒ battles of the Russian campaign
- ☒ battles of the War of Liberation from French rule
- ☒ battles in the defence of France
- ☒ battles in the War of the 100 Days

On 14th July 1789 a crowd of Parisians stormed the Bastille fort to release a handful of political prisoners housed there (below). The incident sparked off a more widespread revolt against the authority of Louis XVI, which led, four years later, to his imprisonment and execution. Bastille Day became the symbol for liberation struggles worldwide.

The industrial revolution in Europe

1 The pattern of industrial expansion, 1800
population per sq. mile in 1801

- under 50
- 50–100
- 100–150
- 150–200
- 200–260
- 260–390
- 390–800

— canal
■ expanding port
● expanding town
coalfields

▲ iron ore mining
C copper mining
— lead mining
tin mining
salt mining
slate mining

James Watt's rotative steam engine. In 1765 Watt developed his first steam engine, used initially to drive pumps. In 1776 it was applied to the iron industry, but with the rotative steam engine in 1781 it was possible to power machinery, making possible the shift to large scale production.

alism (page 118). Britain's precedence rested upon many factors. On the one hand, unlike much of the rest of Europe, it boasted abundant coal, iron and other basic materials, and it enjoyed an advantageous position in the Atlantic trade which generated much capital. On the other hand, it possessed several unique advantages. First, it escaped direct damage from the various wars that ravaged Europe between 1690 and 1815; second, unlike most continental states which bristled with customs barriers and internal frontiers, after the union of England and Scotland in 1707 Great Britain formed a single economic unit; third, again in contrast to continental Europe, the early disappearance of serfdom in England meant that the surplus labour released by rising agricultural productivity could move, without legal obstacles, to the growing industrial centres. Finally,

The Industrial Revolution, which began in England in the later 18th century, became the catalyst of the modern world. Nevertheless the speed of change can be exaggerated. Even in continental Europe its impact remained limited before 1850 to a few enclaves; and not until the last quarter of the century did the great surge forward occur. Outside Europe, except for the United States, industrialization took place even later (page 120). In 1895, even in Germany, one-third of the population still worked on the land, and most of eastern and southern Europe remained virtually untouched by industry.

Until 1900, when its lead began to be challenged by Germany and the United States, Great Britain remained the workshop of the world and its industrial strength, which enabled it to dominate world markets, explains its pre-eminence in the age of imperi-

England possessed a unique network of navigable rivers and canals (map 1), which proved of immense importance before the railway age for moving both raw materials and finished goods.

In its earliest phase, English manufacturers had also relied on water as a source of energy; but in the century to 1870 industrial power depended on steam, generated by the combustion of coal. At first, except in Britain and (from 1820) Belgium, steam power came only slowly, held back by political fragmentation, lack of capital and, above all, poor communications which severely limited markets. The steel firm of Krupp, founded in 1811 and later to be a giant of German industry, still employed only 7 men in 1826 and 122 in 1846. The pace of industrialization only accelerated with railway development. Between 1830 and 1870 the rail networks of Britain, Belgium and Germany became virtually complete, and construction began elsewhere. At much the same time, barriers to trade came down: France demolished her internal tariffs in 1790, Prussia followed suit in 1818 and in 1834 joined the German Customs Union, which included 17 states and some 26 million people.

A new period, sometimes called the Second Industrial Revolution, opened in the 1870s (see map 2). The new German empire (page 116) led the way, increasing its coal output from 38 million tons in 1871 to 279 million tons in 1913, and its iron output from 1.5 million tons to 15 million tons. But it also led in new areas of industrial enterprise, especially chemicals, electricity and steel. By 1910, Krupp employed 70,000 men. At a time of growing international tension (page 124), such rapid economic growth was bound to produce a reaction among Germany's neighbours and Russia began a campaign of rapid industrialization in 1890 (page 114), France in 1895 and Italy in 1905. In all these states, much heavy industry was keyed to armaments. Although the bulk of the population of Europe remained largely untouched, industrialization had both changed the face of the continent and rendered its future uncertain.

2 The industrialization of Europe, 1870–1914

- ▒ areas of industrial concentration 1870–1914
- + centres of textile industry
- ○ coalfields
- ⊞ centres of engineering, armaments and metal industries
- △ iron ore fields
- ◑ lignite fields
- ◔ potash fields
- ▮ centres of petroleum industry
- ── railway network, 1870

The emerging global economy

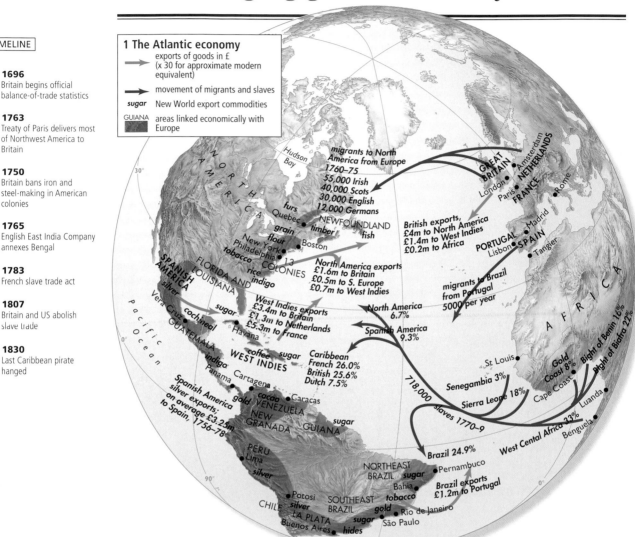

1 The Atlantic economy
exports of goods in £
(x 30 for approximate modern
equivalent)

movement of migrants and slaves

sugar New World export commodities

GUIANA areas linked economically with
Europe

In 1775, the areas of Spanish conquest and settlement in central and south America still ranked as the most valuable European overseas possession, thanks to the silver production of Mexico and Peru and the gold exports of Brazil, most of which went to Europe in return for manufactured goods. Along the Atlantic coast from Brazil to the Chesapeake, but above all in the Caribbean islands, plantation societies had developed to meet the rising demand both in Europe and in British North America (where over 2 million whites now dwelt) for tropical agricultural produce: cacao, tobacco, cotton and (especially) sugar. Since most plantations depended on the labour of African slaves, increased consumption in Europe meant increased shipments of slaves from Africa.

A closely integrated Atlantic economy had thus emerged. By 1775 the mainland colonies throughout the Americas were generally self-sufficient in food

and some supported limited manufacturing. But their white populations consumed prodigious quantities of imported European manufactured goods, and prosperity almost everywhere depended on the ability to export to Europe. Transatlantic commerce, in turn, contributed substantially to the economic development of Spain, France and Britain (almost 40 per cent of whose total exports in 1775 went to America).

In Asia, although the volume of European trade also greatly increased in the 18th century, it remained largely confined to ports or small coastal enclaves to which Asian merchants delivered goods. The Dutch and English East India Companies, founded in 1600-2 (page 80), still dominated trade with maritime Asia, but the shipment of spices to Europe had by the 18th century been overtaken by a boom in textiles (above all silks and cottons) and new drinks (tea and coffee). Since, however, in contrast to the Americas, few European manufactures proved competitive in Asia (except in the Mediterranean ports of the Ottoman empire), increased imports of Asian goods generally depended on shipments of American silver, either re-exported from Europe or carried across the Pacific to the Philippines and thence to China.

European trade also stimulated the demand for export commodities from, and injected large quantities of silver into, India and China; but most of Asia's economic life remained relatively unaffected by contact with the West, and much of its long-distance trade continued to be conducted by Asian merchants using their own pack-animals or ships. However, conditions were changing rapidly in two areas of great economic importance: the British had gained control of Bengal, a major centre of textile

The loading plan of a slave ship *(below)* shows how many slaves could be crammed below decks. The crowding marked a callous compromise between the slavers' desire to ferry as many slaves as possible and the need to ensure as many as possible of those embarked survived the voyage. By the late 18th century most ships lost less then 10 per cent of their human cargo. In earlier times, however, losses had sometimes exceeded 30 per cent, leading the Portuguese to refer to their slave ships as *tumbeiros* – coffins.

manufacture, in the 1760s and now used its huge tax revenues to maintain a substantial army ready to annex other areas of the subcontinent; and the Dutch in Java could impose commercial controls and receive commodities (above all coffee) as tribute.

Only Africa remained almost totally resistant to European penetration. Although the slave trade reached its apogee in the 18th century, with some 2.3 million slaves shipped out between 1770 and 1800, the prices paid by the Europeans for each slave steadily rose – suggesting that the African rulers who dealt in slaves more than held their own, despite the disruption arising from wars and slave-raiding, and the sustained loss of population.

In short, Europe's rapid commercial expansion overseas (for better or worse) hastened the economic integration of the world. The Americas outside the plantations enjoyed a degree of self-sufficiency, but Europe still determined the economic development of much of the continent. Although, except in Bengal, Java and the Philippines, the West could not yet shape the economies of Asia and Africa, with Britain now poised to conquer India (page 96) and with the Industrial Revolution underway in Europe (page 100), the stage was set for the creation of an integrated global economy.

2 The trading worlds of Asia and Africa

— routes of European trade

— routes of trade primarily of African and Asian merchants

coffee African and Asian export commodities

• centres of European trade in Africa and Asia

1775–1865
The United States

The disputes and difficulties leading to the American War of Independence and the foundation of the United States began almost immediately after the English victory over France in the Seven Years' War (page 86). Britain began to reorganize her vastly expanded North American possessions, establishing a huge Indian reserve west of the Alleghenies (1763) and extending the boundaries of Quebec (formerly French Canada) to the Mississippi and Ohio rivers (1774). The 'thirteen colonies' bitterly resented both this check to their westward expansion and the simultaneous insistence by Britain that its colonies should henceforth bear a greater share of the costs of their defence. Armed opposition began at Lexington and Concord in Massachusetts in 1775 (map 1). The colonies' representatives declared Independence in 1776, compelled the main British field army to surrender at Yorktown (1781), and fought on until the Treaty of Versailles (1783) recognized their sovereignty and extended the frontiers of the 'United States of America' to the Great Lakes and the Mississippi.

Expansion now proceeded rapidly. In 1783 the new republic comprised some 800,000 square miles (2,072,000 km^2) of territory, but the purchase of Louisiana from France (1803) more than doubled its size. West Florida was taken by force in 1812 and East Florida (60,000 square miles, 155,400 km^2) during the presidency of James Monroe. Thereafter extensive territories in the south and west were added, largely at the expense of Mexico (map 2), and in 1846 a compromise with Britain was reached over Oregon, increasing the number of states from 13 to 34. The population expanded from 3 million in 1783 to 31 million in 1860, fuelled by the arrival of a new wave of European immigrants, predominantly German and Irish.

These developments had important political consequences. The ruling elites of the southern states, with their plantation economy and large black slave population, felt increasingly threatened by the industrializing north and the growing Midwest. This, rather than the issue of slavery, underlay the American Civil War (1861-5); but the issues in fact proved inseparable because, with over 90 percent of

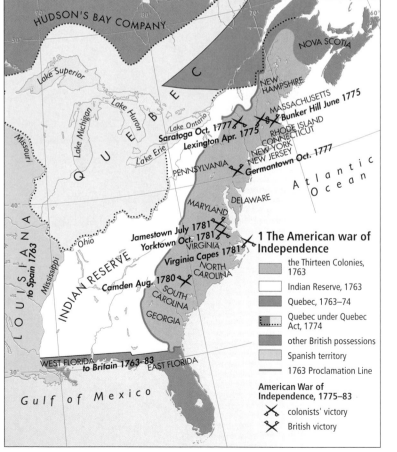

1 The American war of Independence

- the Thirteen Colonies, 1763
- Indian Reserve, 1763
- Quebec, 1763–74
- Quebec under Quebec Act, 1774
- other British possessions
- Spanish territory
- 1763 Proclamation Line

American War of Independence, 1775–83
- ✗ colonists' victory
- ✗ British victory

Dead soldiers at Gettysburg
(below). The small market town of Gettysburg, Pennsylvania, was the scene of the greatest battles of the war. Lee, advancing into the North to force Lincoln to negotiate peace on the basis of Southern independence, attacked General Meade's Union army, but in the course of a three-day battle was comprehensively beaten. The Union lost 23,000 men, the Confederacy 28,000.

the black population living in the South, the moral question was also a regional question. Abraham Lincoln, elected President in 1860 by the votes of the Northern states, was right to claim that the nation could not permanently remain 'half slave and half free'.

Soon after Lincoln's election, South Carolina seceded from the Union and was quickly joined by ten other states which came together as the Confederate States of America with their capital at Richmond, Virginia (map 4). For Lincoln the fundamental issue was whether a constitutional republic could preserve its territorial integrity; he recognized no constitutional right of secession. By 1863, however, pressure from radical Republicans added the aim of freeing the slaves in the rebel states to the commitment to restore the Union. Thanks to the superior military skill of their commanders, and to their shorter lines of communications, the confederacy fought on for four years (1861-5). The Northern strategy was to deny the South vital resources by a naval blockade, to gain control of key river routes and forts in the west and to capture Richmond. Eventually the superior demographic and economic resources of the North prevailed – albeit at the cost of 635,000 Union and 383,000 Confederate military casualties – and created the 'second American Revolution' which, by crippling the southern ruling class and liberating its labour force, determined that the thrusting, urban, industrialized North, with its creed of competitive capitalism, would stamp its pattern (for good or ill) on the entire United States.

4 Comparative resources: Union and Confederate states, 1861

Union States   Confederate States

Total pop.: 2.5 to 1
Male adult pop.: 4.4 to 1
Free men 18–60 yrs in military service: 1864   44%   90%
Wealth produced: 3 to 1
Railroad mileage: 2.4 to 1
Merchant ship ton.: 9 to 1

Naval ship ton.: 25 to 1
Factory prod.: 10 to 1
Textile prod.: 17 to 1
Iron production: 20 to 1
Coal production: 38 to 1
Firearms prod.: 32 to 1

Farm acreage: 3 to 1
Draft animals: 1.8 to 1
Livestock: 1.5 to 1
Wheat prod.: 4.2 to 1
Corn production: 2 to 1
Cotton prod.: 1 to 24

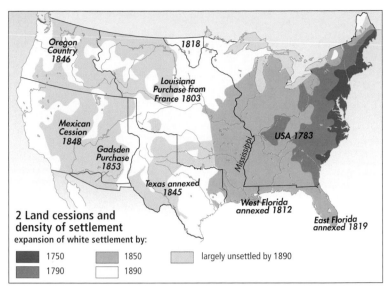

2 Land cessions and density of settlement
expansion of white settlement by:

1750	1850
1790	1890

largely unsettled by 1890

Oregon Country 1846
1818
Louisiana Purchase from France 1803
USA 1783
Mexican Cession 1848
Gadsden Purchase 1853
Texas annexed 1845
West Florida annexed 1812
East Florida annexed 1819
USA 1783
Mississippi

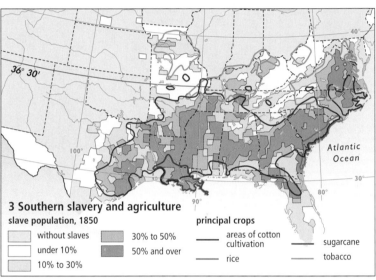

3 Southern slavery and agriculture
slave population, 1850

without slaves
under 10%
10% to 30%
30% to 50%
50% and over

principal crops
— areas of cotton cultivation
— rice
— sugarcane
— tobacco

36° 30'
Atlantic Ocean

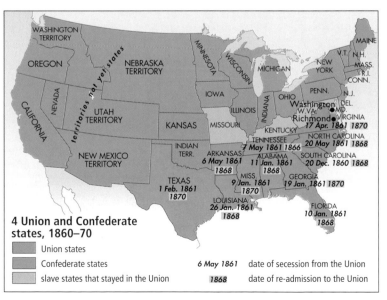

4 Union and Confederate states, 1860–70

Union states
Confederate states
slave states that stayed in the Union

6 May 1861   date of secession from the Union
1868   date of re-admission to the Union

WASHINGTON TERRITORY
OREGON
CALIFORNIA
NEVADA
UTAH TERRITORY
NEBRASKA TERRITORY
MINNESOTA
WISCONSIN
MICHIGAN
MAINE
V.T. N.H.
NEW YORK
MASS.
R.I. CONN.
PENN.
N.J.
OHIO
INDIANA
ILLINOIS
IOWA
KANSAS
MISSOURI
KENTUCKY
territories not yet states
INDIAN TERR.
NEW MEXICO TERRITORY
ARKANSAS 6 May 1861 1868
TEXAS 1 Feb. 1861 1870
LOUISIANA 26 Jan. 1861 1868
MISS. 9 Jan. 1861 1870
ALABAMA 11 Jan. 1861 1868
TENNESSEE 7 May 1861 1866
GEORGIA 19 Jan. 1861 1870
NORTH CAROLINA 20 May 1861 1868
SOUTH CAROLINA 20 Dec. 1860 1868
FLORIDA 10 Jan. 1861 1868
Washington
W.VA. DEL. MD.
Richmond 17 Apr. 1861 1870
VIRGINIA

Australia and New Zealand

1 The European settlement and development of Australia

- native land rights claims, Jan. 1997
- more than 2 persons per square mile 1961 (by statistical division)
- no significant use, c. 1960
- ■ penal settlements
- ● settlements

railways
- —— before 1881
- ----- 1901–1920
- -·-·- 1881–1900
- ········ after 1920

minerals
- gold
- copper
- lead
- natural gas
- T tungsten
- ■ tin
- U uranium
- ⊕ blast furnace
- iron ore
- silver
- zinc
- ▲ oil
- N nickel
- A alumina/bauxite
- M manganese

Although Australia and New Zealand were reconnoitred by the Dutch explorer Abel Tasman in 1642, colonization only began in 1770 when James Cook raised the British flag at Botany Bay. New South Wales served as a penal colony from 1788 to 1839, as did van Diemen's land (later Tasmania) from 1804 to 1853, but in 1829 the British government, in order to forestall the French, claimed the whole Australian continent. Fear of France also led to the annexation of New Zealand in 1840. However, the geographical

obstacles, the lack of exportable goods (at first chiefly seal products and sandalwood), and (especially in the case of New Zealand) the opposition of the indigenous population complicated the colonization process in both territories. In 1850, the total white population of Australia still numbered only 350,000, and that of New Zealand was less than 100,000.

The discovery of gold in New South Wales and Victoria in 1851 initiated a new phase, and encouraged the growth of the inland population. Even more important was the rapid growth of sheep-farming: in 1850 Australia sent 17,000 tons of wool to Great Britain, but 134,000 tons in 1879. Nevertheless, as centralizing systems of communications and transportation developed, the dominance of the coastal cities – especially Sydney and Melbourne – increased. By the 1890s, two-thirds of Australia's population lived in urban areas along the coast (a pattern that steadily intensified throughout the 20th century.) In New Zealand, where wool remained largely a South Island product, exports rose in value from £67,000 in 1853 to £2.7 million twenty years later. The development of the North Island, which was held back by the bitter Maori Wars (1860-71), only came after the introduction of refrigeration, which made possible the export of frozen lamb, butter and cheese. Dairy farming developed rapidly, and the North Island now drew ahead of the South in population.

Political development kept pace with economic growth. In 1855 New South Wales, Victoria, South Australia and Tasmania became self-governing colonies, followed by Queensland in 1859; in 1901 they joined together to form the Commonwealth of Australia. New Zealand, which had been divided in 1852 into six provinces, each with an elected council, became a united Dominion (after measures had been taken to safeguard the rights of the Maori population) in 1876. Both countries achieved sovereign status under the Statute of Westminster in 1931. The economy of both dominions remained heavily dependent on primary exports – wool, meat, grain and dairy products – which enjoyed preferential treatment in the British market. Even the spectacular discoveries of minerals, coal, oil and gas in and about Australia after 1950 went largely into exports. However Britain's decision to join the European Economic Community and dismantle 'imperial preference' in 1973 (page 166), coupled with the conviction that the countries of the Pacific Rim would become the economic hub of the world in the 21st century, drove both Australia and New Zealand to develop new economic activities and to foster trade with countries outside the British Commonwealth.

This romanticized picture of an attack on a Maori *pa* (fort) during the first New Zealand War suggests the storming of a castle. In fact, recent research has revealed that the *pa* evolved rapidly into sophisticated trench and bunker systems which anticipated those of the Western Front by over 50 years. By the end of the conflict large tracts of Maori land had been confiscated by the colonial government.

2 The development of New Zealand to c. 1875

- pioneer sheep regions 1840s
- sheep
- timber
- gold rushes

1850 date of foundation of city

NORTH ISLAND

Marsden's first mission 1814
Russell first capital 1840-1
Auckland second capital 1841-65
Thames 1867-71
New Plymouth 1841
TARANAKI (NEW PLYMOUTH)
Cook's landfall 1769
AUCKLAND
WELLINGTON
Napier 1855
HAWKE'S BAY
Nelson 1841
Blenheim 1855
Wellington capital since 1865
NELSON
MARLBOROUGH
West Coast 1864-68
Hokitika
Tasman's landfall 1642
WESTLAND
Christchurch 1850
Akaroa French colony 1840
CANTERBURY
SOUTH ISLAND
OTAGO
SOUTHLAND
Dunedin 1848 NZ's largest city 1861-c. 83
Invercargill 1857
Stewart Island

3 The development of New Zealand since 1875

- major sheep regions
- coal c. 1880–1914
- dairying (periods shown)
- gold-dredging 1880s–1960
- forest products since 1950
- wine
- horticulture
- hydro-electricity since 1930
- main trunk railways

NORTH ISLAND majority of population since 1901

Marsden Point oil refinery 1965
since 1920s
Polynesian migration since 1950s
Auckland largest city since mid 1880s
Glenbrook steel mill 1969
since 1920s
Hamilton
Arapuni first major h.e. station 1929
75% of Maoris north of line 1980s
New Plymouth
Wellington–New Plymouth railway 1886
since 1880s
North Island main trunk railway 1908
Napier
since 1900
Palmerston North
Wellington–Napier railway 1891
Wellington urban area second largest since 1906
Westport
Nelson
Picton
Cook Strait
rail ferry 1962, h.e. cable 1965
Greymouth
Christchurch–Picton railway 1945
Lake Coleridge first government h.e. station 1914
Cheviot
Christchurch largest South Island city since 1895
Christchurch–Bluff railway 1879
SOUTH ISLAND majority of population 1861-1901
Manapouri
N.Z.'s largest h.e. station 1971
Port Chalmers first export of frozen meat 1882
Dunedin
Edendale first dairy export factory 1882
Bluff aluminium smelter 1971

The decline of the Ottoman empire

The period between 1798 and 1923 saw the disintegration and final collapse of the Ottoman Empire, the major power in West Asia since the 16th century (see page 70). Plagued by foreign invasions, wars, and the revolts of subject peoples demanding national independence, the empire steadily lost territory.

In 1798 a French army led by Napoleon Bonaparte invaded Egypt and Syria, only to be defeated by the British. Peace was arranged in 1802 and three years later the sultan appointed Mohammed Ali governor of Egypt. Under his rule, however, the province gained de facto independence and in 1841 Mohammed was recognized as hereditary viceroy. Meanwhile, between 1830 and 1847 the French conquered Algeria, and in 1881 they annexed Tunis; the following year the British occupied Egypt. There were also wars with Russia, rebellions in the Arab provinces and almost constant revolts in the Balkans – starting with the Greek War of Independence in 1821, which resulted (following the pressure of foreign powers) in the recognition of a sovereign Greek state in 1830. Foreign intervention also

1 The Ottoman empire, 1798–1923

Ottoman empire, 1798
lost by 1886
lost by 1914
eastern limit of nominal Ottoman control, 1913
frontiers, 1914
lost by 1920
Ottoman empire under the Treaty of Sèvres, 1920
Turkey under the Treaty of Lausanne, 1923

precipitated the Crimean War (1853-6) and the Lebanese crisis of 1860-1, while Russian and Austrian demands helped secure the independence of Montenegro, Serbia and Romania by 1878. By 1882, the Ottomans had lost 40 per cent of their empire.

Their finances also deteriorated rapidly until in 1875 the state became virtually bankrupt and the Sultan suspended payment of the interest due on the Ottoman debt. In 1881, he agreed to supervision of his treasury by European bankers: the empire's survival became dependent on foreign governments which preferred the preservation of a weakened Ottoman state to the dangerous power vacuum that would follow Turkish collapse. Nevertheless, further territorial losses followed: Italy annexed Libya in 1911 and, at the end of the Balkan wars in 1913 (page 124), the Ottomans surrendered Crete, most of the Aegean islands, Thrace, Macedonia and Albania. In all, between 1908 and 1911, the Turks lost 30 per cent of their remaining possessions.

Throughout the 19th century the sultans made various attempts to modernize their empire, but not always successfully: Selim III, who aimed to create a modern army, was deposed in 1807 when his troops mutinied against the proposed reforms. The Janissaries rebelled in 1826 against reforms decreed by Mahmud II, but this provoked their abolition.

After a decade of agitation, in 1876 Sultan Abdul Hamid II introduced a constitution, and a Parliament met the following year; but it was dissolved almost immediately and only pressure by the Ottoman Society for Union and Progress (the 'Young Turks') forced its restoration in 1908. The following year Abdul Hamid abdicated, and the Young Turks came to dominate the administration. However, their nationalist policies and opposition to any further surrender of territory contributed substantially to the Arabs' willingness to seek accommodation with the Turks' enemies, once the Ottoman empire entered World War I on the side of Germany and Austro-Hungary (page 132).

Despite tenacious resistance, the Turks were eventually defeated and West Asia (despite earlier promises to the Arabs) came under the control of the victorious French and British governments. The Sultan collaborated with Great Britain after his defeat, and in 1920 agreed to the treaty of Sèvres which would dismember the empire. However, the arrival of Greek troops at Izmir provoked a nationalist uprising which crystallized around the Turks' only undefeated general, Mustafa Kemal. The sultanate was abolished and, after some reverses, Turkish forces drove back the Greeks and their allies and secured recognition of the sovereignty of the Turkish Republic at the treaty of Lausanne in 1923.

Mustafa Kemal, or Atatürk (above), – 'father of the Turks', as he styled himself – was an Ottoman commander in the First World War. His effective leadership of Turkish forces in 1922 led to his becoming president of the new Turkish republic that year. He was determined to turn Turkey into a modern, industrialized, Western-style secular state.

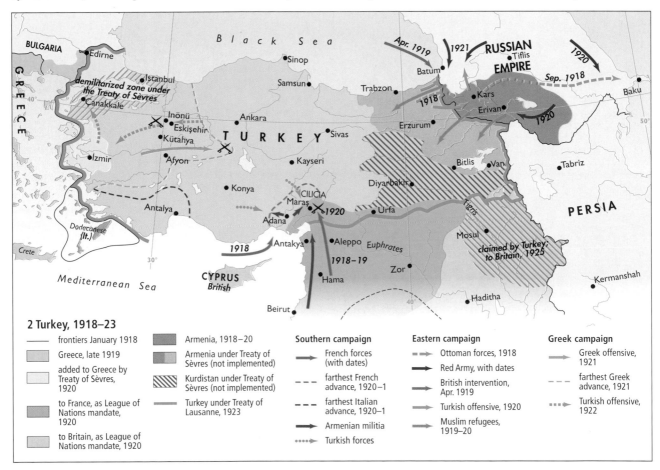

2 Turkey, 1918–23

——	frontiers January 1918
▨	Greece, late 1919
▨	added to Greece by Treaty of Sèvres, 1920
▨	to France, as League of Nations mandate, 1920
▨	to Britain, as League of Nations mandate, 1920

▨	Armenia, 1918–20
▨	Armenia under Treaty of Sèvres (not implemented)
▨	Kurdistan under Treaty of Sèvres (not implemented)
——	Turkey under Treaty of Lausanne, 1923

Southern campaign
→ French forces (with dates)
- - - farthest French advance, 1920–1
- - - farthest Italian advance, 1920–1
→ Armenian militia
•••• Turkish forces

Eastern campaign
- -▶ Ottoman forces, 1918
➜ Red Army, with dates
→ British intervention, Apr. 1919
→ Turkish offensive, 1920
→ Muslim refugees, 1919–20

Greek campaign
→ Greek offensive, 1921
- - - farthest Greek advance, 1921
•••• Turkish offensive, 1922

Africa in the 19th century

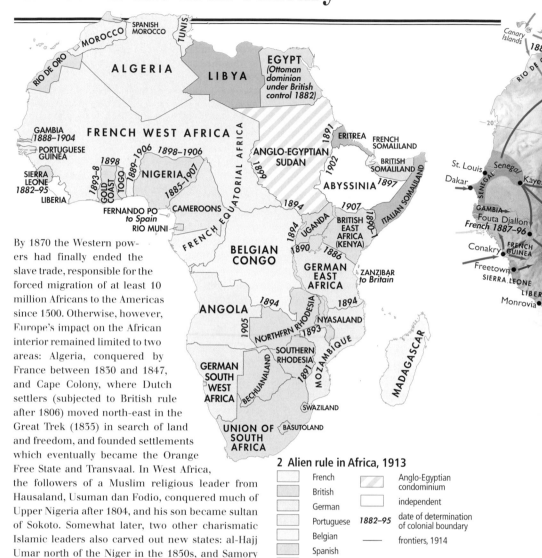

By 1870 the Western pow-
ers had finally ended the
slave trade, responsible for the
forced migration of at least 10
million Africans to the Americas
since 1500. Otherwise, however,
Europe's impact on the African
interior remained limited to two
areas: Algeria, conquered by
France between 1830 and 1847,
and Cape Colony, where Dutch
settlers (subjected to British rule
after 1806) moved north-east in the
Great Trek (1835) in search of land
and freedom, and founded settlements
which eventually became the Orange
Free State and Transvaal. In West Africa,
the followers of a Muslim religious leader from
Hausaland, Usuman dan Fodio, conquered much of
Upper Nigeria after 1804, and his son became sultan
of Sokoto. Somewhat later, two other charismatic
Islamic leaders also carved out new states: al-Hajj
Umar north of the Niger in the 1850s, and Samory
south of it in the 1870s and '80s. In the north-east,
Mohammed Ali of Egypt conquered northern Sudan
in 1820, and his grandson Ismail consolidated

2 Alien rule in Africa, 1913

French		Anglo-Egyptian condominium
British		
German		independent
Portuguese	1882–95	date of determination of colonial boundary
Belgian	——	frontiers, 1914
Spanish		
Italian		

Egyptian control over much of the littoral of the Red
Sea. Finally, in the south, the formation of the Zulu
kingdom by Shaka in 1818 led to widespread disruption as neighbouring peoples moved away from the
aggressive new state.

Meanwhile, the progress of industrialization in
Europe (page 100) created a demand for new sources
of raw materials and new markets, while the mass-
production of quinine (which offered protection
against the malaria endemic in Africa) and machine-
guns gave the Europeans the ability to satisfy these
demands by force. In the 1870s the French advanced
inland from Senegal while the British began the
conquest of Nigeria. In 1882 the British invaded
and occupied Egypt, and the Belgians advanced up
the Congo river. Next, Germany laid claim to
Togoland, the Cameroons, Southwest Africa and

The Battle of Isandhlwana
on 22 January 1879 was the first
major engagement of the Zulu
war *(right)*. A British force of
1700 white and African troops
under Lord Chelmsford was
routed by 20,000 Zulu, the
consequence rather of British
arrogance and carelessness than
of overwhelming numbers. It
demonstrated the continuing
possibility that African tactics
and weaponry could triumph
over well-armed European
forces.

1 The partition of Africa

colonies or settlements, 1880

French
British
Portuguese

★ anti-European resistance

African states or empires

colonial penetration

→ French
→ British
→ Portuguese
→ German
→ Italian
→ Spanish
→ Belgian

Tangier
international zone 1923
MOROCCO 1912 French protectorate
Marrakesh
SPANISH SAHARA 1912
Algiers French occupation 1830
ALGERIA 1870
Tunis
TUNIS
Tripoli 1911
TRIPOLITANIA
Benghazi 1912
CYRENAICA Alexandria
British invasion and occupation 1882
Cairo
EGYPT
Ghadames
In Salah French 1901
FEZZAN
S a h a r a
Taoudenni French occupation 1906
Tamanrasset French 1902
Bilma
Red Sea
SUDAN Anglo-Egyptian Condominium established 1899
Suakin
Massawa
FRENCH SUDAN 1894
Empire of Ahmadu Sefu (son of al-Hajj Umar)
Timbuktu
Gao
NIGER
Agadès
Zinder French 1899
Omdurman Khartoum
Adowa 1896 Italian invasion defeated
Aden (British)
Berbera
Ségou
Bamako French 1883
UPPER VOLTA
Sokoto
Say French 1896
Sokoto British 1903
Kano British 1902
Niger
Fort Lamy
RABIH'S DOMAIN
Mahdist state in the Sudan 1881-98
Fashoda British 1898
ABYSSINIA SHOA
Djibouti Addis Ababa
Samory's empire
IVORY COAST 1891
Kumasi 1896
GOLD COAST 1874
Accra
SOKOTO CALIPHATE
Nikki French 1894
NUPE
ILORIN
YORUBA
Lokoja
IBO
Northern Nigeria claimed by Royal Niger Company (1886-1900)
failed attempt by Marchand to take Fashoda for France, 1898
Gondokoro
Ethiopian expansion under Emperor Menelik
SIDAMA KINGDOMS
ITALIAN SOMALILAND 1889-92
Mogadishu
TOGO DAHOMEY
Lagos
CAMEROONS
Fernando Po Spanish
Principe Portuguese
Sao Tomé Portuguese
Douala German occupation 1884
RIO MUNI
GABON
Congo
CONGO FREE STATE penetration by King Leopold's agents (became Belgian Congo in 1908)
TIPPU TIB'S DOMAIN
UGANDA 1893 Kampala British 1890
Nairobi
BRITISH EAST AFRICA (KENYA)
Imperial British East Africa Company 1888-93
Lake Victoria
GERMAN EAST AFRICA (TANGANYIKA)
Mombasa
Zanzibar British 1890
Dar es Salaam German occupation 1888
Indian Ocean
FRENCH CONGO
Cabinda
Lake Tanganyika
Lake Nyasa
KATANGA
ANGOLA
Benguela
Luanda
Moçâmedes
NORTHERN RHODESIA
British Central Africa (Nyasaland) Protectorate 1891
Zomba
Ruvuma
Mozambique
Quelimane
Zambezi
Salisbury
MOZAMBIQUE
Beira
SOUTHERN RHODESIA
Tamatave
Tananarive
MADAGASCAR
MERINA KINGDOM
Swakopmund
Walvis Bay British 1878
GERMAN SOUTH WEST AFRICA
Rhodes British South Africa Company 'Pioneer Column' 1890
Pretoria TRANSVAAL
Johannesburg Vaal
Delagoa Bay
Lüderitz German 1884
BRITISH BECHUANALAND
Orange
Kimberley
ORANGE FREE STATE
NATAL
Durban
CAPE COLONY
Cape Town
East London
Port Elizabeth

East Africa, each move provoking parallel actions by other powers. Portugal revived her effort to colonize the interior of Angola and Mozambique, while Britain claimed parts of East Africa (later Kenya and Uganda) and, on the initiative of the Cape politician and industrialist Cecil Rhodes, central Africa (later Zimbabwe, Zambia and Malawi).

Even larger gains accrued to the French, who swept into sub-Saharan Africa from three directions and gained control over almost one-third of the continent (map 1). With the conquest of Libya and Cyrenaica by Italy in 1911 and the partition of Morocco between France and Spain in 1912, of the 40 political units into which Africa had been arbitrarily divided, only two could claim any real independence: Ethiopia, which had defeated an Italian attempt at annexation in 1896, and Liberia, which enjoyed financial support from the United States. In little more than a generation, the Europeans had gained control over an additional 12 million square miles (31 million km²) of territory.

Latin America

TIMELINE

1808
Napoleonic invasion of Portugal and Spain stimulates independence movements in Latin America

1819
Battle of Boyacá leads to independence of Colombia

1821
Battle of Carabobo finally secures Venezuelan independence

1822
Brazil declares independence

1823
Mexican Republic declared

1879
War of the Pacific (Chile, Bolivia, Peru)

1910
Start of Mexican revolution

Napoleon's invasion of Spain and Portugal in 1808 (page 98) enabled these countries' American colonies to gain independence. The revolt began in Argentina in 1810 and in Venezuela in 1811, helped by the decision of Great Britain and the United States to oppose intervention by the Iberian powers. The fall of Lima (1821) and Simón Bolívar's victory at Ayacucho (1824), deprived Spain of control over South America. In the North, early rebellions in Mexico were suppressed, but in 1823 a republic was proclaimed, and a last Spanish attempt at reconquest in 1829 met with defeat. Only Brazil made the transition to independence peacefully, as Portugal agreed to provide a constitution and in 1822 the Portuguese king's eldest son became Emperor Pedro I of Brazil. Only in 1889 when, following the abolition of slavery (1888), disgruntled plantation owners rose in revolt, did a federal republic replace the empire.

Independence remained in essence a political movement confined to the colonial aristocracy, who desired a transfer of authority without social change. The next half-century was dominated by military dictators who ruled in the interests of the privileged classes and squandered their assets on repeated territorial disputes. Mexico lost most, forfeiting vast territories to the United States (see page 104); but it was also the first state to introduce limited social reforms after the election of the Indian Benito Juarez as President in 1861.

A subsistence economy still prevailed in most areas. Although Brazil with its slave-operated coffee plantations offered an exception, elsewhere the great rural estates showed little interest in producing for the market. After 1880, overseas investment increased rapidly, but selectively, concentrated mainly in Argentina, Brazil, Mexico and Chile. Moreover, even there, the foreign stimulus shifted those economies sharply towards the export of primary products: grain and meat from Argentina, nitrate from Chile, coffee and rubber from Brazil, oil from Mexico, and fruit from the so-called 'Banana Republics' of the central isthmus.

Most of these countries modernized and commercialized their production, and built docks and railways to expedite the export of food and raw materials. This attracted a new wave of immigrants and created a new urban and industrial proletariat as well as a middle class prospering from the export trade; but it left the majority of the rural population in abject poverty. Mexico under the repressive regime of Porfirio Díaz (1876-1911) exemplified these trends until in 1910 the country erupted in revolution: eventually, in 1917, a constitution incorporating major social and political reforms was adopted. Elsewhere, as long as prosperity continued – that is, until the Great Crash of 1929 (see page 138) – political and social pressures remained under control (albeit sometimes only thanks to armed intervention by the United States); but rapid and unbalanced economic expansion steadily undermined the regimes that promoted it.

abbreviations to map below

A	AGUASCALIENTES	N	NUEVO LEÓN
C	CAMPECHE	P	PUEBLA
G	GUANAJUATO	Q	QUERÉTARO
H	HIDALGO	S	SAN LUIS POTOSÍ
ME	MÉXICO	T	TLAXCALA
M	MORELOS	V	VERACRUZ

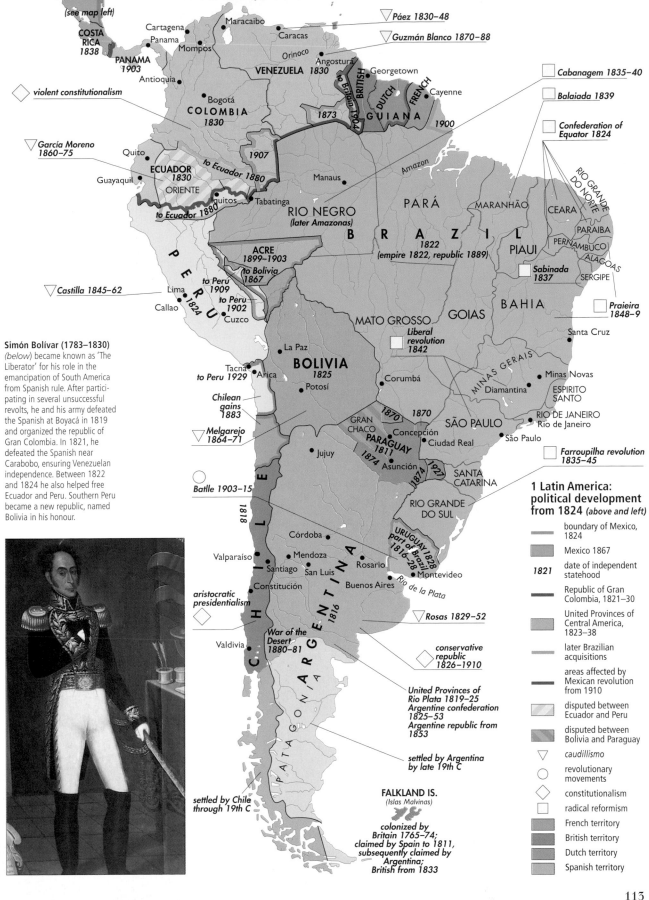

Páez 1830–48

Guzmán Blanco 1870–88

COSTA RICA 1838

PANAMA 1903

Cartagena
Panama
Mompos
Maracaibo
Caracas
Orinoco
Angostura
Georgetown

VENEZUELA 1830

to Britain 1904

BRITISH
DUTCH
FRENCH
GUIANA
Cayenne

Cabanagem 1835–40

Balaiada 1839

Confederation of Equator 1824

◇ violent constitutionalism

Antioquia
Bogotá
COLOMBIA 1830

1873

1900

▽ García Moreno 1860–75

Quito
Guayaquil
ECUADOR 1830
ORIENTE
to Ecuador 1880

1907

to Ecuador 1880
Iquitos
Tabatinga
Manaus

Amazon

RIO NEGRO
(later Amazonas)

PARÁ

MARANHÃO
CEARÁ

RIO GRANDE DO NORTE

PARAIBA
PERNAMBUCO
ALAGOAS
SERGIPE

BRAZIL
1822
(empire 1822, republic 1889)

PIAUI

Sabinada 1837

ACRE
1899–1903
to Bolivia 1867

▽ Castilla 1845–62

Lima
Callao
to Peru 1909
to Peru 1902
Cuzco

P E R U

1824

Praieira 1848–9

BAHIA

Santa Cruz

Simón Bolívar (1783–1830) (below) became known as 'The Liberator' for his role in the emancipation of South America from Spanish rule. After participating in several unsuccessful revolts, he and his army defeated the Spanish at Boyacá in 1819 and organized the republic of Gran Colombia. In 1821, he defeated the Spanish near Carabobo, ensuring Venezuelan independence. Between 1822 and 1824 he also helped free Ecuador and Peru. Southern Peru became a new republic, named Bolivia in his honour.

La Paz
BOLIVIA 1825
Potosí
Corumbá
MATO GROSSO
GOIAS
Liberal revolution 1842

MINAS GERAIS

Diamantina
Minas Novas
ESPIRITO SANTO

Tacna
Arica
to Peru 1929

Chilean gains 1883

▽ Melgarejo 1864–71

○ Batlle 1903–15

Jujuy

GRAN CHACO
PARAGUAY 1811
Concepción
Ciudad Real
Asunción

1870
1870

SÃO PAULO
Rio de Janeiro
São Paulo
RIO DE JANEIRO

1874
1874
1927

SANTA CATARINA

Farroupilha revolution 1835–45

RIO GRANDE DO SUL

1818

Córdoba
Valparaíso
Mendoza
Santiago
San Luis
Rosario

URUGUAY 1828 part of Brazil 1816–28

Montevideo
Rio de la Plata
Buenos Aires

◇ aristocratic presidentialism

C H I L E

A R G E N T I N A

1816

▽ Rosas 1829–52

Valdivia

War of the Desert 1880–81

◇ conservative republic 1826–1910

United Provinces of Rio Plata 1819–25
Argentine confederation 1825–53
Argentine republic from 1853

P A T A G O N I A

settled by Argentina by late 19th C

settled by Chile through 19th C

FALKLAND IS.
(Islas Malvinas)

colonized by Britain 1765–74; claimed by Spain to 1811, subsequently claimed by Argentina; British from 1833

1 Latin America: political development from 1824 (above and left)

- boundary of Mexico, 1824
- Mexico 1867
- 1821 date of independent statehood
- Republic of Gran Colombia, 1821–30
- United Provinces of Central America, 1823–38
- later Brazilian acquisitions
- areas affected by Mexican revolution from 1910
- disputed between Ecuador and Peru
- disputed between Bolivia and Paraguay
- ▽ caudillismo
- ○ revolutionary movements
- ◇ constitutionalism
- ☐ radical reformism
- French territory
- British territory
- Dutch territory
- Spanish territory

113

The expansion of the Russian empire

For 40 years after the Congress of Vienna (1815) Russia remained the strongest military power in Europe, focusing her interests on the Balkans and on the straits leading from the Black Sea. Since most Balkan subjects of the Ottoman empire were Orthodox Slavs, Russia considered herself their natural protector; and because Turkey lay in the way of Russia's access to the Mediterranean, it desired Constantinople to remain amenable to Russian influence alone. However, France and Austria also had imperial ambitions in these areas, while Britain opposed any further Russian expansion. In 1854, therefore, following Russia's invasion of Turkey's Danubian provinces and destruction of the Ottoman fleet, France and Britain (supported by Austria) declared war and invaded the Crimea, eventually forcing Russia to evacuate the Balkans and to dismantle its Black Sea fleet. A further Russian attempt to liberate the Balkan Slavs from Turkish rule in 1877-8 also failed (page 108).

Russia proved far more successful in Asia (map 1). Her forces subdued the Kazakhs (1816-54), completed Russian control of the Caucasus (1857-64) and annexed the khanates of central Asia (1865-76). The imperial frontier now reached – and sometimes penetrated – the great mountain chains that separated it from Persia, Afghanistan, India and China. The colonization of North America also continued into the early 19th century, and forts were built as far

south as California; but most were soon abandoned and Alaska was sold to the United States in 1867. On the other hand, China ceded to the Tsar the Amur basin and parts of the Pacific coast (where Vladivostok was founded in 1860), and leased Port Arthur (1898). This warm-water harbour, unimpeded by winter ice, was soon linked to the main Trans-Siberian railway (completed in 1903). But Russian expansion conflicted with Japanese designs. The two powers had already clashed over their interests in Korea and south Manchuria, following Japan's victory over China in 1894-5 (page 130), and in 1904-5 Japan attacked Russia, forcing her to abandon most of her gains in the Far East and to cede south Sakhalin.

This humiliating defeat fanned the flames of domestic unrest. Shaken by the backwardness exposed in the Crimean War, Tsar Alexander II (1855-81) had initiated a number of reforms in the 1860s: new local government organizations; educational improvements; and radical changes to the legal system. The emancipation of the serfs in 1861 was the cornerstone of the reforms (map 2). However, still confined to their villages, many peasants felt aggrieved that they often had to acquire by purchase less land than they had previously worked. From 1890 the government embarked on an industrialization programme with railways at its centre. Many of the lines aimed to facilitate the movement of troops to frontier areas in case of war, but they allowed not

1 Russia in Asia, 1815–1900

- the Russian empire, 1815
- acquisitions 1816–56
- acquisitions 1856–76
- acquisitions 1877–1900
- vassal khanates
- railway

3 The revolution of 1905

→ voyage of the battleship *Potemkin*

peasant unrest and land seizures

▲ workers' soviets

■ army mutinies

🚩 naval mutinies

★ major strikes and armed workers' uprisings

2 Serfdom in Russia, 1860

serfs as a percentage of the population

over 50

30–50

10–30

under 10

— boundary of Russia, 1871

serfs' obligations

◆ *obrok*: dues in kind or cash

◇ *barshchina*: labour service to landlord

⬥ both *obrok* and *barshchina* dues

ALASKA
sold to USA 1867

Port Alexander

Pacific Ocean

only migration from overcrowded central Russia to western Siberia, but also the movement of peasants to urban areas to man a growing number of factories. Between 1863 and 1914 Russia's urban population increased from 6 to 18.6 million.

In 1905, in the wake of Japan's victory, revolutionary parties proved quick to exploit the low incomes and general hardships created by these rapid changes, while the new professional classes pressed for political reform (map 3). Unrest in the towns spread to the countryside, to the army and even to the Black Sea fleet, led by the battleship Potemkin, forcing Tsar Nicholas II (1894-1917) to grant a constitution, including a duma, or parliament; but by 1907 the government had regained full control. Nevertheless the 1905 revolution irreparably weakened the old order, and after 1912 another wave of social unrest swept the empire. Internally, Russia was in no position to meet the challenge of the First World War in 1914.

Although mobilization took place with a rapidity that took the Germans by surprise (page 132), the tsar's government proved incapable of supplying its millions of troops with equipment, munitions or (eventually) with food.

'It is better to abolish serfdom from above than wait for it to abolish itself from below,' declared Alexander II *(left)* in 1857. Four years later Alexander did indeed free the serfs. He soon found that it was one thing to emancipate them, another to feed, clothe and educate them. Radical though they were in Russian terms, Alexander's reforms failed to address the core problems facing his country.

Nationalism in Europe

Nationalism flourished in Europe in the wake of the French Revolution (page 98), but it remained confined largely to the middle classes and proved relatively short-lived. The Great Powers at the Congress of Vienna in 1815 aimed to restore Europe (as far as possible) to its pre-war condition by combating both liberalism and nationalism and by creating a barrier around France. To that end Holland received the Austrian Netherlands (later Belgium); Prussia took over Westphalia and much of the Rhineland; Sardinia-Piedmont annexed Genoa; Russia retained Finland and most of Poland; and Austria gained Venetia and Lombardy.

By 1830, however, when a new wave of liberal and national agitation arose, the Great Powers no longer worked in unison, enabling Greece (page 108) and Belgium to obtain independence. In 1848-9, when an outburst of nationalism erupted into full-scale revolution, the solidarity of the conservative powers – coupled with divisions among the nationalists themselves – still sufficed to maintain the status quo. Shortly afterwards, a new generation of statesmen began to use nationalism for their own ends. Cavour

Known as the 'Iron Chancellor', Otto von Bismarck *(above)* became minister-president of Prussia in 1862. After wars against Denmark (1864) and Austria (1866), he formed the North German confederation (1867) and after the Franco-Prussian war (1870-1) inaugurated the German empire. As German chancellor (1871-90) he played a leading role in the European alliance systems of the 1870s and 1880s.

2 The unification of Germany, 1815–71

- Prussia in 1815
- acquired by Prussia, 1815–66
- German Confederation, 1815
- North German Confederation, 1867
- Imperial territory of Alsace-Lorraine, 1871
- ● free city
- German Empire, 1871
- Austro-Prussian forces attack on Denmark, 1864
- Prussian armies in the war with Austria, 1866
- German armies in the Franco-Prussian war, 1870–71

1 The unification of Italy, 1859–70

	French from 1768, formerly Genoese
	Kingdom of Sardinia in 1815
	territory annexed 1859
	territory annexed March 1860
	territory annexed November 1860
	territory lost to France 1860
	territory annexed 1866
	territory annexed 1870
	Austrian empire, 1815
	Italian border, 1914

SWITZERLAND

AUSTRO-HUNGARIAN EMPIRE

TYROL

Bergamo

Trent (Trento)

VENETIA

Udine

Görz (Gorizia)

Trieste

Aosta

Como

Monza

Brescia

Verona

Venice

Fiume

SAVOY

PIEDMONT

LOMBARDY

Magenta 1859

Milan

Padua

Novara 1849

Solferino 1859

Custoza 1848, 1866

Mantua

Pola

Susa

Turin

KINGDOM OF SARDINIA

Alessandria

Parma

PARMA

Guastalla

MODENA

ROMAGNA

Ferrara

SAN MARINO

Zara

OTTOMAN EMPIRE

FRANCE

Genoa

Pontremoli

LIGURIA

Modena

Bologna

Rimini

Pesaro

Dalmatia

NICE

Monaco

La Spezia

Lucca

Arno

Pisa

Florence

Urbino

Ancona

Castelfidardo

Lissa 1866

Nice

Livorno (Leghorn)

Arezzo

Siena

MARCHES

PAPAL STATES

CORSICA

Elba

TUSCANY

UMBRIA

Spoleto

Rieti

Adriatic Sea

Civitavecchia

Tiber

Mentana

Rome

Pontecorvo

KINGDOM

Bari

Terracina

Gaeta

Volturno 1860

Benevento

NAPLES

Mediterranean Sea

Sassari

KINGDOM OF SARDINIA

Cagliari

Tyrrhenian Sea

Castellammare

Naples

Salerno

Potenza

Taranto

OF

THE

Cosenza

TWO

Lipari Is.

Aspromonte 1862

Messina

Reggio

Palermo

SICILIES

Marsala

Catania

Syracuse

sought a unification of Italy along conservative lines, in the interests of Piedmont-Sardinia, and was hostile to the more revolutionary nationalism of Garibaldi and Mazzini. Bismarck in Prussia wanted unification to achieve his aim of a conservative, Prussian-dominated German state. Both used diplomacy and war to achieve their objectives: Cavour allied with France before attacking Austria in 1859, securing the unification of Italy (except for Venetia and the Papal States) by 1861 (see map 1). Bismarck allied with Austria in order to defeat Denmark (1864), then in concert with Italy attacked Austria (1866), and finally defeated France (1870-1), achieving in the process the unification of Germany (map 2).

Liberal nationalists later endorsed both achievements, but neither satisfied the nationalism they had aroused. Italy still laid claim to the Alto Adige and Istria; Bismarck's 'Small German' solution, which excluded Austria, disappointed those who hankered after a Greater Germany. Nevertheless, the four short wars fought between 1859 and 1871 solved the Italian and German questions, and re-drew the map of Central Europe. Moreover, the Great Powers now remained at peace for over four decades and although nationalist grievances continued to fester, territorial disputes within Europe ceased to divide most governments.

1830–1914
Imperialism

Until 1830, the search for oriental luxuries remained the driving force behind European imperialism, and (with the important exception of India: page 96) the European stake in Asia and Africa remained confined to trading stations and the strategic outposts necessary to protect trade. Thereafter two new factors transformed the situation. First came the enforced 'opening' of key markets – Turkey and Egypt (1838), Persia (1841), China (1842), Japan (1858) – to European, particularly British, commerce. Then, from the 1870s, a new phase of the Industrial Revolution (page 100) provoked a search for raw materials to feed the new industries. In the scramble for these resources between 1880 and 1914, Europe added almost 9 million square miles (23.4 million km^2) – one-fifth of the land area of the globe – to its overseas colonial possessions.

France and Britain took the lead. The former conquered Algeria after 1830, annexed Tahiti and the Marquesas in the 1840s, expanded its colony in Senegal in the 1850s and began the conquest of Indo-China in 1859. Britain, both to forestall the French and to safeguard its position in India, claimed sovereignty over Australia and New Zealand (page 106), and acquired Singapore (1819), Malacca (1824), Hong Kong (1842), Burma (1852), and Lagos (1861) (map 1).

1 Colonial penetration, 1815–70
see key right

Pacific Ocean

Marshall Is.
1888

Marianas
(Ladrones)
1899

Pacific Islands
to Germany

Gilbert Is.
1892

Ellice Is.
1886

Guam
1898

MANCHURIA
Russian 1900–1905
Port Arthur
Russian 1898–1905

KOREA
(to Japan 1910)

Weihaiwei *1898*
Tsingtao

Caroline Is.
1899

Solomon Is.
1893

to Germany

JAPAN

MONGOLIA

Shanghai
Ningpo

C H I N A

Foochow
Amoy
Canton
Hong Kong
Macao
TONGKING

TAIWAN
(to Japan 1895)

PHILIPPINES
(to USA 1898)

BISMARCK
ARCHIPELAGO
1885

to UK

Samoa
1888–9

New Hebrides
1906

Fiji
1874

Tonga
1900

to USA

Heligoland
1814–90

NETHER-
LANDS

DENMARK

GERMANY

GREAT
BRITAIN

BELGIUM

FRANCE

ITALY

1895

TURKESTAN

1873 *1884–5*

TIBET

LAOS
1893
UPPER
BURMA
1886
LOWER
BURMA

SIAM

ANNAM

CAMBODIA

INDO-
CHINA

1884

NORTH
BORNEO
1881

BRUNEI

SARAWAK
1888

NEW
GUINEA

PAPUA
(to Australia 1902–6)

NEW CALEDONIA

Azores

PORTUGAL
SPAIN

Gibraltar

MALTA

CYPRUS
(leased by UK 1878)

OTTOMAN EMPIRE

PERSIA

KUWAIT

Aden

OMAN

ARABIA

Diu

Goa

I N D I A

Andaman
Is.

Nicobar
Is.

DUTCH
BORNEO

TIMOR

Norfolk I.

Madeira

Ceuta
Melilla

TUNISIA
1881

MOROCCO
1912

ALGERIA

EGYPT
1882

LIBYA
1912

Penang
Singapore

SUMATRA

MALAYA
1875–95

JAVA

COMMONWEALTH
OF AUSTRALIA
1901

Canary Is.

IFNI

RIO DE ORO

Cape Verde Is.

FRENCH
WEST AFRICA
1876–98

ANGLO-
EGYPTIAN
SUDAN
1898

ABYSSINIA

ERITREA
1889

BRITISH
SOMALILAND
1884

FRENCH SOMALILAND *1884–8*

ITALIAN
SOMALILAND
1889–92

Socotra 1876

Laccadive
Is.

Maldives

CEYLON

Cocos Is.

Chagos Archipelago

Seychelles

NEW
ZEALAND

TASMANIA

SENEGAL

GAMBIA

PORTUGUESE
GUINEA

SIERRA LEONE
1896

TOGOLAND
1884

IVORY
COAST
1893

GOLD COAST
1874–96

LIBERIA

NIGERIA
1884–1900
Porto
Novo

DAHOMEY
1890

Fernando Po

São Tomé

CAMEROONS
1884

FRENCH
CONGO
1875–92

CONGO
FREE
STATE
1885

UGANDA

BRITISH
EAST
AFRICA
1886

GERMAN
EAST
AFRICA
1886

Comoro Is.

Mauritius

Réunion

MADAGASCAR
1895–9

Ascension I.

ANGOLA

NORTHERN
RHODESIA
1891

SOUTHERN
RHODESIA
1890

NYASALAND *1891*

PORTUGUESE
EAST AFRICA

St. Helena

GERMAN SOUTH-
WEST AFRICA

Walvis Bay
1878

1884

BECHUANALAND *1885*

SWAZILAND *1895*

BASUTOLAND *1871*

Tristan da Cunha

UNION OF SOUTH AFRICA
1910

South Georgia

Gough I.

2 The closing of the world system

major powers

British	Ottoman
French	Dutch
German	Italian
Portuguese	Spanish

Belgian
Russian
USA
Danish
Japanese

1893 date of European control
1902 date of independence
princely states of India
○ treaty ports
----- sphere of effective

.... proposed spheres of
influence

🏴 major investments of
European colonial
powers outside Europe

—— major sea routes

**major raw materials
exported to Europe**

✎ grain	▬ jute
◑ meat	◀ silk
T tea	○ rubber
▥ cane sugar	⊖ veg oil
🐄 dairy produce	◍ copra
▶ cotton	◠ wool

The same imperatives underlay British expansion after 1880, except that the number of competitors to forestall increased. Thus the French empire grew between 1871 and 1914 by nearly 4 million square miles (10.4 million km²) and 47 million people (mainly in north and west Africa and Indo-China, where Laos and Tongking were added to Cambodia and Cochin-China, but it also secured Madagascar and some Pacific islands); Germany also acquired an empire of 1 million square miles (2.6 million km²) and 14 million colonial subjects (in South-West Africa, Togoland, the Cameroons, Tanganyika and the Pacific islands); Italy obtained several outposts in Africa; the United States annexed the Philippines, Guam, Hawaii and some Caribbean islands; and Russia began to expand in central Asia. Britain too managed to acquire extensive new territories in Africa which almost linked Cape Town with Cairo, more Pacific islands (including Fiji), and parts of the Indonesian archipelago (map 2). It added 88 million subjects to her empire and, by 1914, exercized authority over a fifth of the world's landmass and a quarter of its peoples.

In retrospect, the fragility of these European empires, so hastily assembled, is obvious. None of the imperial powers possessed the resources to govern them effectively and European imperialism proved more ephemeral than anyone at the time imagined; yet it left an indelible mark on the peoples of Africa and Asia, propelling them willingly or unwillingly into the 20th century.

Advertisements often unconsciously reflect the assumptions on which societies operate. The Victorian tobacco advert *(left)* shows the wealthy European manufacturers receiving the raw material from crudely parodied native growers, to whom the finished product will eventually be resold.

1865–1929
North America

TIMELINE

26 Apr. 1865
The South surrenders; end of Civil War; Reconstruction begins

1867
Canadian Federation formed; USA purchases Alaska from Russia

1869
First trans-continental railroad in USA completed

1870-1
Manitoba and British Columbia join Canadian Federation

1877
Reconstruction formally comes to an end

1885
Canadian-Pacific railroad completed

1898
USA annexes Hawaii: Cuba and the Philippines seized from Spain

1914
Canada and (1917) USA join World War I

Although the United States made a remarkably rapid recovery after the Civil War (page 104), development remained very uneven. In the defeated South, the period of Reconstruction (1865-77) proved a bitter experience. South Carolina, which in 1860 had ranked third in the nation in per capita wealth, ranked 40th ten years later; and other once-prosperous states did scarcely better. The 4 million liberated black slaves fared worst, being left (as Frederick Douglass wrote) without money, property or friends. Although the population of the Union surged from 31 million in 1861 to 92 million in 1910, most of the increase by-passed the South and concentrated wealth and power in the north-east and the upper Mid-West. Only around 1920 did cheap labour attract textile industry to the South (map 1).

The settlement of the Great Plains, made possible by the railway boom after 1870, constituted perhaps the most striking achievement of the post-war period. The track in operation increased from 30,000 miles (48,000 km) in 1860 to 163,000 (262,000 km) in 1890 (at which point it exceeded the size of the entire European rail system); the number of farms rose from 2 million in 1860 to 6 million in 1910; and the population living west of the Mississippi grew from 6 million to 26 million. Yet the bulk of the population remained concentrated in the north-east (map 3), and most of the 25 million immigrants arriving between 1870 and 1914 stayed there, providing cheap labour for American industry.

Railways played an even more prominent role in the development of Canada. The United States made no secret of its hope to absorb the provinces and thus create a continent-wide empire. After the acquisition

Pittsburgh, Pennsylvania, surrounded by huge coal-fields and beds of iron and at the confluence of two important rivers, became the leading centre of iron and steel production in the United States. So vast and dramatic was the sight of its blast furnaces and coke ovens at work that early 20th-century artists and commentators began to refer to it as 'Hell with the lid off.'

2 Canada, 1867–1929

land occupied;
- prior to 1851
- 1851–1871
- 1871–1901
- 1901–1921

population of towns, 1871;
- 25,000-100,000 people
- over 100,000 people

population of towns, 1911;
- 25,000-100,000 people
- over 100,000 people

railways 1916:
- —— Canadian Pacific Railway
- ---- Canadian Northern (Main Line)
- .... National Trans-continental Railway
- —— main industrial regions

ALBERTA date of accession to
1905 Dominion of Canada

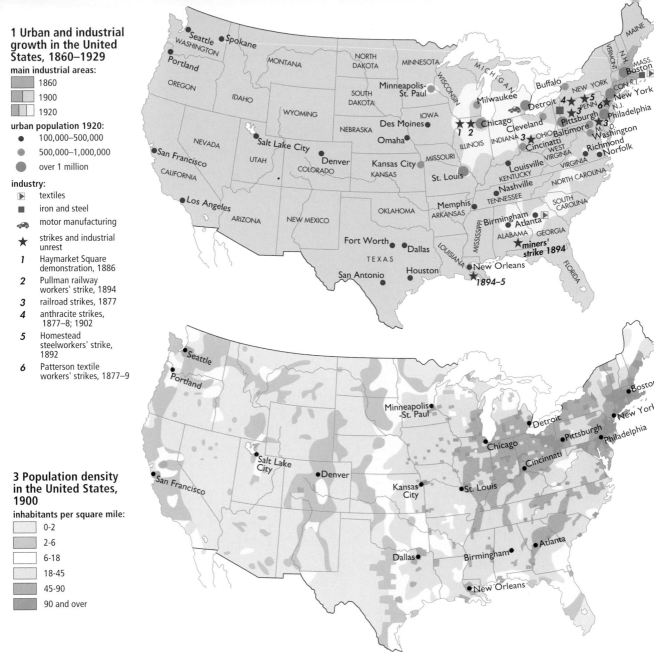

1 Urban and industrial growth in the United States, 1860–1929

main industrial areas:
- 1860
- 1900
- 1920

urban population 1920:
- 100,000–500,000
- 500,000–1,000,000
- over 1 million

industry:
- ▷ textiles
- ■ iron and steel
- 🚗 motor manufacturing
- ★ strikes and industrial unrest

1 Haymarket Square demonstration, 1886
2 Pullman railway workers' strike, 1894
3 railroad strikes, 1877
4 anthracite strikes, 1877–8; 1902
5 Homestead steelworkers' strike, 1892
6 Patterson textile workers' strikes, 1877–9

3 Population density in the United States, 1900

inhabitants per square mile:
- 0-2
- 2-6
- 6-18
- 18-45
- 45-90
- 90 and over

of Alaska by the United States (1867), this pressure grew, but the Canadians frustrated their neighbours' intentions by forming the Canadian Federation in 1867, completed by the purchase of Rupert's Land from the Hudson's Bay Company (1869) and the adhesion of Manitoba (1870) and British Columbia (1871). The great transcontinental railways – the Canadian Pacific (completed 1885) followed by the Canadian Northern and the National Trans-continental – became the lifeblood of the new Dominion, opening Manitoba and Saskatchewan, and turning Canada into one of the world's leading wheat producers. It also facilitated the exploitation of rich mineral deposits, particularly copper and nickel (map 2). Overall, Canada's industrial output increased from $190 million in 1890 to over $500 million in 1914.

This achievement was dwarfed, however, by the economic and territorial growth of the United States. Output of iron and steel increased 20-fold between 1870 and 1913, by which time steel production exceeded that of Britain and Germany combined, and the United States remained the world's leading agricultural producer. Meanwhile, in 1898 (following a successful war with Spain), the Philippines, Guam, Puerto Rico and Hawaii were annexed, the latter after many years of American encroachment in the islands' affairs; and in 1903 Cuba and the Panama Canal Zone became protectorates. The United States now possessed the political and economic might to intervene almost anywhere on the world stage: in Mexico in 1914 and again in 1916, and – on a far greater scale – in Europe in 1917-18 (page 132).

Japan

The Tokugawa shoguns (page 88) gave Japan over two centuries of peace and prosperity. In 1868, however, internal tensions, combined with the pressure of Western powers to open Japan to foreign trade, resulted in a revolution (known as the Meiji Restoration) which replaced the shogun and the feudal structure with a modern system of government. The new Japanese leaders implemented widespread reforms in the belief that a modern economy and military would ensure Japan's international independence and equality. They instituted a national education system (which by 1900 provided teaching for 90 per cent of children), a conscript army, and a navy with modern ships. Legal codes, largely based on French and German models, were introduced from 1882. The economic reforms were wide-reaching; the first railway opened in 1872 and by 1906 the system linked most parts of the country; up to one-third of state expenditure went on developing commerce and industry (map 1); and a land tax reform in 1873 provided a secure source of revenue for the government. The shifting structure of Japanese foreign trade (see table 3) illustrates the dramatic impact of these changes. Whereas by 1878-82, manufactured goods represented half of all imports but only 7 per cent of exports, in 1918-22 the ratio had reversed:

1 Industrial Japan

town population, 1918
● less than 50,000
● 50,000–100,000
● 100,000,–500,000
■ 500,000–1 million
■ over 1 million

〜 railways in 1906
- - - additions to railways 1906–1918
■ main manufacturing areas

KYOTO   prefecture

industries:
■ metal   ᛁ ceramics
ᛩ shipbuilding   ▌ chemicals
+ textiles   ◆ food
▮ wood   ⊞ machinery
◀ silk   ▪ manufac-turing industry

minerals:
● coal
C copper
▲ iron
▯ oil

The battle of Tsushima Strait, in May 1905, was one of the most complete naval victories in history *(right)*. The Russian fleet, in dire need of mechanical overhaul, was outmanœuvred by the Japanese Togo, and forced to surrender after the sinking of six of its battleships. The war was over – the first time that an emerging Asian power had defeated a Western one; the news resounded throughout the colonial world.

finished manufactures now accounted for over 40 per cent of sales and only 15 per cent of purchases. Moreover the total value of Japan's exports rose in this period from 30 million to 1.8 billion yen.

International recognition of Japan's new status was nevertheless slow in coming: consular jurisdiction survived until 1894, and the unequal treaties negotiated in the 1850s with the Western powers remained in force until 1911. As Japan's strength and confidence grew, however, so did nationalist and imperialist ambitions. In 1894-5 a victorious war against China, arising from disputes in Korea, ended in a treaty granting Taiwan to Japan. Russo-Japanese rivalry over Manchuria culminated in Japanese victory in the war of 1904-5. The Treaty of Portsmouth (1905) gave Japan a lease of territory in China and extensive rights in South Manchuria. In 1910 she acquired Korea. Japanese support for the victorious Western powers in World War I brought few further rewards, however, and the country's military leaders became frustrated. After 1931, under the impact of the Great Depression (page 138), Japan overran first Manchuria and then – despite strong opposition from the United States – northern China in an attempt to achieve economic self-sufficiency (map 2). Germany's victory over France and the Netherlands in 1940 offered an opportunity to expand southwards – thereby gaining control over valuable oil fields in Borneo and Burma – precipitating full-scale war with the Western powers (page 142). Paradoxically, Japan's total defeat and the ensuing American occupation propelled her even more decisively into the modern world than the Meiji restoration had done.

2 Japanese expansion from 1914

- Japanese territory by 1914, with dates of acquisition
- spheres of Japanese influence, 1918
- expansion to 1933
- expansion to Nov. 1941
- ✷ Japanese conflict with USSR
- → Japanese attacks
- ■ Chinese capitals
- ▪ Allied bases
- — railways

3 Structure of Japanese trade

food, drink raw materials semi-manufactured goods finished goods other

1878-82 export
1878-82 import
1918-22 export
1918-22 import

0%   25%   50%   75%   100%

Map labels

KARAFUTO 1905
USSR
MANCHURIA
Manchukuo (Japanese protectorate proclaimed 1932)
Nomonhan 1939
Japanese forces defeated by Red Army under Zhukov
Amur
Vladivostok
Changkufeng 1938
Sea of Japan
1933
SOUTH MANCHURIA
Changchun
Mukden
KOREA (CHOSEN) 1910
Pusan
Tokyo
JAPAN
Russian support for China, 1935
Yellow R.
Peking
Tientsin
Kwantung leased territory 1905
SHANTUNG
Tsingtao
Yellow Sea
Russian support for China, 1935
CHINA
1932
1937
Shanghai 1937
Nanking
Nanchang
Ryukyu (Loochoo) Is.
Pacific Ocean
1941
Chungking
Yangtze
Burma Road
Kunming
Nanning
Hanoi
Hainan
FUKIEN
Amoy
Swatow
Canton
Hong Kong 1941
TAIWAN (Formosa) 1895
8 Dec. 1941
PHILIPPINE IS. (USA)
Japanese support for independence movements
Manila
South China Sea
occupied by Japan, 1940
FRENCH INDO-CHINA
Franco-Japanese agreement permitting occupation, 1941
SIAM under Japanese influence, 1941
BURMA
Bangkok
Saigon

European rivalries and alliances

The unification of Germany and Italy (page 116) seemed for a time to have resolved the major questions which had disturbed the peace of Europe since 1848. Bismarck, the architect of German unification, concentrated after 1871 on building a system of alliances that would ensure the future of the new empire, mainly by isolating France, which proved unable to reconcile itself to the rise of the new German empire, and for almost 20 years he succeeded in convincing the rest of Europe of Germany's conservative and pacific intentions. In time, however, the alliances that had seemed defensive became aggressive and destabilizing.

Meanwhile, although the achievements of Bismarck and Cavour reduced nationalist fervour in central Europe, they stirred up a hornet's nest in the Balkans, where the struggles of various national groups for independence from the Turks inevitably involved the neighbouring powers, Russia and Austria (which, after its exclusion from Germany in 1866 became far more interested in the Balkans).

Revolts in the Balkans between 1875 and 1878, culminating in Russian intervention and war with the Turks, resulted in the treaty of Berlin (brokered by Bismarck) which either confirmed or established the independence of Serbia, Montenegro, Romania and Bulgaria and granted Austria a mandate to govern Bosnia and Herzegovina. In 1879 Germany and Austria signed a defensive alliance, expanded to include Italy in 1882 (map 1). Russia, satisfied that Slav interest had been met in the Balkans, turned increasingly to Central Asia and the Far East. The main European rivalries were now between Britain and Russia in Asia, and Britain and France in Africa. Britain remained isolated in Europe, while France and Russia signed an alliance in 1894 as a counterweight to the strength of the alliance bloc based around Germany.

The situation changed after 1897, however, when Germany began to seek a 'place in the sun'. This was not unreasonable; but by then most places in the sun had been occupied by others, and German policy – which involved building a High Seas Fleet to rival that of Britain – therefore seemed to constitute a threat to the established imperial powers. As a result, Britain resolved its differences with France in 1904,

1 European alliance systems, 1882–1914

— frontiers, 1912

The Triple Alliance, 1882

The Triple Entente, 1912

The Balkan League, 1912

UNITED KINGDOM
1904: Entente Cordiale (with France)
1907: conciliation of interests with Russia

1879: Dual Alliance with Austria-Hungary
1882: Triple Alliance with Austria-Hungary and Italy
1883: alliance with Romania

RUSSIA
1894: Dual Alliance with France
1897: Entente with Austria-Hungary (to 1909)
1907: conciliation of interests with Britain
1909: secret treaty with Italy

FRANCE
1894: Dual Alliance with Russia
1902: neutrality agreement with Italy
1904: Entente Cordiale (with Britain)

AUSTRO-HUNGARIAN EMPIRE
1879: Dual Alliance with Germany
1882: Triple Alliance with Germany and Italy
1883: alliance with Romania

ROMANIA 1883: alliance with Germany and Austria

ITALY
1882: Triple Alliance with Austria-Hungary and Germany
1902: neutrality agreement with France
1909: secret treaty with Russia

AUSTRO-HUNGARIAN EMPIRE

Budapest

Lake
Balaton

Sava

BOSNIA-
HERZEGOVINA
administered by Austria-
Hungary 1878; annexed 1908

Banja Luka

Belgrade

Sarajevo

SERBIA

principality 1817;
independent 1878

Nish

MONTENEGRO

Kotor
(Cattaro)

Cetinje

Scutari

to Serbia
1913

Tirana

Uskub
(Skoplje)

ALBANIA
principality
1913

Koritsa

Monastir

Adriatic
Sea

EPIRUS

Corfu

Yannina

to Greece 1864

Preveza

Arta

THESSALY
to Greece 1881

Larissa

KINGDOM OF GREECE

to Greece
1864

to Greece
1864

independent 1830

Ionian
Sea

Patras

Ionian Islands

Tripolis

to Greece 1864

Athens

Piraeus

CRETE
independent 1898
to Greece 1913

Candia

WALLACHIA
semi-independent
1829

ROMANIA
united 1859; independent 1878;
kingdom 1881

Carpathian Mts

MOLDAVIA
semi-independent
1829

Jassy

Galatz

Vidin

Bucharest

Sofia

BULGARIA
principality 1878
independent 1908

Danube

EASTERN
RUMELIA
to Bulgaria 1885

Maritsa

Balchik

Varna

Burgas

Black
Sea

to Bulgaria 1913

Macedonia

Kavalla

to Bulgaria 1913

to Greece 1913

Salonica

Thasos

Thrace

Adrianople

Constantinople

Lemnos

to Greece 1913

Mytilene

OTTOMAN
EMPIRE

Aegean
Sea

Chios

Smyrna

to Greece 1913

Nikaria

Dodecanese

Rhodes

occupied by Italy
1912

**2 The Balkans,
1878–1913**

- - - frontier of Ottoman
empire, 1800

─── frontier of Ottoman
empire, 1885

─── national frontiers
after the Balkan
wars 1912–13

HMS Temeraire, depicted on a
pre-war postcard. Britain
responded to Germany's
increased warship building after
1900 with a rival programme
based on the most modern
Dreadnought battleships. The
Royal Navy was fully mobilized
for exercises at the outbreak
of war.

and with Russia in 1907,
and France settled its long-standing dispute with Italy in 1902. Thereafter,
the Triple Entente with France and Russia
became the lynch-pin of British foreign policy,
the only firm assurance against the German 'threat'.
Germany, on the other became concerned with the
danger of 'encirclement' by a hostile ring constructed
by Great Britain (map 1).

As a result, a dangerous simplification of align-
ments occurred into a bi-polar system: the Triple
Alliance and the Triple Entente drew tighter, and
Germany in particular grew closer to its only
dependable ally, Austria. When Austria annexed
Bosnia and Herzegovina in 1908, Germany gave her
qualified support, though it rekindled Austro-Russian
antagonism in the Balkans. During the Balkan wars
(1912-13), in which a Russian-sponsored Balkan
League consisting of Serbia, Greece and Bulgaria
attempted to drive the Turks out of Europe, the two
diplomatic systems still cooperated; but Austria
stood aghast at the consequent enlargement of
Serbia – which almost doubled its size – and feared
Serb agitation for an independent south Slav state
(map 2).

The assassination of the heir to the Austrian
throne in Sarajevo (Bosnia) in June 1914 provided
what seemed to the Austrian government like its last
chance to deal with Serbia before it grew too powerful, and Germany threw its entire weight behind its
ally. Russia, however, could not afford to leave Serbia

in the lurch and began to mobilize against Austria.
Germany regarded this as a direct threat, and also
began to mobilize. However, to forestall an attack
from Russia's allies in the West, German Grand
Strategy called for an immediate attack on France –
in the hope that it could be knocked out of the war
before Russia advanced in force. On 28 July, Austria
declared war on Serbia; on 1 August 1914 Germany
declared war on Russia, and two days later on
France. The diplomatic system created by Bismarck,
coupled with the volatile situation in the Balkans,
had produced a world war (page 132).

The formation of a world economy

The integration of the global economy into a single interdependent whole formed one of the principal developments of the period 1870-1914. Europe (and to a lesser extent the United States) stood at the heart of this process, emitting the impulses that opened up the remaining areas of the globe to Western exploration and exploitation.

Three interrelated aspects deserve special attention. First came the development of better means of communication. In 1870, railways remained largely confined to Europe (60,400 miles, 97,250 km of track) and North America (56,300 miles, 90,600 km): the rest of the world could boast only 9100 miles (14,650 km). By 1911, however, the total network of tracks had increased to 657,000 miles (1.06 million km) – 175,000 miles (280,000 km) of them outside Europe and North America – and included some spectacular transcontinental links: across the United States (four between 1869 and 1893), Canada (1885), Russia (1904) and the Andes (1910). The expansion of world shipping was equally striking, with not only a spectacular rise in the total tonnage, but a shift from sail to steam which increased the speed and regularity of shipments. However, the main shipping traffic, both passenger and freight, took place among the advanced countries and the white dominions, or between them and the producers of the raw materials they required. Canal construction also continued apace – above all the Suez Canal, completed in 1869, which carried 437,000 tons in 1870 and over 20 million in 1913; and the Panama Canal, completed in 1914, which carried 5 million tons of cargo in its first year. These spectacular totals reflected the enormous savings in distance – 41 per cent for vessels sailing from Liverpool to Bombay, 60 per cent for vessels sailing from New York to San Francisco.

Finally, messages travelled around the world with increasing speed. Cables laid beneath the oceans linked the continents – between Britain and North America (1866); from Vancouver to Brisbane (1902) – followed by telephones (with international lines from 1887) and wireless stations (from 1897).

These developments paralleled a boom in commerce. Foreign trade tripled in volume between 1870 and 1914, although (again) most of the activity occurred among the industrialized countries, or between them and their suppliers of primary goods or their new markets. In 1913, only 11 per cent of the

1 The development of the world economy

foreign investment, 1914
(in $ million)

- 535 United Kingdom
- 420 United States
- 3180 France
- 1050 Germany

—— busiest shipping routes
—— other major shipping routes, c. 1900
—— international telegragh cables

Colonial empires in 1900

- Belgian
- British
- Danish
- Dutch
- French
- German
- Italian
- Japanese
- Ottoman
- Portuguese
- Russian
- Spanish
- USA
- other countries

Panama canal, 1914

3 The share of world trade

1860 total $8 billion

Others / United Kingdom / USA / France / Russia / Spain / Austria-Hungary / Italy / Scandinavia / Germany / Holland and Belgium / Switzerland world's trade took place between the primary producers themselves. Britain ranked as the world's largest trading nation in 1860, but by 1913 it had lost ground to both the United States and Germany: British and German exports in that year each totalled $2.3 billion, and those of the United States exceeded $2.4 billion.

Britain remained the world's financial capital, however, as well as its largest lender, with almost $20 billion in foreign investments by 1914 – slightly more than those of France, Germany, Holland and Belgium combined. The United States and Russia were in fact net borrowers of foreign capital. Investments within Europe and North America on the whole assisted and accelerated economic advancement, helping to create the costly infrastructure (such as railways and other public works) for developing nations that would in time repay these debts. By contrast, investments in non-industrial regions (such as the Russian and Ottoman empires) and overseas territories that lacked both the knowledge and the power to direct the capital flow, served to colonize rather than develop them, destroying native industries and creating dangerous political and economic pressures which would, in time, produce conflict between rich nations and poor nations and demands for a new economic order (page 174).

Miners at the Republic Gold Mining Company in the Transvaal, South Africa, fuelled the economic engine that drove the Gold Standard. This originated in Britain in 1821, but until Germany joined the system in 1871, most other countries remained on a bi-metallic standard, gold and silver.

2 Foreign Investment in 1914 (in $ million)

Russia	500
Belgium	900
USA	3,510
Holland	4,100
Germany	5,650
France	9,280
United Kingdom	19,935

Map labels:

300 NEW ZEALAND
COMMONWEALTH OF AUSTRALIA 1700
GERMAN NEW GUINEA
DUTCH NEW GUINEA
DUTCH BORNEO
SARAWAK
JAPAN 500
MONGOLIA
CHINA 200 200 600
INDO-CHINA
SIAM
BURMA
INDIA 1850
RUSSIAN EMPIRE 550 400 2400
GREENLAND
investment in the rest of Europe
420 535
NORWAY SWEDEN
180 1050
UK GERMANY 750
FRANCE
AUST-HUNGARY 450
ITALY
OTTOMAN EMPIRE 650
PERSIA
Suez canal, 1869
ARABIA
SPAIN
Mediterranean Sea
200 500
200
ALGERIA LIBYA EGYPT
100
ABYSSINIA
ANGLO EGYPTIAN SUDAN
BRITISH EAST AFRICA 600
FRENCH WEST AFRICA
all of Africa 500
NIGERIA
GERMAN E. AFRICA
CONGO FREE STATE
MADAGASCAR
Indian Ocean
ANGOLA RHODESIA
1550
GERMAN SOUTH WEST AFRICA
UNION OF SOUTH AFRICA from 1910

FOUR

The Modern World

By making the world one, the European powers stirred up forces that eventually caused their own eclipse. The world wars between 1914 and 1945 whittled away their resources and Europe's exhaustion benefited the Soviet Union and the United States, the two superpowers on the eastern and western flanks, whose rivalry produced an age of bipolarity. But bipolarity, too, proved to be temporary. The recovery of Europe, the emancipation of Asia and Africa, the rise of Japan and finally the collapse of the Soviet empire brought a new constellation into being, and with it the threat of confrontation between rich and poor nations and of the exhaustion of global resources through overpopulation. No one can foretell the shape of things to come. All this section can do is show, in historical perspective, how the world of the 20th century changed and chart the emergence of significant new factors.

Devastation inflicted by the first atomic bomb
Hiroshima, 1945

The Chinese Republic

1 The Nationalist (Kuomintang) regime, 1928–37

occupied by Japan by 1933

area in which Japan attempted to establish a puppet North China state, 1935

areas of effective control of Nationalist government

from 1928

added 1929–34

added 1935–7

brought under Nanking influence, 1935–7

By 1911 the imperial government of China was thoroughly discredited (page 94) and an army mutiny led to the emperor's abdication. But the Republic proclaimed in 1912, with Sun Yat-sen as its first president, was overwhelmed by its inherited problems, and Sun was soon deposed by Yuan Shih-k'ai, the most powerful general of the old regime. After Yuan's death in 1916 power passed to provincial warlords, whose armies caused untold damage and millions of casualties. Compounding this misery were the expansionist policies of Japan and the foreign powers, based in the Treaty Ports (page 88), which interfered in the Chinese economy and in Chinese politics.

In 1919, the refusal of the Paris Peace Conference to abrogate foreign privileges provoked spontaneous urban uprisings (the 'May 4th' movement). These provided a new opportunity for Sun Yat-sen, who in 1923 reorganized his Nationalist (Kuomintang; KMT) Party, allied with the Chinese Communist Party (founded 1921), and prepared to reunite the country. But Sun died in 1925 and it was Chiang Kai-shek, the Moscow-trained general of the KMT army, who in 1926 marched northwards to eliminate the warlords. Helped by peasant and workers' uprisings along his route, Chiang proved remarkably successful, but in 1927 he turned on his allies, massacring the Communists in

Shanghai. However KMT direct rule remained limited to the lower Yangtze (map 1). Nevertheless, the Japanese, fearing the potential challenge from a reunited China, decided to reinforce their hold in the north and overran Manchuria (1931) and Jehol (1933).

Although KMT purges had virtually eliminated Communism from the cities, peasant disaffection – arising from the absence of land reform – offered an alternative constituency. From his base at Chingkang Shan, Mao Tse-Tung and others created a new centre of revitalized communism, developing a peasant-based party rather than an urban, proletarian party on the Russian model. In 1929 KMT pressure

2 The Chinese Communist movement to 1945

✊ abortive urban insurrections after the break with Kuomintang 1927

⭕ position of early Communist army groups *(dashed)*

⭕ early Soviets (self-governing Communist areas) 1927–35

➜ route of the 'Long March', Oct. 1934–Oct. 1935, of Chinese Communists after Kuomintang assaults on Kiangsi Soviet area

■ main Communist base area, governed from Yenan 1935–45

■ area occupied by Japan end 1941

■ area occupied by Japan during 1944 offensives

■ 'liberated areas' dominated by local Communist groups by 1945

— railways in 1937

▨ main industrial areas 1937

■ main industrial centres 1937

◆ other industrial centres 1937

USSR

MANCHURIA

Manchouli · Hailar · Tsitsihar · Kiamusze

OUTER MONGOLIA (independent 1921)

Harbin · Kirin · Changchun

Mukden · Fushun · Penki · Chinchow · Anshan · Yingkow · Antung

KOREA Japanese 1910–45

Kalgan · Tatung · Peking · Tangshan · Dairen · Port Arthur (Lüshun) · Tientsin · Paotow

SHEN-KAN-NING

Yenan · Pao-an: Soviet 1930–5

Taiyuan · Tsinan · Tsingtao · Yellow Sea

Lanchow · Sian · Yellow River (Hwang Ho) · Loyang · Chengchow · Kaifeng · Hsü-chou (Suchow) · Lienyünkang

C H I N A

Chengtu · Chungking · Wuhan · Nanking · Soochow · Shanghai

4th army group, Chang Kuo-tao, Hsü Hsiang-ch'ien

Tsunyi Jan. 1935 · W. Hunan · Changsha · Hengyang · Kiukiang · Nanchang Aug. 1927 · Hangchow · Ningpo

10th army group, Fang Chih-min

East China Sea

Kweiyang · Chingkang Shan, Mao Zedong and Chu Teh, 1927–9 · Ju-chin (Juikin) · Foochow · Kiangsi Soviet under Mao Zedong and Chu Teh, 1929–34

Kunming · Amoy

TAIWAN Japanese 1895–1945

Canton Dec. 1927 · Swatow · Hailufeng Soviet under P'eng P'ai, 1927–8

Hong Kong British

BURMA

FRENCH INDO-CHINA

THAILAND

Hainan · South China Sea

INDIA

compelled Mao and his followers to move first to Kiangsi, and then in 1934 to the north-west (the 'Long March': map 2).

In 1937 Japanese forces invaded northern and central China and the KMT retreated to the interior, where they remained until the Japanese surrender in 1945. A race to occupy the liberated areas now ensued, with the Communists gaining much of the north and most of Manchuria, and the KMT re-occupying the south. In 1946 hostilities between the two sides erupted into a civil war from which the Communists emerged victorious. The People's Republic of China was proclaimed in October 1949, and soon afterwards the KMT fled to Taiwan. For the first time in a century, a strong regime controlled all of mainland China – albeit most of the country had been devastated by the warlords, the Japanese occupation and the civil war.

A poster from c.1927 showing Sun Yat-sen (top centre) and Chiang Kai-shek (on horse) about to set out with Kuomintang forces on the 'Northern Expedition' of 1926–8.

All the war-plans of the Great Powers in 1914 envisaged a short war. The German Schlieffen Plan called for an attack on northern France through Belgium, leading to the rapid collapse of the French government before Russia had time to mobilize (page 125). It almost succeeded: the Germans came within 40 miles of Paris, but not before Russian armies had invaded East Prussia. Although their advance was halted at Tannenberg (August), important German reserves were diverted from the Western front just as a spirited counter-attack by French and British troops began at the Marne (September). The two sides now spread their forces out and dug in, until their trenches stretched from the Channel coast to Switzerland.

The war in the west (map 2) turned into a war of attrition. Each side launched repeated offensives, with appalling casualties but little gain, for railways were able to bring up reinforcements before the slow-moving front-line troops could make good any advantage. In 1916 the British, under Sir Douglas Haig, made a major frontal assault on German lines at the river Somme. On the first day of the battle 60,000 British casualties were mowed down as they advanced through the barbed wire. Haig threw his forces into an unwinnable conflict for another four months. Both sides experienced terrible losses and achieved little. Neither side could break the trench

stalemate by pursuing alternative strategies. The British and French attempted a series of attacks from the rear: in the Dardanelles and Mesopotamia against the Ottoman empire, which entered the war in November 1914 on the side of the Central Powers (Germany and Austria); on Austria's southern frontier after Italy declared war in May 1915; at Salonika in Greece in support of Serbia. All failed. The Germans countered by building a fleet of submarines with the express intention of bringing Britain to its knees by attacking vulnerable food imports on which Britain relied. In 1917 unrestricted submarine warfare failed to halt Britain's food supply, but provoked the United States into war with Germany.

On the eastern front, which stretched for twice the distance of that in the west, warfare remained more mobile and both Germany and Austria scored major successes. In 1915 the former overran a huge area of Poland, whose resources it ruthlessly exploited, while the latter occupied most of Serbia. In 1917 the combination of huge losses and economic chaos broke the fighting spirit of the Russian forces and provoked revolution and military collapse (page 134). At the peace of Brest-Litovsk in March 1918 Germany gained the Ukraine, Poland, Finland and the Baltic provinces.

1 The Great War in Europe, 1914–18

Entente Powers

Central Powers

major Entente Power offensives

major Central Power offensives

farthest advance by Entente Powers: (east 1914, west 1918)

farthest advance by Central Powers: (west 1914, east 1918)

★ battle

✪ battle costing over 250,000 lives

⚓ naval base

Map labels include:

naval blockade of Germany effective end 1916

1916: Battle of Jutland

1914: Tannenberg counter-offensive

1914: Russian offensive in East Prussia

1917: Riga offensive

1918

1914

1915: Gorlice campaign

1916: Brusilov offensive

1918: Central Powers advance through Ukraine

Kiev 1918

1917

1916: Asiago offensive

1917

1918

1915: Isonzo

1915: conquest of Serbia

1916: Central Powers conquest of Romania

1916

1914

1918: Allied advance into Serbia

1915: British land at Salonica to support Serbia

1915: Gallipoli offensive

see inset below left

Instead of moving its forces across to the West, however, Germany sent its troops to occupy these new territories – even Finland – and at the same time launched a final, all-out offensive in the West, in an attempt to break the deadlock. Once again it came close to success but the Allied line held and in July, aided by tanks and reinforced by American forces and money, a counter-attack began that pushed the German army back towards the German frontier. Morale collapsed: by October 1918, with Austria close to disintegration and with Germany facing a grave political crisis at home, the Berlin government sued for an unconditional armistice, granted on 11 November 1918.

At the peace conferences held in and around Paris in 1919, the victors imposed upon Germany, Austria, Hungary, and Bulgaria notable losses of territory, huge reparations and stringent reductions in their armed forces. The draconian nature of the settlement made it inevitable that, although over 9 million men had perished in the fighting, and the financial cost of the war totalled over $186 billion worldwide, it would not be (as so many had hoped) 'the war to end all wars'.

The Menin Road (left), vividly recalled by the British painter Paul Nash, saw some of the Western Front's worst fighting. In the second half of 1917, a British campaign to re-capture seven miles of Flanders towards Menin and Passchendaele floundered in heavy rain and mud. The British lost 265,000 men and Menin remained in German hands

The USSR from Lenin to Stalin

2 Collectivization, 1923–39

- 2-10% of all farms collectivized by 1928
- 25-50% of all farms collectivized by 1933
- 50-70% of all farms collectivized by 1933
- 70-85% of all farms collectivized by 1933
- famine areas, 1932
- *Kraslag* labour camp admin. zone
- corrective labour camps, 1932

By 1917 the strain of war had fatally weakened the Tsarist government: liberals, businessmen, generals and aristocrats all plotted its overthrow. In the end sheer hunger turned a general strike and bread queues into a revolutionary movement which in February forced the Tsar to abdicate, and power passed to a provisional government of prominent *duma* (parliament) politicians. The revolutionary committees (soviets) did not disband, however, and gradually the 'peace, bread and land' programme of the Bolshevik group, led by V. I. Lenin, gained support. In October, the Bolsheviks seized control of strategic points in Petrograd (formerly St Petersburg), arrested the Provisional Government, and assumed power in the name of the soviets. The same soon happened in other cities (map 1).

No one thought they would retain power for long. The overriding need was for peace, and Lenin accepted the onerous terms imposed by Germany in the treaty of Brest-Litovsk (March 1918: page 133); but almost immediately the Bolsheviks (who now took the name 'Communists') faced massive invasions by forces loyal to the Tsar and assisted by troops from Britain, France, Czechoslovakia, Poland and other anti-Bolshevik powers. Nevertheless, by 1920 the civil war had been won, albeit at the cost of 13 million lives and immense damage to property. Lenin now introduced his 'New Economic Policy', which by 1925 allowed the Russian economy to regain its pre-war industrial level. In 1928 Lenin's successor, Joseph Stalin, introduced a Five Year Plan of industrialization, and the following year embarked on the forced collectivization of agriculture, which transformed small, individual peasant holdings into huge state collective farms. The results of the policy proved disastrous, however. It was implemented without adequate machinery, and poorly organized. Crop yields fell, and a great famine in 1932-3 claimed millions of victims. This rural catastrophe caused some 40 million people to move into the cities, where their fresh labour was used mainly for construction, making the industrial growth rates of the Soviet economy under the first and second Five Year Plans (1928-37) look both startling and unique amid the Great Depression that prevailed elsewhere.

This industrialization took place against a background of state-directed terror as Stalin consolidated the Communist dictatorship. The security forces (the NKVD) executed perhaps 12 million people, while a further 10 million suffered imprisonment in forced labour camps (see map 2). Russia survived the German invasion in 1941 (page 140), partly because over 1500 factories were moved to safety further east, but the setback remained undeniable. A further 20 million Soviet citizens died in the conflict and, although the USSR mobilized more fully than any other state in World War II, its industrial output in 1946 stood at only 70 per cent of the 1940 level.

A poster of Stakhanov, a model mine-worker who exceeded his norm through exceptional efforts. He became a hero of the Soviet State and a propaganda tool in Communist efforts to increase worker participation.

1 Russia in war and revolution

——	Russian empire, 1914
- - -	front between Russia and Central Powers, 12 Mar. 1917
✊	serious Russian mutinies, Aug. 1917
★	principal towns where Bolsheviks took power, Nov. 1917–Feb. 1918 (dates in new calendar)
——	boundary of Russian territory occupied by Central Powers following the Treaty of Brest-Litovsk, Mar. 1918
⋯⋯	area controlled by the Bolsheviks, Aug. 1918
▲	towns occupied Entente forces, Aug. 1918–19
- - -	eastern boundary of area controlled by Bolsheviks, Apr. 1919
▧	area controlled by Bolsheviks, Oct. 1919
⟶	areas controlled by anti-Bolshevik forces, May 1920
➡	White Russian armies
➡	non-Russian anti-Bolshevik forces (Entente Powers)
——	boundary of Soviet territory, Mar. 1921
——	frontiers, 1923

Norwegian Sea

Barents Sea

White Sea

Entente fleet
Murmansk
British French Canadians Italians Serbs
Canadians Americans
Archangel 17 Feb. 1918
British French
Finns
Mezen
Onega
Sukhona

NORWAY

Narvik

SWEDEN

FINLAND
independence of Finland recognized Dec. 1917

Lake Onega
Petrozavodsk 17 Jan. 1918

Lake Ladoga

Trondhjem

Stockholm
Åbo
Helsingfors

Revel 8 Nov. 1917
Yudenich
ESTONIA
British/French naval assistance

Baltic Sea

Riga
LATVIA
Letts
Baltic Germans

Dvinsk

LITHUANIA

Königsberg
Vilna

Danzig

GERMANY (E. PRUSSIA)

Minsk 7 Nov. 1917

POLAND
Warsaw
Brest-Litovsk
Poles

Łódź
Cracow
Lemberg

CZECHOSLOVAKIA

HUNGARY
Debrecen
Kolozsvár
Temesvár
Brassó

Romanians
Jassy

BESSARABIA

ROMANIA
Bucharest

Danube
Ruse

BULGARIA
Sofia
Plovdiv
Adrianople
Varna
Burgas

Salonica
Constantinople
Angora

GREECE
Athens
Smyrna

TURKEY

Petrograd 7 Nov. 1917
Novgorod 27 Nov. 1917
Kornilov's attack on Petrograd Sep. 1917
Pskov 15 Nov. 1917
10 Nov. 1917
Tver 9 Nov. 1917
Government moved from Petrograd Mar. 1918

Vologda 8 Feb. 1918

Yaroslavl 9 Nov. 1917

Kostroma 15 Dec. 1917

Ivanovo 7 Nov. 1917

Vyatka 8 Dec. 1917

Perm 14 Nov. 1917

Nicholas II and family shot by Bolsheviks July 1918

BOLSHEVIK

Vitebsk 12 Nov. 1917
Smolensk 9 Nov. 1917
Mogilev 1 Dec. 1917

Moscow 15 Nov. 1917

Kaluga 11 Dec. 1917
Tula 20 Dec. 1917
Orel 14 Nov. 1917

Nizhniy Novgorod 10 Nov. 1917

Izhevsk 9 Nov. 1917
Kazan 8 Nov. 1917

RUSSIA

Yekaterinburg 8 Nov. 1917

Kolchak 1918–19

Ufa 8 Nov. 1917

Trans-Siberian Railway

Samara 9 Nov. 1917

Czechs

Gomel 12 Nov. 1917

Kursk

Tambov 13 Nov. 1917
Penza 4 Jan. 1918

Saratov 9 Nov. 1917

Orenburg 31 Jan. 1918

Don

Volga

Ural

Zhitomir 22 Jan. 1918
Kiev 8 Feb. 1918
Vinnitsa

Denikin 1919
Poltava 19 Jan. 1918

Kharkov 24 Dec. 1917

Voronezh 12 Nov. 1917

Don Cossacks 1917–19

Ural Cossack Army 1918–20

Yekaterinoslav 11 Jan. 1918

Don

Tsaritsyn 27 Nov. 1917

Kishinev 10 Dec. 1917

Nikolayev 27 Jan. 1918

Dniester
Dnieper

Odessa 31 Jan. 1918

Wrangel 1920
Simferopol 26 Jan. 1918

Novocherkassk 25 Feb. 1918

Rostov 10 Nov. 1917

Cossacks

Astrakhan 7 Feb. 1918

Kuma

Caspian Sea

French
Sebastopol 29 Dec. 1917
Novorossiysk 14 Dec. 1917

Sea of Azov

French
British

Black Sea

British

Georgians 1919–20

Batum

Caucasus

Mensheviks

Baku 15 Nov. 1917

Tiflis
Erivan

Trebizond

PERSIA

British 1918–19

Entente fleet

Volga

1929–1939
The Great Depression

The New York Stock Market crash in October 1929 reflected deep weaknesses in the world economy. Commodity prices world-wide had been falling since 1926, reducing the capacity of exporters such as Australia and Latin America to buy products from Europe and the United States. Within the latter, wages lagged behind profits, impairing the development of domestic markets and limiting the potential of new industries, such as automobiles, to replace old ones, such as textiles. International finance never recovered from the strains of World War I, which caused a dramatic increase in productive capacity, particularly outside Europe, without a corresponding increase in sustained demand. Fixed exchange rates and free convertibility gave way to a compromise – the Gold Exchange Standard – that lacked the stability necessary to rebuild world trade.

In the scramble for liquidity that followed the Great Crash, funds flowed back from Europe to America and Europe's fragile prosperity crumbled. In many industrial countries one-quarter of the labour force was thrown out of work. Prices and wages plummeted, industrial production fell to 53 per cent of its 1929 level in Germany and world trade sank to 35 per cent of its 1929 value (see map 1). Early attempts to solve the problem did more harm than good. In 1930 the United States imposed the highest tariff in its history; in 1932 Britain responded with the Ottawa agreements, a series of preferential tariffs for the Commonwealth. Britain also left the Gold Standard in 1931, followed by other countries, dividing virtually the entire world into closed currency blocs which inhibited trade still further. Only Soviet Russia, largely isolated from the world economy, continued to increase its industrial production (page 134).

Economic nationalism fostered political nationalism, just as mass unemployment and the erosion of middle-class living standards fostered political extremism. In Japan, the fall of the Hamaguchi government in 1931 marked the end of constitutional democracy and the beginning of aggression in

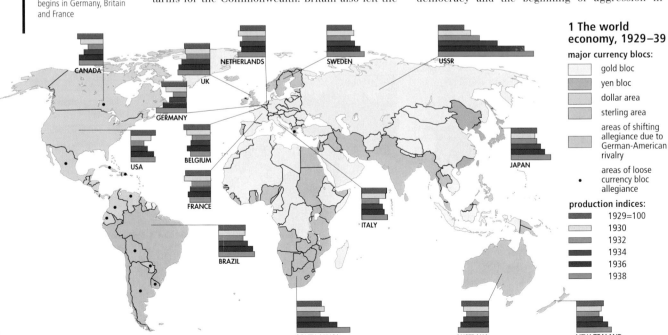

1 The world economy, 1929–39

major currency blocs:
- gold bloc
- yen bloc
- dollar area
- sterling area
- areas of shifting allegiance due to German-American rivalry
- areas of loose currency bloc allegiance

production indices:
- 1929=100
- 1930
- 1932
- 1934
- 1936
- 1938

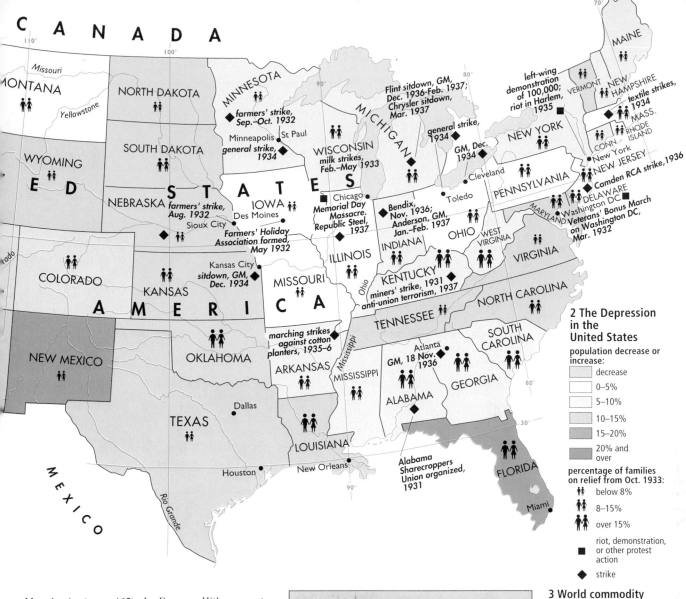

2 The Depression in the United States

population decrease or increase:

- decrease
- 0–5%
- 5–10%
- 10–15%
- 15–20%
- 20% and over

percentage of families on relief from Oct. 1933:

- below 8%
- 8–15%
- over 15%
- riot, demonstration, or other protest action
- strike

Map labels:

CANADA

MONTANA
NORTH DAKOTA
MINNESOTA
 farmers' strike, Sep.–Oct. 1932
Minneapolis general strike, 1934
St Paul
WISCONSIN milk strikes, Feb.–May 1933
MICHIGAN
Flint sitdown, GM, Dec. 1936-Feb. 1937; Chrysler sitdown, Mar. 1937
MAINE
VERMONT
NEW HAMPSHIRE
left-wing demonstration of 100,000; riot in Harlem, 1935
textile strikes, 1934
MASS.
RHODE ISLAND
CONN.
NEW YORK
general strike, 1934
GM, Dec. 1934
Cleveland
New York
NEW JERSEY
Camden RCA strike, 1936
PENNSYLVANIA
Toledo
DELAWARE
MARYLAND
Washington DC
Veterans' Bonus March on Washington DC, Mar. 1932
WYOMING
SOUTH DAKOTA
UNITED STATES
NEBRASKA
 farmers' strike, Aug. 1932
IOWA
Des Moines
Sioux City
Farmers' Holiday Association formed, May 1932
Chicago Memorial Day Massacre. Republic Steel, 1937
INDIANA
Bendix, Nov. 1936; Anderson, GM, Jan.–Feb. 1937
OHIO
WEST VIRGINIA
VIRGINIA
COLORADO
KANSAS
AMERICA
Kansas City sitdown, GM, Dec. 1934
MISSOURI
ILLINOIS
Ohio
KENTUCKY miners' strike, 1931
anti-union terrorism, 1937
NORTH CAROLINA
TENNESSEE
NEW MEXICO
OKLAHOMA
marching strikes against cotton planters, 1935–6
ARKANSAS
Mississippi
Atlanta GM, 18 Nov. 1936
SOUTH CAROLINA
GEORGIA
MISSISSIPPI
ALABAMA
TEXAS
Dallas
LOUISIANA
Houston
New Orleans
Alabama Sharecroppers Union organized, 1931
FLORIDA
Miami
MEXICO
Missouri
Yellowstone
Rio Grande

Manchuria (page 123). In Europe, Hitler rose to power in 1933 partly in response to the deflationary policies of his predecessors that raised unemployment from 3 million in 1930 to 6 million in 1932 (page 137). Even in Britain and the United States, fascist movements exercised considerable pressure. In the former, a right-wing National Government, formed in 1931, preserved democratic rule; in the latter, President Franklin Roosevelt, elected in 1932, implemented a 'New Deal' that laid the foundations for recovery. Nevertheless in 1934 some 20 billion days were lost in the US through industrial action and in 1938 over 10 million Americans remained out of work (map 2). Only World War II, and the boost it gave to production, pulled the United States out of the Depression.

By 1932 two out of every five Germans were out of work, and many of the rest were on short time. Here (*right*) the unemployed queue for newspapers carrying lists of jobs. Official efforts were made to limit the employment of women and to give preference to unemployed men.

3 World commodity production, 1926–38

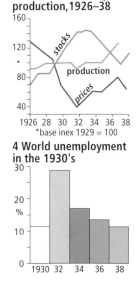

(graph showing stocks, production, prices)
160
120
80
40
1926 28 30 32 34 36 38
*base inex 1929 = 100

4 World unemployment in the 1930's

30
%
20
10
0
1930 32 34 36 38

The Second World War: the West

Hitler's accession to power in 1933 added a new dimension to international politics. At first his expansionist designs had to await economic recovery, but his virtually unopposed annexation of Austria and Czechoslovakia (1938-9) and the Nazi-Soviet Pact of August 1939 (page 137) led him to expect similar acquiescence when, the following month, he invaded Poland. This time he miscalculated: the western democracies declared war (though this did nothing to aid the Poles).

Over the next two years, Germany rapidly secured first Denmark and Norway, then France and the Low Countries, and finally Yugoslavia and Greece, while Italy annexed Albania and invaded Egypt (map 1). Despite the Nazi-Soviet pact, however, Hitler's ultimate goal was the conquest of Russia: his operations in the West, like the Schlieffen Plan in 1914 (page 132),

merely aimed to eliminate Germany's western enemies before the main struggle began in the east. In this Hitler failed because Britain – though defeated on the continent and subjected to sustained aerial bombing – refused to concede defeat. Nevertheless, in June 1941 Hitler launched his forces on Russia and, thanks to the

1 The Axis advance, 1939–41

- Axis territory, 1 Sep. 1939
- Axis co-belligerents
- occupied by Axis after Sep. 1939
- Vichy France and territories
- Soviet annexed territory, 1939–41
- neutral powers
- frontiers, 1 Sep. 1939
- ← Axis advances, 1939
- ← Axis advances, 1940
- ← Axis advances, 1941
- Axis airborne landings
- ← Allied forces
- ← Soviet advances, 1939–40
- ◄-- Allied retreat and withdrawal
- major cities severely damaged by bombing

combination of strategic surprise and tactical superiority, made rapid progress, taking over 3 million Russian prisoners-of-war. But the winter killed many Germans, who had far outrun their logistical support and lay stranded outside Moscow, Leningrad and Rostov. At precisely this point, on 7 December 1941, Japan attacked the United States (page 142), and Hitler – in an act of egregious folly – also declared war.

Although Germany launched another major thrust in Russia in 1942, reaching the Volga at Stalingrad, that too failed, with the loss of a major army, and its troops fell back in the face of superior Soviet forces, supplied both by the industrial complex built up beyond the Urals (page 134) and by the United States. Meanwhile, Anglo-American troops cleared Axis forces first from Africa and then from Sicily in 1942-3, leading Italy to make peace (though German forces there fought on); partisans gradually took over Yugoslavia; and from June 1944 allied armies liberated France and Belgium before moving into Germany. They met the Soviets on the Elbe in May 1945.

The costs of the war were appalling: 15 million military personnel and 35 million civilians perished, 20 million of them Soviet citizens. The Germans murdered prisoners of war

(Canadians, Americans and Britons in the West as well as Russians in the east); they murdered all captured partisans and members of the communist party; and they murdered all Jews they could find, many in mass shootings and at least 6 million in special extermination camps. However, they also lost heavily: the Anglo-American strategic bombing offensive reduced most of their major cities to rubble, and the Soviet troops carried out a systematic campaign of destruction as they advanced in 1944-5. By war's end, almost all Europe lay in ruins, yet already the differences between the victors had appeared which would darken the post-war years (page 164).

German troops fighting on the Eastern Front in June 1943. From early in 1943 the Soviet army experienced an almost uninterrupted run of successes against the Germans. In 1944 the Red Army pushed as far west as Warsaw, and in 1945 into Germany itself. Nearly 3 million German soldiers died during the war.

2 The defeat of Germany, 1942–5

☐ Grossdeutches Reich, 1942

⟵ Axis attacks

⟵- - Axis withdrawals

⟵ Allied attacks

✊ major cities under heavy air attack

✴ major battle with date

✊ partisan/resistance movements

● commando raids

◤ V1 launching sites

◤ V2 launching sites

— frontiers 1942

Map labels: Kirkenes · Petsamo 1944 · Murmansk 1944 · 1944 · NORWAY · SWEDEN · FINLAND · Leningrad 1941-2 · Narva 1944 · Helsinki · Novgorod · Oslo · Stockholm · Baltic Sea · ESTONIA · Moscow Dec. 1941 · UNION OF · Smolensk · Tula 1941-2 · SOVIET · North Sea · GREAT BRITAIN · IRELAND · DENMARK · Copenhagen · 1940-4 · Riga · LATVIA · LITHUANIA · Orel · Saratov · SOCIALIST · 1940-5 · Königsberg Feb.-Apr. 1945 · E. PRUSSIA · Minsk 1944 June-Aug. 1944 · Gomel · Kursk July-Aug. 1943 · 1944-5 · Hamburg · Hanover · Bremen · Berlin May 1945 · Warsaw Jan. 1945 · 1943-4 · REPUBLICS · NETH. · Arnhem · 1944-5 · Düsseldorf · Cologne · Dresden · 1941-4 · Kiev Nov.-Dec. 1943 · Kharkov · Stalingrad 1942-3 · June-July 1944 · London · BEL. Brussels · Frankfurt · Prague · Lemberg · 1942-3 · Nov.-Feb. 1943 · Cherbourg · Dieppe Dec. 1944 · Mannheim · May 1945 · UKRAINE · Volga · Caen · Paris 1944 · Stuttgart · Munich · Vienna Apr. 1945 · Budapest 1944-5 · Krivoy Rog · Rostov 1942-3 · St. Nazaire · FRANCE · Lyon · SWITZERLAND · AUSTRIA · HUNGARY · Transnistria · Odessa · Kerch · 1942-4 · VICHY FRANCE · Milan 1944-5 · Trieste · 1941-4 · CROATIA · Belgrade 1941-4 · Jassy · Sebastopol · Yalta · Marseilles · 1943-5 · Livorno · Florence · MONTENEGRO · SERBIA · Bucharest · ROMANIA · Ploesti · PORTUGAL · SPAIN · Madrid · Corsica · Rome taken June 1944 · Aug. 1944 · Anzio 1944 · Cassino Jan.-March 1944 · ALBANIA · Sofia · BULGARIA 1944 · Istanbul · Balearic Is. · Sardinia · July 1943 · Jan.-March 1944 · Salerno Sep. 1943 · 1941-4 · Thessaloniki · Nov. 942 · Gibraltar (Br.) · Nov. 1942 · Nov. 1942 · Mediterranean Sea · Nov. 1942 · Messina · Sicily July 1943 · GREECE · Oct. 1944 · Athens · Leros · Nov. 1942 · Oran · Algiers · Bougie · Bizerta · Tunis · April-May 1943 · Feb.-May 1943 · Malta · Sep. 1943 · Crete 1941-5 · Kos · Rhodes · MOROCCO · ALGERIA · TUNISIA · Tripoli · LIBYA · Benghazi · Tobruk · 23 Oct. 1942 British offensive · Alexandria · El Alamein · Cairo · El Agheila · Cyrenaica · Jan.-June 1942 · EGYPT · Oct.-Nov. 1942

The Second World War: Asia and the Pacific

Japanese expansion in Asia after 1931 (page 123) stemmed from a desire for economic self-sufficiency, military security and a self-imposed leadership of East Asia. By 1940, however, with no end in sight to the Chinese war, Japan widened its ambitions to include the empires of the colonial powers – those of France and the Netherlands, recently defeated by her ally Germany, and those of Britain, at war with Germany (page 140) – as an alternative source of raw materials and markets that would free Japan from economic dependence on an increasingly unfriendly United States.

In September 1940 Japan occupied French Indo-China and the United States promptly placed an embargo on sending all iron and steel scrap to Japan. Next, following a sharp defeat in summer 1939 at Nomonhan (Kalkhin Gol), Japan

concluded a neutrality pact with Russia – which had been seen as the empire's principal potential enemy since the Russo-Japanese war (page 122) – and prepared to occupy the rest of the European colonies in South-East Asia. But first she felt it necessary to forestall a counterstrike by the United States: at dawn on 7 December 1941 her aircraft attacked and partially destroyed the US Pacific fleet at Pearl Harbor, Hawaii.

Japan hoped to fight the world's greatest industrialised power to a stalemate that would result in a negotiated peace recognizing Japanese hegemony in east Asia. Within six months, her forces had conquered the American outposts of Guam and the Philippines, and occupied the British and Dutch colonies throughout South-East Asia. Their forces also overran the Bismarck archipelago and much of New Guinea, and captured most of the island redoubts necessary to create a defensive perimeter in the mid-Pacific (map

On 2 September 1945
Japanese representatives finally signed the act of surrender (below) on board the battleship USS Missouri in Tokyo Bay.

Map labels

U S S R

Nomonhan May-Aug. 1939 — MANCHURIA (MANCHUKUO)

INNER MONGOLIA

C H I N A

KOREA

JAPAN · Tokyo

Sea of Japan

East China Sea

Tsingtao

Yangtze · Nanking · Shanghai

Changsha

Kunming

BURMA — Laokai

Imphal — Hanoi

Hong Kong captured 1941

Japanese take Rangoon 8 Mar. 1942

Rangoon

SIAM

FRENCH INDO-CHINA

Saigon

MALAY STATES — Japanese land on Malay coast 8 Dec. 1941

Medan

Singapore — Japanese take Singapore 15 Feb. 1942

Sumatra

Borneo

DUTCH EAST INDIES

Battle of the Java Sea 27 Feb. 1942

Batavia — Java

Macassar

Lombok · Sumba · Flores · Timor

Celebes

Banda Sea

Ceram · Tanimbar Is. · Aru Is.

Halmahera

New Guinea

Port Moresby — Buna

Battle of the Coral Sea May 1942

US forces land 9 Feb. 1942

Coral Sea

New Caledonia

US forces land 12 Mar. 1942

Japanese attack on Philippines 8 Dec. 1941

Manila

Corregidor surrenders 6 May 1942

Philippine Is.

Mindanao — Zamboanga

Palau

Saipan

Guam

Caroline Is.

Truk

Kwajalein

Makin — Gilbert Is.

Abemama — Christmas

Admiralty — Manus Is.

Bismarck Arch. — New Ireland — Green Is.

Rabaul — Bougainville

Solomon Is.

Guadalcanal — Santa Cruz Is.

Espiritu Santo · New Hebrides · Fiji Is.

Ellice Is.

Pacific Ocean

Volcano Is.

Bonin Is.

Sea of Okhotsk · Kamandorski Is. · Bering Sea

Aleutian Is. · Attu · Kiska

Kurile Is.

Japanese perimeter July 1942

Japanese forces repulsed 3-6 June 1942 — Midway

Hawaiian Is.

attack on Pearl Harbor, 7 Dec. 1941 — Pearl Harbor

Wake I.

A U S T R A L I A
US commit ground forces to defence of Australia from Feb. 1942

Melbourne · Sydney

Map legend

1 The Japanese advance, 1941–2

- - - Japanese empire, 1941
→ Japanese advance or strike
● Japanese base
■ Allied base
✕ battle

1). In June 1942, however, at Midway Island, aggressive tactics shaped by superb intelligence allowed the aircraft carriers of the US Pacific fleet (which had not been in Pearl the previous December) to destroy a major Japanese carrier force. The United States, although following a 'Europe first' policy in the world war, still possessed abundant resources to advance on two distinct axes against Japan: in the south Pacific, an island-hopping strategy (by-passing the major centres of Japanese resistance and executed by amphibious forces) aimed for the Philippines; in the central Pacific, carrier-borne forces advanced towards the Marianas, from whose airbases bombing raids could be launched on Japan itself. At the same time, Allied forces moved from India into Burma; and in August 1945 Russia finally broke her neutrality pact and invaded Manchuria (map 2).

But Japan, though utterly exhausted, succumbed to none of these conventional threats: rather two atomic bombs, dropped on Hiroshima and Nagasaki in August 1945, precipitated the unconditional surrender of the millions of her troops still in arms. The brief Japanese colonial adventure had caused almost as much destruction as Hitler's war in Europe; but it also unleashed forces of revolutionary nationalism that would shape events throughout Asia over the next five decades (page 162).

Map labels

U S S R

Soviet army attacks 9 Aug. 1945

Sea of Okhotsk

Kamchatka 17 Aug. 1945

Komandorski Is.

Attu · Kiska — Aleutian Is. · Amchitka

Bering Sea

10 Oct. 1943

May–Aug. 1943

MANCHURIA (MANCHUKUO)

Khabarovsk

Kurile Is.

Hokkaido

INNER MONGOLIA

Peking

Tientsin · Dairen

Seoul

Sea of Japan

JAPAN

Tokyo

Japanese perimeter Mar. 1944

Japanese perimeter Oct. 1944

inese advance into rma after Oct. 1943
panese offensive into E. India Feb.–June 1944
itish offensive into rma after Nov. 1944
ngoon retaken May 1945

C H I N A

KOREA

Fusan

Hiroshima 6 Aug. 1945

fighters sweep over Japan from May 1945

Nanking

Nagasaki 9 Aug. 1945

Shikoku

Shanghai

Kyushu

bombing raids from June 1944

Pacific Ocean

40°

Chinese counter-offensive Apr.– June 1945

1944 Japanese Ichi-Go Offensive

Okinawa

direct air attack on Japan from Okinawa from May 1945

Bonin Is.

Volcano Is.

Iwo Jima Feb.–Mar. 1945

20th Air Force begins direct air attack on Japan from 24 Nov. 1944–14 Aug. 1945

Midway

Hawaii Is.

BURMA

Kunming

Amoy

Formosa

Laokai · Hanoi

Canton

Hong Kong

Luzon landings Jan. 1945

Battle of Philippine Sea. Japanese carrier aviation annihilated June 1944

Saipan June 1944

Tinian

Guam July 1944

Marianas

Eniwetok Feb. 1944

Wake I.

Oahu Pearl Harbor

20°

FRENCH INDO-CHINA

Mandalay

Hainan

Gulf of Tongking

Philippine Is.

Manila

25 Oct. 1944 Battle of Leyte Gulf. Heavy Japanese naval losses

Leyte

Leyte landing 20 Oct. 1944

Ulithi Sep. 1944

Caroline Is.

Truk

Marshall Is.

Kwajalein Feb. 1944

Majuro Jan. 1944

Pacific Ocean area forces

SIAM

Rangoon

Bangkok

Phnom Penh

Saigon

Gulf of Siam

Sulu Sea

Mindanao May 1945

Palau Sep. 1944

Makin

Gilbert Is.

Tarawa Nov. 1943

Christmas I.

0°

MALAY STATES

Kuala Lumpur

Singapore

SARAWAK

BRUNEI June 1945

Tarakan May 1945

Borneo July 1945

Morotai Sep. 1944

Halmahera

Sansapur

Noemfoor July 1944

Sorong

Manus Feb. 1944

Admiralty Is.

Bismarck Arch.

New Ireland

Rabaul

Bougainville Nov. 1943

Battle of Santa Cruz Oct. 1942

Eastern Solomons Aug. 1942 Japanese forces repulsed

Abemama

Ellice Is.

D U T C H   E A S T   I N D I E S

Sumatra

Palembang

Bandjarmasin

Celebes

Amboina

Ceram

Aru Is.

Macassar

Banda Sea

Tarimbar Is.

May 1944

Hollandia

New Guinea

Saidor Jan. 1944

Solomon Is.

Tulagi

South Pacific area forces

Espiritu Santo

Fiji Is.

New Hebrides

Japanese perimeter Aug. 1945

Batavia

Surabaya

Java

Lombok

Flores

Sumba

Timor

Timor Sea

Darwin

Cape York

Buna

Port Moresby

Guadalcanal 7 Aug. 1942– 9 Feb. 1943

Coral Sea

New Caledonia

20°

17–25 Sep. 1942 Japanese ground forces repulsed

A U S T R A L I A

Sydney

Melbourne

Legend

2 The Allied counter-offensive

→ Allied advance

—✈ Allied air attack

■ Allied base

✹ atomic bomb target

● Japanese base

◉ Japanese base bypassed or neutralized

✕ battle

Japanese perimeters

······ March 1944

—·—· October 1944

– – – August 1945

The United States since 1945

The requirements of wartime production solved the unemployment problem (page 138) of the United States at last, and the gigantic output achieved and allies demonstrated the economic potential which, when realized, would create an era of unprecedented prosperity for the United States. Gross National Product almost trebled in real terms between 1950 and 1990, while real income per head nearly doubled.

A number of factors brought about the economic surge: rapid population increase (from 132 million in 1940 to 281 million in 2000); technological advances coupled with the emergence of new consumer goods; the sudden spending of wartime savings; and the rearmament programmes connected with the Cold War and the Korean War (page 164 and 154). Affluence came to seem entirely normal and business confidence was seldom less than buoyant: on this basis of wealth and hope most American people began to transform their entire way of life. The expansion of the suburbs constituted perhaps the most obvious change. Easy credit, cheap fuel (both for homes and cars), mass production of housing and automobiles, and giant road-building programmes (40,000 miles of interstate highways by 1980), all helped encourage Americans in their millions to move off the farms and out of the cities into endless miles of suburbs. So although the population of the central cities grew from 48 million to 79 million between 1950 and 1990, that of their urban fringes also rose from 21 million also to 79 million (map 1).

By 1990, less than one-third of the US population lived in non-metropolitan areas, but the flight from the farms did not reduce productivity: on the contrary, the number of people fed by one farm worker doubled from 15 in 1950 to 30 in 1970. Thanks to mechanization,

improved seeds and fertilisers and government subsidies, the United States provided a significant proportion of the world's staple foods, such as wheat, maize and soya beans. The economy at large grew steadily, with the service sector (as in western Europe: page 166) expanding far more rapidly than manufacturing.

But beneath the prosperity lurked tensions. American capitalists tended to spend their profits rather than re-invest them, and industrial workers claimed higher wages and easier conditions of work without regard to the effect such claims (if successful) might have on prices and on the international competitiveness of American industry. The Vietnam War (1965-73: page 162) created high inflation and bitter internal divisions. Explicit discrimination against Blacks and Asians exploded in urban riots during the 1960s and gave rise to a widespread movement for civil rights led by Dr Martin Luther King (map 2). Then came the policies of Presidents Ronald Reagan (1981-9) and George Bush (1989-93), who cut taxes by a third (releasing a flood of spending power on the markets), slashed welfare programmes (turning the inner cities into ghettoes), increased expenditure on armaments (so creating the biggest deficit in history), and failed to remedy the structural defects of American industry (so that the new purchasing power went overwhelmingly into imports, creating an equally unprecedented trade deficit).

Under the presidency of Bill Clinton (1993-2001), Americans rediscovered their national self-confidence. The United States played a decisive role in the conflicts in the Middle East and the Balkans and its economy boomed. Much of this prosperity depended on sales of computers and satellite communications, however, and when demand for these slackened in 2000, recession threatened. The terrorist attacks of September 2001, by shaking public confidence and precipitating a decline in consumer spending, turned the threat into reality.

On 11 September 2001, two planes hijacked by Islamic extremists were deliberately crashed into the World Trade Centre in New York, killing thousands of people. A third plane crashed into the Pentagon in Washington. The shock to a nation which had never suffered a peace-time atrocity on this scale was profound. Defence and the need to secure the nation against similar attacks immediately rose to the top of the political agenda. The blame for the assault was squarely laid on the Islamic al-Qaeda network led by Osama bin Laden and based in Taleban-ruled Afghanistan. An American-led bombing campaign which began in October led, by December, to the collapse of the Taleban regime and the destruction of much of al-Qaeda's infrastructure in Afghanistan.

3 Growth of consumer durables, 1950–98

Phone   TV   VCR
Radio   Cable TV

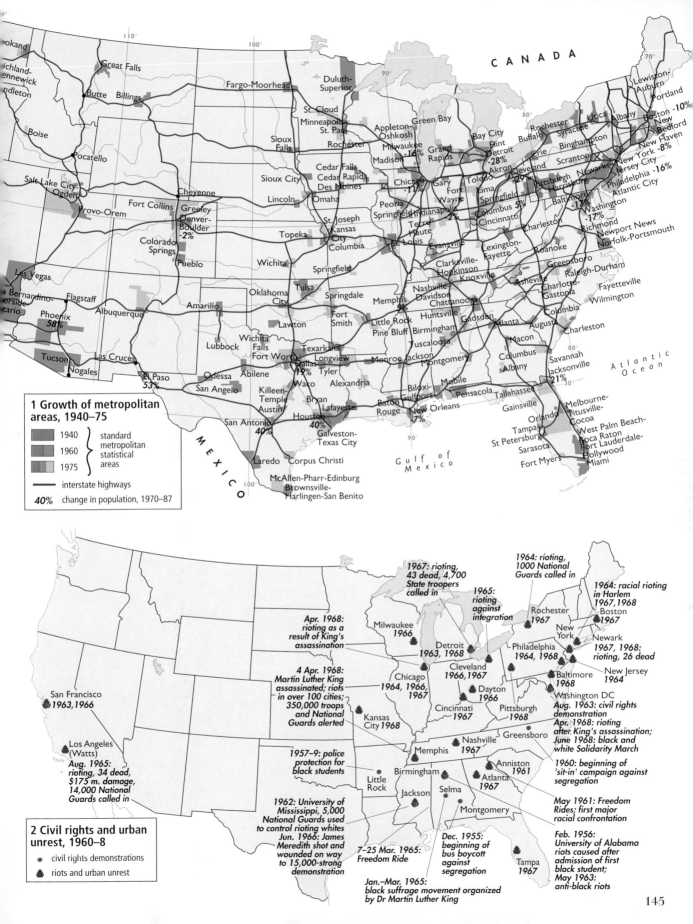

1 Growth of metropolitan areas, 1940–75

- 1940 ⎫
- 1960 ⎬ standard metropolitan statistical areas
- 1975 ⎭
- —— interstate highways
- **40%** change in population, 1970–87

Map labels (Map 1):

Spokane, Richland-Kennewick, Pendleton, Great Falls, Butte, Billings, Boise, Pocatello, Salt Lake City-Ogden, Provo-Orem, Fort Collins, Cheyenne, Greeley, Denver-Boulder -2%, Colorado Springs, Pueblo, Las Vegas, San Bernardino-Riverside-Ontario, Flagstaff, Phoenix 58%, Albuquerque, Tucson, Nogales, Las Cruces, El Paso 53%, Laredo, Nogales, McAllen-Pharr-Edinburg, Brownsville-Harlingen-San Benito, Corpus Christi, San Antonio 40%, Austin, Killeen-Temple, Bryan, Houston 40%, Galveston-Texas City, Lafayette, Baton Rouge, New Orleans 7%, Biloxi-Gulfport, Pensacola, Mobile, Tallahassee, Gainsville, Melbourne-Titusville-Cocoa, West Palm Beach-Boca Raton, Fort Lauderdale-Hollywood, Miami, Fort Myers, Sarasota, St Petersburg, Tampa, Orlando, Jacksonville 21%, Savannah, Charleston, Columbia, Augusta, Macon, Albany, Columbus, Montgomery, Jackson, Monroe, Longview, Tyler, Waco, Dallas 19%, Fort Worth, Texarkana, Abilene, San Angelo, Odessa, Lubbock, Wichita Falls, Lawton, Fort Smith, Springdale, Amarillo, Oklahoma City, Tulsa, Wichita, Springfield, Topeka, Kansas City, St. Joseph, Columbia, Lincoln, Omaha, Sioux City, Sioux Falls, Fargo-Moorhead, Duluth-Superior, St. Cloud, Minneapolis-St. Paul, Rochester, Cedar Falls, Cedar Rapids, Des Moines, Appleton-Oshkosh, Green Bay, Bay City, Madison, Milwaukee -16%, Chicago -11%, Gary, Peoria, Springfield, Terre Haute, Indianapolis 2%, Evansville, St. Louis, Clarksville-Hopkinson, Nashville-Davidson 3%, Memphis, Little Rock, Pine Bluff, Birmingham, Tuscaloosa, Huntsville, Gadsden, Chattanooga, Knoxville, Lexington-Fayette, Asheville, Charlotte-Gastonia, Greensboro, Raleigh-Durham, Fayetteville, Wilmington, Charleston, Roanoke, Richmond, Newport News, Norfolk-Portsmouth, Columbus 5%, Cincinnatti, Lima, Springfield, Fort Wayne, Toledo, Akron -29%, Cleveland, Detroit -28%, Flint, Grand Rapids, Erie, Pittsburgh, Harrisburg, Scranton, Binghampton, Utica, Syracuse, Rochester, Buffalo, Baltimore -1%, Washington -17%, Philadelphia -16%, Atlantic City, Jersey City, New York, Newark, New Haven, New Bedford -8%, Boston -10%, Albany, Portland, Lewiston-Auburn

CANADA, MEXICO, Gulf of Mexico, Atlantic Ocean

---

2 Civil rights and urban unrest, 1960–8

- ● civil rights demonstrations
- ♠ riots and urban unrest

Map annotations (Map 2):

San Francisco 1963, 1966

Los Angeles (Watts): Aug. 1965: rioting, 34 dead, $175 m. damage, 14,000 National Guards called in

Apr. 1968: rioting as a result of King's assassination

4 Apr. 1968: Martin Luther King assassinated; riots in over 100 cities; 350,000 troops and National Guards alerted

1957–9: police protection for black students

1962: University of Mississippi, 5,000 National Guards used to control rioting whites
Jun. 1966: James Meredith shot and wounded on way to 15,000-strong demonstration

Little Rock

Kansas City 1968

Milwaukee 1966

1967: rioting, 43 dead, 4,700 State troopers called in

Detroit 1963, 1968

Chicago 1964, 1966, 1967

Cincinnati 1967

Dayton 1966

Cleveland 1966, 1967

Memphis 1967

Nashville 1967

Birmingham

Jackson

Selma

Montgomery

1965: rioting against integration

Rochester 1967

1964: rioting, 1000 National Guards called in

1964: racial rioting in Harlem 1967, 1968

Boston 1967

New York

Newark 1967, 1968: rioting, 26 dead

New Jersey 1964

Philadelphia 1964, 1968

Baltimore 1968

Pittsburgh 1968

Washington DC Aug. 1963: civil rights demonstration; Apr. 1968: rioting after King's assassination; June 1968: black and white Solidarity March

1960: beginning of 'sit-in' campaign against segregation

May 1961: Freedom Rides; first major racial confrontation

Feb. 1956: University of Alabama riots caused after admission of first black student; May 1963: anti-black riots

Greensboro

Anniston 1961

Atlanta 1967

7–25 Mar. 1965: Freedom Ride

Dec. 1955: beginning of bus boycott against segregation

Jan.–Mar. 1965: black suffrage movement organized by Dr Martin Luther King

Tampa 1967

145

World War II left Europe politically disorganized and economically prostrate, a situation greatly exacerbated by large-scale population movements. The German collapse released millions of incarcerated prisoners-of-war and slave-workers, and a further 5 million Russian prisoners, refugees and servicemen were repatriated. Two more lasting shifts of population also occurred: some 12 million Germans abandoned (voluntarily or forcibly) their pre-war homes in the east, especially in lands annexed by the Nazis after 1938; and over 2 million Russians moved into the territories annexed by the Soviet Union during its westward advance (map 1).

The political frontiers of the new Europe were established at conferences between the victors (USA, USSR, Britain and France) held at Yalta and Potsdam in February and July 1945: the union of Germany and Austria decreed by Hitler in 1938 was dissolved and Germany lost territory to Poland and the Soviet Union; both countries were divided into occupation zones under four power control. In Austria the system worked relatively smoothly, and in 1955 the country achieved independence, albeit as a permanently neutralized state; but co-operation between the USSR and her allies in Germany broke down in 1948. Britain and the United States had already amalgamated their

1 Post-war population movements and territorial change

Territorial change, 1945–9

- cities divided into four occupation zones
- frontiers, 1949
- Germany, 1937
- Allied control zones of Germany and Austria
- annexed by Soviet Union 1940–5
- states which became Communist, 1945–8
- Yugoslav gains from Italy, 1945
- Federal Republic of Germany from 1949
- German Democratic Republic from 1949

Population movements: peoples resettled, evacuated or expelled (with numbers):
- Germans
- Finns driven from area bordering Russia
- Baltic peoples
- Russians
- Russians forcibly repatriated
- Poles
- Czechs
- peoples settled by International Refugee Organisation

zones in 1947 and, in conjunction with France, they now prepared for the formation of a West German government (the Federal Republic: BRD). After an attempt to prevent this by means of a blockade on Berlin, the Soviets prepared their zone for quasi-independence as the German Democratic Republic (DDR): the two states came into existence in 1949 (map 1).

They immediately took their place in the two political blocs into which Europe had become divided. The eastern republics had all come under communist rule by 1948 and economic growth, though continuous, remained slow thanks to Stalinist methods of production. In the western democracies, thanks largely to lavish American aid (the Marshall Plan from 1947; map 3), an economic miracle took place, with smooth and rapid growth year after year. The two blocs had their own military groups – NATO in the west (1949) and the Warsaw Pact in the east (1955) – and their own economic organizations – in the east Comecon (1949) and in the west the European Community (six members 1957; 9 by 1973) and the less successful European Free Trade Association (map 4). However the growth surge suffered a serious check in 1973 when the Arab-led Organization of Petroleum Exporting Countries (OPEC) increased the price of oil by 250 per cent.

4 European military and economic trading blocs, 1947–73

military partitions
Nato 1949– (including United States and Canada)

Warsaw Pact 1948–91

economic blocs
Benelux customs union, 1947

joined EEC, 1973

founder members of European Free Trade Association (EFTA), 1960

subsequent EFTA members

Council for Mutual Economic Assistance (COMECON) members, 1949

subsequent COMECON members

original European Economic Community (EEC) members, 1957

On 23 June 1948, the Soviet Union set up a blockade of the Western sectors of Berlin. The Western states mounted an airlift *(left)* until May 1949, which brought in 2.3 million tons of supplies.

3 The Marshall Plan

applied for and received Marshall aid, with amounts (in US$)

applied for Marshall aid but withdrew application

did not apply

14.0% Net Marshall aid as percentage of national income 1948–9

ICELAND $24 m 5%

NORWAY $236 m 5.8%

SWEDEN $118 m 0.3%

IRELAND $116 m 7.8%

UNITED KINGDOM $2,825 m 2.4%

DENMARK $257 m 3.3%

NETH. $979 m 10.8%

BELGIUM $546 m 0.6%

WEST GERMANY $1,297 m 2.9%

FRANCE $2,445 m 6.5%

AUSTRIA $560 m 14.0%

applied for Marshall aid but received nothing

PORTUGAL $50 m

ITALY $1,314 m 5.3%

denied Marshall aid because of Franco's pro-Axis sympathies

GREECE $515 m

TURKEY $152 m

2 Berlin, 1945–90

American sector
British sector
French sector
Soviet sector
city borders
the Berlin Wall, 1961–89

Autobahn
international railway
airport
headquarters
allied HQ
air corridor

REINICKENDORF
Falkensee
Tegel
SPANDAU
PANKOW
WEDDING
WEISSENSEE
TIERGARTEN
PRENZLEUER-BERG
Neuenhagen
LICHTENBERG
Checkpoint Charlie
Gatow
Tempelhof
TEMPELHOF
ZEHLENDORF
STEGLITZ
NEUKÖLLN
Rüdersdorf
KÖPENICK
Potsdam
Schönefeld
Schmöckwitz
Havel
Spree

China since 1949

The establishment of the People's Republic of China in 1949 (page 130) marked a fundamental turning point in the modern history of China. After a century of severe internal conflict and disintegration, usually provoked or exacerbated by external aggressors, China was now reunified and strongly governed by leaders who possessed a decisive vision of the society they wished to create. Whatever the excesses and failures since 1949, not least the systematic repression of much of the population, that remains a fundamental achievement.

For a time, China closely followed the Soviet model of directed economic planning and achieved modest progress in developing heavy industries and raising agricultural production. In 1958, however, the communist leader Mao Zedong became impatient and sought to mobilize the revolutionary energies of China's vast population, launching the 'Great Leap Forward'. Rural China was divided into 26,000 communes, each required to abolish private property and meet huge targets in agricultural and industrial production. Some 600,000 backyard furnaces sprang up across the countryside. The experiment proved an unmitigated disaster: production declined sharply, 20-30 million people died from starvation or malnutrition, and the project was abandoned in 1961.

This failure strengthened the hands of moderate communists who preferred a more centrally-planned, Soviet-style development. Mao responded by forming an alliance with the People's Liberation Army (PLA) and with Chinese youth who, as 'Red Guards', faithfully supported his policies. In 1966 Mao launched the Great Proletarian Cultural Revolution. Red Guards were set loose to prevent the development of 'vested interests' and careerism in party and state by establishing permanent revolution. The guards killed thousands and forcibly resettled millions. Chaos followed throughout China, forcing Mao to call on the PLA to restore order (map 1).

Mao died in 1976 and his widow Jiang Qing with three allies (later denounced as the 'Gang of Four') tried to seize power; but by this time the PLA and the elite had had enough of revolution. The 'Gang of Four' were arrested, tried and expelled from the Communist Party.

In the late 1970s Deng Xiaoping became the dominant figure in China's politics. Following the visit of United States President Nixon in 1972, which began the process of re-opening China to the capitalist West, Deng launched a policy of economic liberalization. He created special economic zones in areas bordering the foreign colonies of Hong Kong and Macao and Taiwan, and in Shanghai, with inducements to encourage foreign investment. By 1992, $36 billion had been invested. Other reforms followed: peasants were permitted to own land and, by 1984, 98 per cent did so. The communes vanished and agricultural output increased by 49 per cent in five years. Private businesses, also now permitted, grew in number from 100,000 in 1978 to 17 million in 1985 (map 2).

Economic reforms led to demands for political liberalization. In December 1986, students demonstrated for democracy in 15 cities. Deng responded

Student demonstrators in Beijing in 1989 *(right)*. Thousands of students occupied Tiananmen square for six weeks in May and June to demonstrate for greater democracy. On 3-4 June the army violently ejected the students. The death toll was later estimated at 400-800.

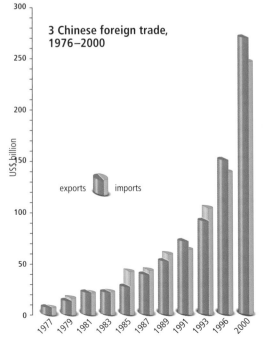

3 Chinese foreign trade, 1976–2000

US$ billion

exports   imports

1977 1979 1981 1983 1985 1987 1989 1991 1993 1996 2000

1 The Cultural Revolution in China, 1966–76

★ fighting involving Red Guards and Army or workers, 1966–9

◼ main areas of activity of Red Guards

→ movement of urban intellectuals to rural areas

with repression: he arrested 'troublemakers' and sacked Hu Yaobang, the liberal secretary-general of the Chinese Communist Party. When Hu died in April 1989, students used the occasion to demand democracy, gathering in Beijing's Tiananmen Square, at times numbering over a million, until in June Deng sent in the PLA and the movement was ruthlessly crushed.

After the Tiananmen massacre China swiftly reassured the world that it was a stable economic partner, and most of the world obligingly ignored human rights concerns in return for a share of China's economic boom. Foreign investment soared, and so did China's foreign trade (table 3). Further economic liberalization now took place as most of China operated a 'socialist market economy'. Growth rates, which averaged 10 per cent or more for the 1980s and 1990s, were only slightly affected by the economic turmoil which hit most of the rest of east Asia in 1997–8. In 1997, Britain returned its colony of Hong Kong, which retained a degree of self-government, and two years later Portugal surrendered Macao. With growing freedom in many areas of life, the issue of democracy remained the unfinished business of China's 20th-century achievement.

2 The Chinese economy, 1983–97

◼ 672 foreign investment, 1983-97, by province, in million US$

◼ Special Economic Zone (SEZ), 1984

☐ GDP per capita <80% of national average, 1997

☐ GDP per capita 80-120% of national average, 1997

☐ GDP per capita >120% of national average, 1997

● open coastal city

● inland city with expanded authority

━ "golden triangle" development areas

▲ major oilfields

■ major coalfields

─ frontiers, 1992

Japan and Korea

In the wake of the Second World War, United States support for Japan, South Korea and Taiwan, perceived after 1948 as its first line of defence in east Asia, transformed their economies.

Japan, like Germany (page 146), ended the war with its economy in ruins: most towns and industrial plants destroyed; nearly all foreign assets lost; domestic capital run down. Moreover, the victors demanded reparations and occupied the country following its surrender. The Far East Commission, which contained representatives of all the countries that had fought Japan but remained an American enterprise, sought to demilitarize Japan and create a peaceful, democratic state. It reformed the education system (removing from the syllabus all material that

had encouraged military and authoritarian values); abolished the divinity of the emperor and made the Diet (parliament) the highest political authority; established an independent judiciary and free labour unions; introduced a programme of land reform; and sought (with little success) to break up the great concentrations of corporate power. With the advance of the Chinese communists after 1948, however, the United States increasingly came to see Japan not only as the key bulwark of Western power in east Asia but also as one whose effectiveness depended on the reconstruction of its economic power. The occupation formally ended in 1951.

Japan's defeat also ended its harsh colonial rule of Korea (since 1910) and led to the peninsula's occu-

Robots on a Toyota assembly plant *(below)*. Car production was an essential component of Japan's post-war economic miracle. The Toyota company produced just 11,000 vehicles in 1950, but by the peak of production (in 1985) this had increased to 5.6 million annually.

Map labels:

EUROPE 33,500
NETH. 800
WEST GERMANY 400
8,124 34,710
2,500
UK
1,800 LUX.
FRANCE 330
SOVIET BLOC
860 2,288
USSR
6,576/11,458
62/482
SOUTH KOREA
ASIA 404,700
4,868/12,456
JAPAN
650
MIDDLE EAST 12,000
54
CHINA 1,200
15,565 57,239
1,413/2,104
AFRICA 27,100
SAUDI ARABIA
TAIWAN 370
HONG KONG 1,100
LIBERIA 267 4,162 4,244
THAILAND 250
MALAYSIA 160
272/3,392
SINGAPORE 500
INDONESIA 550
OCEANIA 26,400
2,163 6,300
AUSTRALIA 1,200

5 Japanese exports, 1960–99 (millions US $)

Chart values (y-axis): 450,000 / 400,000 / 350,000 / 300,000 / 250,000 / 200,000 / 150,000 / 100,000 / 50,000 / 0

Chart years (x-axis): 1960, 1965, 1970, 1975, 1980, 1985, 1990, 1995, 1999 pation by the victors: Japanese forces north of the 38th parallel surrendered to Soviet Russia, those in the south to the United States. The Soviets supported the establishment of a communist state in the north under Kim Il-Sung, a guerrilla leader who had spent considerable time in the Soviet Union; and the Americans retaliated by sponsoring a representative regime under Syngman Rhee, a strong anti-communist. Both new governments entertained strong ambitions to unite the country under their own rule, and in June 1950 the North attacked, pushing the South Korean and remaining United States troops back toward Pusan (map 1). The US forces counterattacked in September with a daring amphibious landing at Inchon, leading to a further offensive that promised to unify Korea. In November, however, the Chinese committed substantial forces and regained most of the north. A stalemate ensued until an armistice was signed in 1953.

The Korean War boosted the Japanese economy and initiated a period of exceptionally high economic

growth – well over 10 per cent a year throughout the 1960s, and over 4 per cent annually between 1974 and 1985, faster than that of any other OECD country. A key feature of Japan's growth was its flexibility in pursuing economic objectives: in the 1950s it emphasized heavy industry, ship-building and iron and steel; in the 1960s it moved into high-technology consumer manufactures largely for export; from the 1970s it concentrated on technological innovation and higher value-added products while transferring the production of lower value-added goods overseas. Industrial production and exports soared (tables 3 and 5) and massive Japanese investment took place in Asia, Europe and North America. Yet by 2002, Japan, for so long boasting the world's strongest economy and the largest per capita GNP, had endured a decade of slow growth or recession, rising unemployment and deflation.

Korea epitomized the relative success of the communist and capitalist projects. Until 1970 North Korea had the higher GNP per capita, but by the 1990s GNP was declining at 5 per cent and the state, still communist, came close to economic and humanitarian disaster. From the mid-1960s South Korea embarked on rapid industrialization and by the 1990s boasted the world's 13th largest economy with great strengths in car manufacture, shipbuilding and semi-conductors (table 4). Its regime showed little tolerance of political dissent, however, and crushed open protest.

Although the economic turmoil that hit the east Asian economies in 1997 exposed serious structural weaknesses, particularly in the inefficient and debt-laden finance and banking sectors, the vast underlying strength of the region suggests that the Pacific Rim will remain a lynchpin of the global economic system.

3 Japanese industrial production

index of industrial production (1945=100)

- 2684.1 — 1980
- 1736.4 — 1970
- 487.8 — 1960
- 112.2 — 1950

2 Japanese investment overseas, 1970–98

15,565 | 57,239 — trade with region, 1970–4 and 1985–9 (billion Yen)

6,576/3,392 — value of Japanese direct foreign investment in region, 1987/1999 (US$ million)

1,200 — value of Japanese direct foreign investment in country, 1987 (US$ million)

404,700 — workers in Japanese-affiliated companies, 1980

CANADA — 650

NORTH AMERICA — 83,900

15,357/21,873

USA — 14,700

17,170 | 75,190

BAHAMAS — 730

CAYMAN ISLANDS — 1,200

4,814/6,479

PANAMA — 2,300

LATIN AMERICA — 128,100

BRAZIL — 230

2,024 | 2,372

4 The two Koreas; per capita GNP growth, 1945–99

thousand US$

$13,300 (1999)

— South Korea
— North Korea

1945 1950 1960 1970 1980 1990 1999

1 The Korean War

CHINA

Chosan

Antung • — Chinese intervention Oct. 1950

• Iwon

• Unsan — Hungnam

US airborne landings 20 Oct. 1950

NORTH KOREA — • Wonsan

landing of US 7 Division, 26 Oct. 1950

• Pyongyang

UN maximum advance 2 Nov. 1950 before start of Chinese counter-attack

armistice line 27 July 1953

38th Parallel

Panmunjom • — • Seoul

• Inchon

Chinese and North Korean maximum advance 25 Jan. 1951

landing of US X Corps 15 Sep. 1950

• Wonju

• Taejon

SOUTH KOREA

North Korean maximum advance 15 Sep. 1950

• Pohang

Taegu

• Pusan

• Mokpo

153

Retreat from empire

The Western empires created in the 19th century (page 118) remained intact in 1939, though most German and Ottoman possessions had passed to Britain, France and Japan as League of Nations mandates. The United States planned to grant independence to the Philippines, acquired in 1898, and did so immediately after World War II; but none of the seven remaining European colonial powers – Britain, France, Spain, Portugal, Belgium, Italy and the Netherlands – surrendered their empires voluntarily. Only Britain even conceived of independence as the ultimate goal, albeit with continued membership of the Commonwealth, a goal already attained in 1939 by Canada, South Africa, Australia and New Zealand. The continental colonial powers thought more in terms of evolution towards a common citizenship, with their colonies as overseas parts of the metropolitan territory. Such plans were complicated, however, by the resistance of European settlers, with consequent inter-racial tensions, and by clashes between the European ideal of evolution along Western lines (in education and economic development) and the powerful Hindu, Muslim, Buddhist and Confucian cultures of the 'subject peoples'.

TIMELINE

1942
Japan overruns Europe's Far Eastern colonies

1947
India partitioned: India and Pakistan independent

1954
Communist Vietnamese defeat French at Dien Bien Phu: start of Algerian War

1957
Suez crisis; abortive French and English invasion of Egypt

1957-68
Independence for British African colonies

1960
Independence for all French sub-Saharan colonies and Belgian Congo

1962
France withdraws from Algeria

1965
Rhodesian white settlers make Unilateral Declaration of Independence resulting in guerrilla war

1975
Portuguese rule in Africa ends

1990
Namibia gains independence from South Africa

1997
Hong Kong returned to China

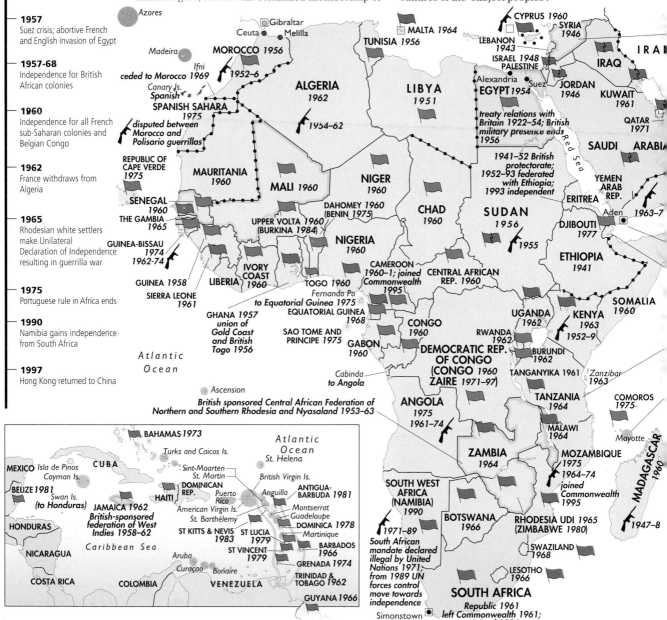

154

France fought stubbornly to maintain its control of Indochina (page 162), and the Netherlands struggled to contain the nationalists of Java, who had proclaimed the Indonesian Republic in 1945. Neither succeeded. Continual unrest forced Britain to grant independence to India and Pakistan (1947), followed in 1948 by Burma and Ceylon (page 162). Nevertheless Britain fought (and won) a long war against communist insurgents in Malaya, and resisted Indonesian attempts to annex Sarawak and Brunei. Only after the evacuation of Aden in 1967 did Britain abandon its presence east of Suez – save only for Hong Kong, retained until 1997, its economic success being of some benefit to Communist China.

In Africa resistance to independence was strongest in colonies with substantial white settler populations. In Algeria, with 1 million whites, a savage war of liberation occurred between 1954 and 1962; but conflict proved bitter, too, in Kenya and Rhodesia. However by 1974 all had achieved independence (page 160). By then, although Britain showed in the Falklands War (1982) its determination to fight on behalf of the few outposts still directly ruled from London, the formal structures of European imperialism had been dismantled and largely replaced by different forms of association such as the British Commonwealth or the French Community.

Mohandas Gandhi (right) became leader of the Indian nationalist movement in 1918, preaching non-violence (satyragha). In 1922 he was imprisoned by the British authorities, but was released in 1924 on becoming president of the Indian National congress. He led a campaign to boycott British cotton imports, and in 1930 encouraged resistance to a proposed salt tax. Although he withdrew from formal politics in 1933 he remained the guiding influence of the nationalist movement, and was a key figure in the eventual negotiations for Indian independence and partition in 1946-8.

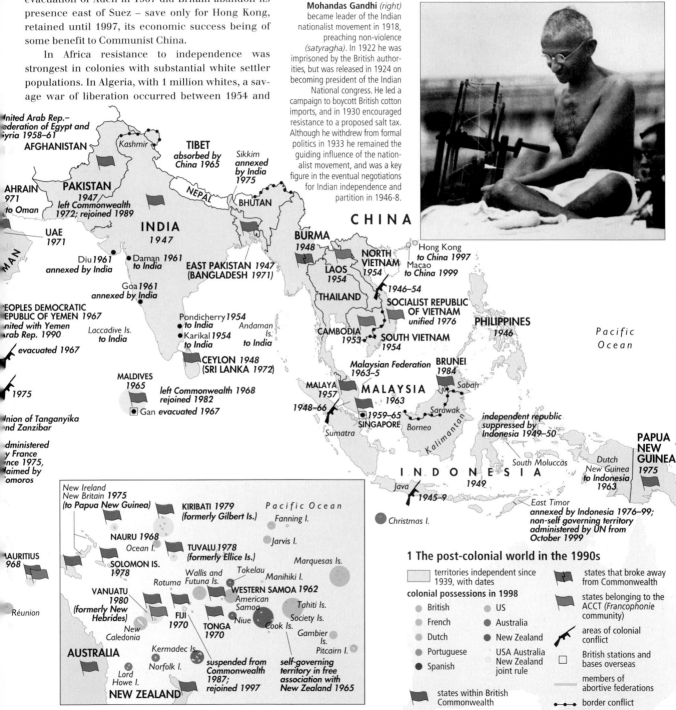

1 The post-colonial world in the 1990s

▢ territories independent since 1939, with dates	◣ states that broke away from Commonwealth
colonial possessions in 1998	◤ states belonging to the ACCT (Francophonie community)

British	US
French	Australia
Dutch	New Zealand
Portuguese	USA Australia New Zealand joint rule
Spanish	

⚔ areas of colonial conflict

▢ British stations and bases overseas

━━━ members of abortive federations

•–•–• border conflict

🏳 states within British Commonwealth

The Middle East since 1917

The Middle East has occupied world attention more consistently than any other region since 1945: Israel and its neighbours have engaged in four full-scale wars; Israel has invaded Lebanon twice; two Gulf wars have been fought; military coups have reinforced a regional pattern of internal repression; waves of refugees have been forced to flee.

American support for the state of Israel (founded in 1948), sponsorship of the Baghdad Pact (1955), and intervention in Lebanon (1958) seemed to threaten the USSR's southern frontier, and so it offered assistance to Syria, Egypt and (after 1958) Iraq. The Soviets also championed the Arab states during the Arab-Israeli war of 1967, despite which Israel occupied the west bank of the Jordan, Sinai and the Golan heights, provoking further large-scale Arab emigration (map 1). In 1973 an Egyptian and Syrian attack on Israel met with limited military success, and opened a new phase of negotiation. Egypt and Israel concluded the Camp David Accords (1978) which resulted in the return of Sinai in 1982; but the Israelis refused to return the other territories occupied since 1967, instead installing large numbers of new Jewish settlements. Moreover in 1982, to counter Palestinian guerrilla activity, they invaded and held south Lebanon. Nevertheless, in the wake of a prolonged period of resistance to Israeli rule in the West Bank and Gaza, which excited much outside sympathy, in 1991 the US succeeded in bringing Israel and its Arab neighbours into extended peace talks, which resulted in limited Palestinian self-rule in 1994-5, although by 2002 relations with the Palestinian leadership had broken down completely. Israel withdrew from south Lebanon in 2000.

As open conflict between Israel and her neighbours abated, it began around the Persian Gulf. The replacement of the Shah of Iran by Ayatollah Khomeini in 1979 seemed to President Saddam Hussein of Iraq to offer the chance of territorial gain. He attacked in 1980. However, eight years of attritional warfare achieved virtually nothing and in 1990 (map 2), in an attempt to gain new resources with which to liquidate his war debts, Saddam invaded and annexed another neighbour, Kuwait. The United Nations, led by the US, put pressure on Saddam to withdraw and, when he refused, in 1991 used armed force to expel him. These events catastrophically reduced oil production in the Gulf area. Its share of global output fell from 41 per cent in 1979 to 26 per cent in 1991, with production in Iraq and Kuwait reduced almost to zero.

1 Israel and Palestine, 1948–95

▮ Israel after Arab invasion and War of Independence, 1948

▯ Israeli conquests, 1967

— Egyptian re-conquests, and Israeli conquests, 1973

→ Jewish immigration, 1948–64

→ Arab refugees, 1948

→ Arab refugees, 1967

Sinai, the Israeli withdrawal:
■ ■ ■ Egyptian frontline under second Sinai agreement, 1 Sep.1975

○ Israeli settlements given up in 1982

✈ Israeli military and civil airports given up in 1982

⌂ Israeli oil wells given up in 1982

ALGERIA
Dec. 1991: Front Islamique de Salut (FIS) score dramatic gains in elections
Feb. 1992: elections cancelled, state of emergency declared, FIS banned
June 1992: President Boudiaf assassinated by FIS
from 1993: government repression of FIS sparks continuing bitter civil war
1995: terror bombing campaign in Paris
1997: ceasefire with FIS
1997–: continued attacks by GIA and GSPC groups

283,000 from M. East

350,000 from Europe

264,500 from n. Africa

Rafah salient: 11 Israeli settlements established by 1978, with Jewish population of 2,000

Sinai Peninsula returned to Egypt 1982

Popular protest played a key role in the fall of the shah of Iran in 1979 and the assumption of power by Ayatollah Khomeini in February that year. The picture was taken in 1987 on the eighth anniversary of the revolution. According to Khomeini, ultimate governmental authority should be vested in a supreme Islamic jurist. Subsequently, a rightly guided Iran should spread the message of true Islam to the rest of the Islamic world. But true Islam had first to be consolidated within Iran: an estimated 10,000 people had been executed by 1985 and 40,000 imprisoned.

3 Islamic fundamentalism 1979–99

- countries with radical Islamic governments
- Islamic parties represented in parliament
- ✳ civil war
- ✊ violent anti-government Islamic campaigns
- ▲ countries with significant Shia populations
- ✳ Islamic terrorist attacks

Mar. 1994: pro-Islamist Welfare Party scores gains in local elections
Dec. 1995: Welfare Party wins largest percentage of votes in general election; subsequent deal between secular parties keeps it out of power
1998 Welfare Party banned. New Islamist party, Virtue, founded
1999 Virtue Party comes 3rd in general elections

1983: foundation of Hezbollah, radical Islamic movement; becomes principal proxy for Iranian-inspired terrorism in Lebanon

Feb. 1982: rioting by Islamic militants in Hama brutally supressed

1979: following overthrow of shah, hardline Islamic fundamentalist government, headed by Ayatollah Khomeini, established
late 1980s: Iranian backing for the formation of HAMAS and Islamic Jihad, militant Palestinian Islamic groupings

continuing anti-Israeli campaign of suicide bombings

2001: radical Islamic Taleban regime overthrown following US-led campaign

1973: Qadhafi publishes Third Universal Theory, declaring Islam the true path
1977 Libyan "cultural revolution" introduces Islamic socialism

original home of Muslim Brotherhood (founded 1920s), the region's most significant and widespread Islamic organization

autumn 1994: civil disturbances among Shia majority, Iranian instigation alleged

1992: emergence of incipient Islamic political opposition
1996: Hizballah attack on US military complex at Khobar Towers

June 1989: military coup brings National Islamic Front (NIF) to power, launches violent attempt to Islamicize rebel south Sudan

1998: Islamic army of Aden kidnaps foreign tourists
2000: Islamist attack on USS Cole

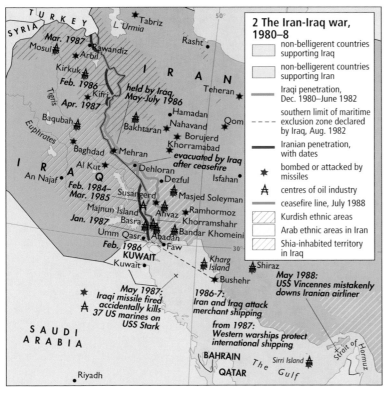

2 The Iran-Iraq war, 1980–8

- non-belligerent countries supporting Iraq
- non-belligerent countries supporting Iran
- Iraqi penetration, Dec. 1980–June 1982
- southern limit of maritime exclusion zone declared by Iraq, Aug. 1982
- Iranian penetration, with dates
- ✳ bombed or attacked by missiles
- ⚓ centres of oil industry
- ceasefire line, July 1988
- Kurdish ethnic areas
- Arab ethnic areas in Iran
- Shia-inhabited territory in Iraq

Mar. 1987
Feb. 1986
Apr. 1987
held by Iraq, May-July 1986
Feb. 1984–Mar. 1985
Jan. 1987
evacuated by Iraq after ceasefire
Feb. 1986

May 1987: Iraqi missile fired accidentally kills 37 US marines on USS Stark

1986-7: Iran and Iraq attack merchant shipping

from 1987: Western warships protect international shipping

May 1988: USS Vincennes mistakenly downs Iranian airliner

Nevertheless, oil remained the most valuable natural asset of the region. Output and revenue both increased dramatically after the OPEC price-rise in 1973, creating some of the highest per capita incomes in the world in the Arab Gulf states. Their prosperity also attracted massive immigration from Egypt, Jordan, Yemen and the Indian sub-continent, creating a potential problem. The rise of Islamic fundamentalism posed another. After 1979 it became a badge of hostility towards the West in Iran and towards Russia in Afghanistan, and elsewhere toward the regime in power – unless, as in Iran, that regime was an Islamic theocracy. In northern Africa, in the 1990s Islamic fundamentalism stimulated terrorist violence, provoking serious conflict in Algeria and Egypt (map 3).

Although the collapse of the Soviet Union (page 168) ended superpower rivalry in the area, the Western powers continued to exert their influence, both to safeguard the oil supplies on which their economies still depended and to protect blatantly persecuted minorities like the Kurds of northern Iraq. Moreover, the enormous concentrations of conventional weapons – and the interest in developing chemical and biological weapons – in so many antagonistic states ensured that the Middle East continued to occupy world attention.

Latin America since 1930

The Great Depression (page 138) struck Latin America a shattering blow, cutting off supplies of foreign capital and lowering the price of its primary products in the world markets. Chile's exports fell by over 80 per cent between 1929 and 1933; those of Bolivia and Peru by 75 per cent. Only oil-exporting Venezuela more or less weathered the storm. The economic collapse led to widespread disillusion with middle-class liberal or radical parties: in 1930 and 1931, 11 of the 20 republics south of the Rio Grande experienced revolutionary changes in government. Mexico, where Lázaro Cárdenas (1934-40) revived the land distribution policies of 1911 (page 112), experienced a shift to the left; but elsewhere the swing was mainly to the right. The new dictators tended to be populists, appealing directly to the masses and cooperating with organised labour. They also introduced programmes of industrialization – following Soviet or, more often, Fascist models – to reduce dependence on overseas markets and hasten economic development.

Manufacturing industry received a further boost during World War II, which cut off imported consumer goods and stimulated the industrial sector. But industrialization made Latin America dependent upon imported capital goods, raw materials, technology and finance – especially from the United States – creating enormous foreign debts (map 2). Multinational corporations exploited the cheap labour of Latin America without stimulating economic development. Social tensions arose from income concentration, unemployment, lack of opportunities, and from the intrusion of foreign interests. Social revolutions were attempted but frustrated in Guatemala, Bolivia and Chile (map 1), underlining the obstacles to change in economies too narrowly based to sustain welfare programmes, where local elites were prepared to collaborate with the United States.

Cuba after 1959 attempted to achieve social change, economic growth and freedom from the United States simultaneously; but although its revolution led to greater social equality and some improvement in the lot of rural workers, it also brought a repressive regime and dependence on the Soviet Union. Moreover its attempts to spread revolution in Central and South America all failed.

In the face of revolutionary change, with some support from the upper and middle classes, the military seized power in many areas and combined political repression with economic liberalization. But by the late 1980s their policies too had largely failed and, in

A government soldier in Peru (below), guards against attacks by the Shining Path guerrillas. The Shining Path (Sendero Luminoso) was founded in 1980 by Abimael Guzmán, a philosophy professor. It adopted a mixture of Maoist political and military tactics and gained control of large areas of the central Andean highlands in the early 1990s. After Guzmán's capture in 1992, the movement fragmented and the level of its attacks diminished sharply.

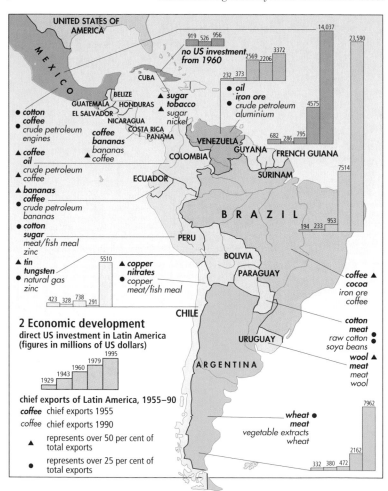

2 Economic development
**direct US investment in Latin America
(figures in millions of US dollars)**

chief exports of Latin America, 1955-90
coffee chief exports 1955
coffee chief exports 1990

▲ represents over 50 per cent of total exports

● represents over 25 per cent of total exports

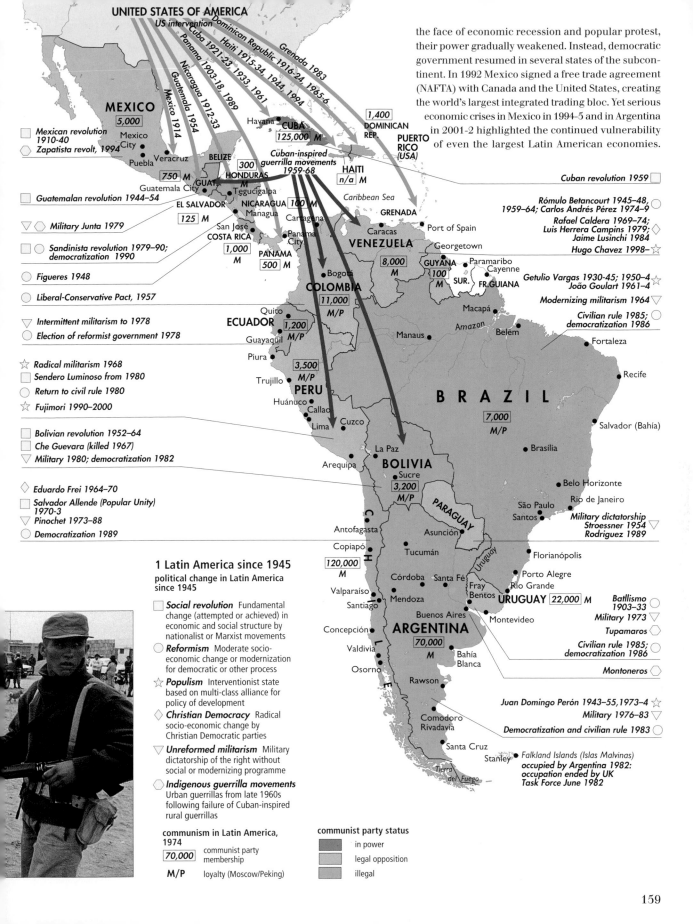

the face of economic recession and popular protest, their power gradually weakened. Instead, democratic government resumed in several states of the subcontinent. In 1992 Mexico signed a free trade agreement (NAFTA) with Canada and the United States, creating the world's largest integrated trading bloc. Yet serious economic crises in Mexico in 1994-5 and in Argentina in 2001-2 highlighted the continued vulnerability of even the largest Latin American economies.

UNITED STATES OF AMERICA
US intervention
Dominican Republic
Cuba 1921-23
Haiti 1915-34, 1944, 1994
Grenada 1983
Panama 1903-18, 1989
Nicaragua 1912-33
Mexico 1914
Guatemala 1954

MEXICO
5,000
Mexico City
Puebla
Veracruz

□ Mexican revolution 1910-40
◇ Zapatista revolt, 1994

Havana
CUBA
125,000 M

1,400
DOMINICAN REP.
PUERTO RICO (USA)

BELIZE
HONDURAS
300 M
Guatemala City
GUAT.
750 M
Tegucigalpa
EL SALVADOR
125 M
NICARAGUA 100 M
San José
Managua

Cuban-inspired guerrilla movements 1959-68

HAITI
n/a M

Caribbean Sea

□ Guatemalan revolution 1944-54

▽◇ Military Junta 1979

□◯ Sandinista revolution 1979-90; democratization 1990

◯ Figueres 1948

◯ Liberal-Conservative Pact, 1957

COSTA RICA
1,000 M
PANAMA
500 M
Panama City

Cartagena

GRENADA
Port of Spain

Caracas
VENEZUELA
8,000 M

Georgetown
GUYANA
100 M
SUR.
Paramaribo
Cayenne
FR.GUIANA

□ Cuban revolution 1959

◯ Rómulo Betancourt 1945-48, 1959-64; Carlos Andrés Pérez 1974-9

◇ Rafael Caldera 1969-74; Luis Herrera Campins 1979; Jaime Lusinchi 1984

☆ Hugo Chavez 1998–

Bogotá
COLOMBIA
11,000 M/P

Macapá
Amazon
Belém
Manaus

☆ Getulio Vargas 1930-45; 1950-4; João Goulart 1961-4

▽ Modernizing militarism 1964

◯ Civilian rule 1985; democratization 1986

Quito
ECUADOR
1,200 M/P
Guayaquil
Piura

Fortaleza

Recife

▽ Intermittent militarism to 1978
◯ Election of reformist government 1978

3,500 M/P
Trujillo
PERU
Huánuco
Callao
Lima
Cuzco

B R A Z I L
7,000 M/P

Salvador (Bahía)

☆ Radical militarism 1968
□ Sendero Luminoso from 1980
◯ Return to civil rule 1980
☆ Fujimori 1990-2000

La Paz
BOLIVIA
Sucre
3,200 M/P
Arequipa

Brasília

Belo Horizonte
Rio de Janeiro
São Paulo
Santos

□ Bolivian revolution 1952-64
□ Che Guevara (killed 1967)
▽ Military 1980; democratization 1982

PARAGUAY
Asunción

▽ Military dictatorship Stroessner 1954 Rodriguez 1989

◇ Eduardo Frei 1964-70
□ Salvador Allende (Popular Unity) 1970-3
▽ Pinochet 1973-88
◯ Democratization 1989

Antofagasta
Copiapó
120,000 M
Tucumán
Córdoba
Santa Fé
Valparaíso
Santiago
Mendoza
Concepción
Valdivia
Osorno

Florianópolis
Porto Alegre
Rio Grande
Fray Bentos
URUGUAY 22,000 M
Montevideo

◯ Batllismo 1903-33
▽ Military 1973
◇ Tupamaros
◯ Civilian rule 1985; democratization 1986
◇ Montoneros

ARGENTINA
70,000 M
Buenos Aires
Bahía Blanca
Rawson

☆ Juan Domingo Perón 1943-55, 1973-4
▽ Military 1976-83
◯ Democratization and civilian rule 1983

Comodoro Rivadavia
Santa Cruz
Stanley
Tierra del Fuego

● Falkland Islands (Islas Malvinas) occupied by Argentina 1982: occupation ended by UK Task Force June 1982

1 Latin America since 1945

political change in Latin America since 1945

□ **Social revolution** Fundamental change (attempted or achieved) in economic and social structure by nationalist or Marxist movements

◯ **Reformism** Moderate socio-economic change or modernization for democratic or other process

☆ **Populism** Interventionist state based on multi-class alliance for policy of development

◇ **Christian Democracy** Radical socio-economic change by Christian Democratic parties

▽ **Unreformed militarism** Military dictatorship of the right without social or modernizing programme

◇ **Indigenous guerrilla movements** Urban guerrillas from late 1960s following failure of Cuban-inspired rural guerrillas

communism in Latin America, 1974

70,000 communist party membership

M/P loyalty (Moscow/Peking)

communist party status
- in power
- legal opposition
- illegal

159

Africa since 1945

After World War II, although some French and British liberals sympathetic to African claims for advancement initiated programmes of social improvement and political reform, the need to exploit every asset in order to assist metropolitan recovery led to attempts to reassert colonial control. Nevertheless in the 1950s both Britain and France began to transfer responsibility to elected governments in their West African colonies.

In Muslim North Africa, longer-established nationalist movements received great stimulus from the overthrow of the Egyptian monarchy in 1952 and the rise to power of Gamal Abdel Nasser. In 1956 an Anglo-French-Israeli invasion failed to topple him. Meanwhile France granted independence to Tunisia and Morocco but tried to incorporate Algeria, the colony with the largest white population, into metropolitan France. This sparked a civil war that lasted until France reluctantly granted independence in 1962.

Elsewhere, white settlers strove to maintain their ascendancy. In South Africa, a Nationalist government dedicated to policies of racial separation ('apartheid') came to power; in Kenya, British troops arrived to suppress the Mau-Mau insurrection directed against the settlers; in Central Africa, a federation of Nyasaland and Rhodesia aimed to preserve white dominance. But in 1963 Kenya achieved independence and the Federation collapsed. Southern Rhodesia's white settlers created their own independent state in 1965, but had to accept black majority rule in 1980. Portugal retained its colonies longest, but in all of them guerrilla warfare eventually led to ignominious withdrawal in 1974-5.

Most of the newly independent African states possessed borders drawn by European governments in the 19th century with insufficient attention to ethnic rivalries. Soon after independence, those rivalries began to tear them apart. In 1960, tribal and regional factions in Zaire (formerly the Belgian Congo) led to demands for a federal constitution and, when these were refused, the army mutinied and the mineral rich province of Katanga seceded. United Nations intervention reunited the country in 1963, but two years later the

Nelson Mandela *(right)* joined the African National Congress in 1944 and helped to found its Youth League. In 1961, frustrated at the failure of civil disobedience to undermine apartheid, he adopted the idea of armed struggle. In 1962 he was sentenced to life imprisonment. Released in 1990, aged 72, he became leader of the ANC and, in 1994, South Africa's first president elected by universal franchise. He retired from the presidency in 1999.

1976 Western Sahara jointly occupied by Morocco and Mauritania; Polisario guerrilla resistance backed by Algeria
1991 cease-fire between Morocco and Polisario
W. SAHARA

1976-79 war with Polisario
1978 military rule
1991 multi-party elections
MAURITAN

1968 civilian government overthrown
1974-85 border conflicts with Burkina

1991 RUF launches civil war
1992 military coup
1996 civilian rule restored under Ahmad Tejan Kabbah
1997 military overthrow Kabbah
1998 Kabbah restored
1999 rebels almost capture Freetown
Nov. 2000 RUF call truce
SENEGAL
GA.
GU.

1989 outbreak of civil war
1993 pan-African peace-keeping force (Ecomog)
intervenes in attempt to halt civil war
GUINEA

1957 first Black African country to gain independence
1966 Nkrumah deposed
1967-85 series of military coups
SIERRA LEONE

1967-70 Nigerian civil war
1981 civilian rule restored
1984, 1985, 1993 military coups
1993 elections declared void; riots;interim government ousted by milit
1999 civilian ruled restored
LIBE

1966 military takeover led by Col. Bokassa, crowned emperor 1976
1980 republic restored
1981 military coup

army seized power and retained it for 34 years. Similarly, in Nigeria the secession of Biafra in 1967 led to a three-year civil war that restored central control, but likewise delivered power to the army. Elsewhere, ethnic violence caused enormous casualties – in the small state of Rwanda, Hutu-Tutsi violence left over 500,000 dead in 1994 – while repeated droughts (compounded by government inefficiency and corruption) caused famine and massive refugee problems in many areas of East Africa. In Algeria, from 1990 Islamic Fundamentalism challenged government control.

By the 1980s, white supremacy survived only in South Africa where the nationalist regime sought to retain its grip by draconian internal repression, by sending troops against guerrillas in neighbouring states, and by granting spurious independence to some black settlement areas set up under apartheid. Eventually, however, economic crisis and international isolation forced concessions. In 1990, the nationalists released Nelson Mandela, imprisoned leader of the banned African National Congress, and within four years the ANC's victory in the first multi-racial elections in South Africa's history swept away white rule. Despite the problems of healing decades of racial tension, the ANC created a more stable political system than under white rule and preserved the most successful economy on the continent. Mandela retired in 2000. Meanwhile in Zimbabwe (formerly Rhodesia) serious racial conflict broke out.

1 Africa: post-independence wars and revolutions

- ✹ civil war
- → invasion
- ✊ guerrilla activity
- ✳ border dispute

MOROCCO
1956 independence

TUNISIA
1956 independence
1984 major rioting
1987 Bourguiba ousted

ALGERIA
1962 independence
1960s border conflicts
with Morocco
1965 Ben Bella deposed
by Col. Boumedienne
1990 election of Islamic
fundamentalist-dominated
chamber of deputies
1991 election results nullified;
anti-government terrorist
campaign by Islamic
Fundamentalists

LIBYA
1969 King Idris deposed; replaced
by military junta under Col. Gadhafi
1986 US bomb Tripoli in retaliation
for terrorist attacks

EGYPT
1952 King Farouk deposed by army
officers led by Neguib
1954-70 Nasser president
1956 Suez crisis
1967, 1973 wars with Israel
1981 Mubarak president on
assassination of Sadat
1991 forces join US-led war against
Iraqi occupation of Kuwait

MALI

NIGER

CHAD
1960 civil war;
FROLINAT guerrillas
supported by Libya
1973, 1981 Libyan invasion
and withdrawal
1984 border war with Libya

SUDAN
1963–72 civil war
1969 General Numeiry takes
power in military coup,
intermittent civil war in
South since independence
1984 severe famine
1985 Numeiry overthrown
(civil war continues)
1989 military coup; National
Islamic Front in effective
control
1994–5 ceasefire between
feuding southern anti-
government forces

ERITREA
1952 federated with Ethiopia
1962 Union
1961-91 armed resistance
to Ethiopian rule in both
Eritrea and Tigre
1991 Eritrean and Tigrean
forces victorious
1993 independence
1998–2000 border war
with Ethiopia

DJIBOUTI

ETHIOPIA
1961- war against Eritrea secessionists
1974 Emperor Haile Selassie
overthrown by army junta
1984-88 severe famine, aid from West
1991 Mengistu's Communist
regime overthrown after civil war

SOMALIA
1964, 1970 border disputes
with Ethiopia and Kenya
1976-78 occupation of Ogaden
and war with Ethiopia
1993 UN military intervention
to halt civil war and famine

BURKINA FASO

BENIN

IVORY COAST

GHANA

TOGO

NIGERIA

CAMEROON

CENTRAL AFRICAN REPUBLIC

E. GABON

CONGO

DEMOCRATIC REPUBLIC

OF CONGO (ZAIRE)

UGANDA

KENYA
1970s border
disputes with
Uganda and Somalia

RWANDA

BURUNDI

TANZANIA

1966 Obote expels Kabaka (King) of Buganda
1970 border dispute with Kenya
1971 Obote overthrown by Amin; Asians expelled;
large-scale repression
1979 invaded by Tanzania, Amin overthrown;
Obote restored (1980), overthrown (Jan 1986)
1986 Yoweri Museveni president

1962 independence
1965 civil war, massacre of Tutsi
(in Rwanda and Burundi)
1994 tribal violence/civil war;
exodus of refugees to Rwandan
borders. Mass killings of Tutsi
civilians; large scale UN
humanitarian assistance

1960-69 civil war
1978 invasion of Shaba province by anti-Mobutu
dissidents, repelled with French assistance
1997 Mobuto overthrown by rebel movement led by
Laurent Kabila
1997–2000 continued civil war
2001 Kabila assassinated

1962 independence followed by
civil war/tribal violence, massive
refugee movement to
neighbouring countries

ANGOLA

ZAMBIA

MALAWI

MOZAMBIQUE

1975- Marxist MPLA government in conflict
with UNITA guerrillas aided by South Africa
1991 peace agreement between MPLA and
UNITA breaks down after elections:
civil war renewed
1992 renewed fighting
1994 agreement between UNITA and
government
1998–9 fighting between UNITA and
government restarts

support for black nationalists
in Angola, Namibia and Rhodesia
1991 Kaunda defeated in democratic
election

South African presence resisted by
SWAPO to 1990
1991 fully independent from South Africa

NAMIBIA

ZIMBABWE

BOTSWANA

MADAGASCAR
1972 military
takeover

1948 implementation of apartheid
1975 invasion of Angola
1976 mounting black urban unrest
1976-81 African homelands (Bantustans) established
in Transkei, Bophuthatswana and Ciskei
1984 new constitution, limited representation
for Indians and coloureds
1985–87 growing African resistance and civil unrest
1986 commando raids on neighbouring countries
1990 Mandela released President de Klerk starts
to dismantle apartheid
1993 multiracial council paves way to free elections
1994 election victory for ANC; Mandela president
1996 National party leaves governing coalition
1999 Mandela steps down as president

SWAZILAND

LESOTHO

REPUBLIC OF SOUTH AFRICA

1975-1993 civil war between Frelimo
government and Renamo guerrillas
1980- South African intervention
in support of Renamo
1994 multi-party elections following
Renamo-Frelimo peace accord

1965-80 independent as Rhodesia under
white-minority rule 1980 black majority rule
established; increasing steps towards
one-party state
2000 resettlement of "war veterans" on
white owned land causes serious unrest

South and South East Asia since 1945

The history of southern Asia since independence has been dominated by three factors. First, the seizure of power by military leaders (Pakistan 1958, Indonesia 1967), with the aim – rarely successful – of abolishing corruption and stabilizing the economy; second, the resurgence of long-standing regional, tribal and religious conflicts (Naga and Sikh unrest in India; nationalist uprisings among the Mons, Shans and other 'hill people' in Thailand and Burma); finally, intervention by the Great Powers (Russia in Afghanistan; China and the United States in Vietnam).

Wars between states also characterized certain areas. The partition of the Indian subcontinent in 1947 left numerous points of friction between the new states of India and Pakistan, particularly Punjab, Kashmir and Bengal, and these erupted into war in 1965 and again in 1971 (in connection with the secession of East Pakistan to form the separate state of Bangladesh). The potential for war became more serious after both countries developed nuclear arms in 1998, and serious clashes over Kashmir in 2002 carried the threat of nuclear confrontation. Indian forces also expelled the Portuguese from their coastal enclaves (1961), fought China over a frontier dispute (1962), and intervened in Sri Lanka to protect the Hindu Tamil minority (1986-90). Civil wars, however, proved far more common (map 1). Malaya suffered a communist insurrection (1948-60), led by ethnic Chinese; the Philippines experienced rebellions by both communists and Muslims from the 1960s; Cambodia was devastated by the civil war between the communist Khmer Rouge and its non-communist opponents.

The most savage conflict, however, occurred in Vietnam (map 2). After the Japanese collapse in 1945 Ho Chi Minh established a communist regime in Hanoi while the French recreated their colonial empire in the south. In 1946 armed conflict began, continuing until a humiliating defeat at Dien Bien Phu in 1954 forced the French to withdraw. Although this left Cambodia and Laos as independent states, it did not create a unified Vietnam: at the Geneva Peace Conference in 1954 Ho accepted a 'temporary' partition of the country at the 17th parallel until nationwide elections, mandated for 1956, took place. However an anti-communist regime in the south, backed by America, refused to hold elections. In 1959 Ho therefore attacked, and the US immediately provided munitions and advisers to the south, with regular troops and air strikes after 1965. Despite saturation bombing and the commitment of 500,000 US ground troops, the communists (supported by both Russia and China) held their own and in 1968 negotiations began between Hanoi and Washington. In 1973 American forces withdrew, although the US continued to supply the south on a massive scale. When the communists launched an orthodox military offensive in 1975, however, the south's army collapsed. Vietnam was now unified, under Hanoi, although its economy was ruined and its invasion of Cambodia in 1978 led to ostracism by the West.

Elsewhere in Asia, however, rapid development occurred. Following the path of Japan (page 152), Taiwan, Malaysia, Singapore, Thailand and eventually Indonesia achieved rapid rates of growth from the late 1960s. Even during the world recession of the 1980s, each experienced an annual growth rate of well over 5 per cent

Indira Gandhi daughter of India's first premier, Nehru, was the country's prime minister from 1972 to 1977 and from 1980 to 1985. She ruled over an India torn by ethnic and religious conflict. Between 1975 and 1977 she imposed a state of emergency following her conviction for electoral malpractice. In 1985 she was assassinated by one of her Sikh bodyguards.

3 Indo-China 1966–8

areas of control, early 1966:

- controlled by the Vietcong
- under Vietcong influence
- controlled by the Government
- under Government influence
- heavily contested area
- 'Tet' offensive, 1968

Vinh
Dong Hoi
NORTH VIETNAM
Vinh Linh
LAOS
Hue
Phu Bai
Da Nang
Ho Chi Minh trail
Chu Lai
Qui Nhon
SOUTH VIETNAM
CAMBODIA
Saigon
7th US fleet 1964
Mekong
South China Sea

1955 supports Baluchistani separatists in Pakistan
Dec. 1979 invaded by USSR; continued resistance by Islamic guerrillas
1988 USSR withdraws
1992 post Soviet-backed regime defeated by Islamic guerrillas
1997 regime overthrown by radical Islamic Taleban movement
2001: Taleban regime collapses after US-led campaign against it

AFGHANISTAN

1948 Democratic People's Republic of Korea proclaimed
1950 invasion of South Korea
1994 death of Kim Il Sung. His son, Kim Jong Il succeeds

NORTH KOREA

SOUTH KOREA

1948 Republic of Korea proclaimed
1950–3 Korean War
1961 military coup followed by dictatorship of Park Chung Hee (assassinated 1979);
mounting opposition from 1974
1979 martial law (relaxed 1981)

1951 peace treaty with USA and end of occupation
1956 agreement with USSR, ending state of war;
1960 widespread demonstrations against US military bases in Japan and Okinawa
1972 normalization of relations with China
1990 agreements with USSR formally ending 1945 war

JAPAN

Okinawa occupied by US after 1945, reverted to Japan 1972

1971 secession from Pakistan; civil war followed in 1975 by murder of Sheikh Mujib and military control

CHINA

TIBET

NEPAL

PAKISTAN

INDIA

spasmodic unrest among Nagas, Sikhs and Tamils
1961 India occupies Portuguese enclaves
1962 Sino-Indian border war
1975–7 state of emergency proclaimed
1984 Sikh separatist uprising suppressed; Indira Gandhi assassinated
1991 Rajiv Gandhi assassinated
1998 nuclear tests conducted
2002 serious confrontation with Pakistan over Kashmir

BANGLADESH

BURMA

guerrilla activity since independence (1948)
1958, 1962 military coups
1974 Socialist People's Republic inaugurated
May 1990 pro-democracy protests lend to free elections; military refuse to recognise result
1990– opposition leader Aung San Suu Kyi and her pro-democracy movement suppressed by military

VIETNAM
LAOS
THAILAND
CAMBODIA

seat of Chinese Nationalist government since 1949
1958 territorial dispute with China over Quemoy and Matsu
1996 China attempts military intimidations as Taiwan holds first free elections

TAIWAN

1954 French withdrawal; civil war
1956–73 US backed South Vietnam and the communist-backed North engaged in escalating conflict
1973 US withdraws all forces
1976 North and South Vietnam reunified under Viet-Minh rule
1978 invasion of Cambodia and border clashes with China
1979 Chinese invasion

1953–73 civil war
1975 monarchy abolished; Pathet Lao seizes power

Communist and Muslim insurgency since 1968, eruption into civil war 1972–8
1986 Marcos regime ousted following general election. Aquino president
1992 Ramos succeeds as president
2001 President Estrada forced to step down by popular protests

PHILIPPINES

1947 military takeover, guerrilla activity since 1960
1976 border clashes with Cambodia
1978 Cambodian refugee camps in E. Thailand become bases for anti-Vietnamese factions
1987 border clashes with Laos

Mindanao

1958 military coup by Ayub Khan
1965 border clashes with India in Rann of Kutch
1965 war with India over Kashmir
1971 war with India over Bangladesh
1972 ceasefire lines established
1977 military coup by Zia ul-Haq
1988 democratic elections;. Benazir Bhutto prime minister (deposed 1990)
1993 Benazir Bhutto returns as prime minister (deposed 1996)
1998 nuclear tests conducted
1999 military under General Musharraf overthrows government of Nawaz Sharif

SRI LANKA

1958, 1961 fighting between Sinhalese and Tamils
1971 government assumes emergency powers after rural guerrilla uprisings; 1983 intercommunal rioting
1986–90 Indian intervention to crush Tamil rebellions
May 1993 President Ranasinghe killed in rebel Tamil attack

MALAYSIA

1970 monarchy abolished
1970–4 civil war; victory of Khmer Rouge who massacre millions of civilians
1978 Vietnamese invasion overthrows Khmer Rouge
1989 Vietnamese forces withdraw
1991 peace agreement leads to May 1993 elections, boycotted by Khmer Rouge which carries on civil war

Aceh

INDONESIA

1967 Sukarno ousted by military coup; suppression of Communists
1976- resistance to Indonesian rule in E. Timor
1977–99 secessionist rising in Irian Jaya
1989– GAM independence movement in Aceh fights guerilla campaign against government
1998 President Suharto steps down in face of rising protests
1999–2001 intercommunal violence in the Moluccas
1999 UN peace-keeping force enters East Timor after violence following vote in referendum for independence from Indonesia

Irian Jaya

East Timor

1948–60 'The Emergency'- civil war with communist guerrillas
1969 rising by Chinese minority groups
1975–8 Communist guerrilla activity
1978- renewed racial and religious conflict

1 Post-independence wars and revolutions

★ civil war　　→ invasion　　✊ guerrilla activity　　✳ border dispute

(table 3). Various factors were responsible: all except Singapore possessed large pools of cheap labour; all created a substantial industrial base oriented towards export markets throughout Asia, Europe and North America; all the governments sought to attract substantial foreign investment through tax incentives and infrastructural development. A major part of that investment came from Japan. Finally, political stability – Lee in Singapore; Mahathir in Malaysia; Suharto in Indonesia – underpinned the economic strategy of industrial development and helped to attract foreign investment.

All these economies suffered in the economic turmoil which hit east Asia in 1997, when a currency crisis was transformed into a general crisis of confidence in the Asian economic model. The Thai economy was seriously affected, while Indonesia was badly hit by a 75 per cent devaluation of the rupiah, again exacerbated by a major political crisis, as the 35-year old Suharto regime finally collapsed under the weight of nationwide protests. In general the region's economies recovered far faster than expected. Yet Indonesia remained gripped by widespread civil and ethnic unrest (including the withdrawal from East Timor in 1999), which threated to destabilize the whole country and in 2001 Suharto's successor, Abdurrahman Wahid, was in turn replaced as President by Megawati Sukarnoputri.

3 The economies of South East Asia

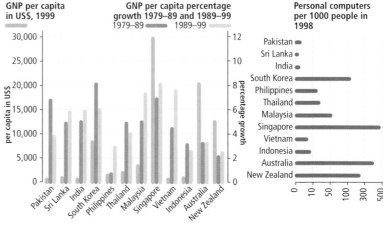

GNP per capita in US$, 1999

GNP per capita percentage growth 1979–89 and 1989–99
1979–89　1989–99

Personal computers per 1000 people in 1998

Pakistan
Sri Lanka
India
South Korea
Philippines
Thailand
Malaysia
Singapore
Vietnam
Indonesia
Australia
New Zealand

The Cold War

The defeat of Germany, Italy and Japan and the weakening of Britain and France in World War II left the USA and USSR as the only 'superpowers'. Their ideological and political confrontation expressed itself as the Cold War. Conflict between the two had already appeared before the final victory: The Western Allies had already agreed (reluctantly) at Yalta (February 1945) to allow Soviet control of eastern Europe after the end of the war. By 1949 Stalin had developed an atomic bomb, thus ending the US monopoly of nuclear weapons. In reply, the USA built up the defence of western Europe with the formation of the North Atlantic Treaty Organization (NATO) in 1949 (page 146). In 1952 the US tested a thermo-nuclear (hydrogen) bomb; Russia followed suit in 1953.

Although it started as a conflict over central Europe, the Cold War soon developed into a global confrontation. The US saw the Korean War (1950-3: page 152) as evidence of a world-wide communist conspiracy, and American policy now became the 'containment' of Communism by a series of encircling alliances. NATO was followed by the South-East Asia Treaty Organization (SEATO) in 1954 and the Baghdad Pact (1955); the US maintained over 1400 foreign bases, including 275 bases for nuclear bombers, in 31 countries around the Soviet perimeter (map 1). As long as nuclear devices could only be delivered by aircraft, possession of these bases conferred an enormous advantage on the US. But when in the early 1960s both sides began to deploy ballistic nuclear missiles

US inspectors at a Soviet nuclear weapons site, 20 kilometres from Saratov *(right)*. Under the terms of the disarmament agreement of 1987 both sides agreed to the decommissioning of a large proportion of their nuclear stockpiles and to a system of inspections.

3 The Cuban missile crisis, 1962

	Soviet missile and jet bomber bases
	US Air Force base
	US naval base

1 The age of bipolarity

JAPAN
US 7th fleet
PHILIPPINES
ALASKA
Okinawa
S. KOREA
KOREA 1950–53
TAIWAN
Quemoy, Matsu 1954–55, 1958
SOUTH VIETNAM 1945–54, 1957–73
LAOS
THAILAND
MALAYSIA
Arctic Ocean
SOVIET UNION
MONGOLIA
CHINA left Soviet bloc, 1960
GREENLAND
ICELAND
NORWAY
W. GERMANY
HOLLAND
BELGIUM
DENMARK
E. GERMANY
UNITED KINGDOM
POLAND
CZECH.
HUNGARY
ROMANIA
BULGARIA
YUGO. 1948–53
ALBANIA
ITALY
GREECE 1946–9
FRANCE
SPAIN
PORTUGAL
TURKEY 1945–7
IRAN
1958 IRAQ
AFGHANISTAN
PAKISTAN
INDIA
EAST PAKISTAN
Indian Ocean
LEBANON 1958
SAUDI ARABIA
US 6th fleet
Suez, 1956
LIBYA
EGYPT

Legend:
- USA and allies, 1958
- USSR and allies, 1958
- Soviet ICBM bases (7000 mile range)
- other Soviet missile sites, 1961
- principal Soviet military airfields
- US ICBM bases (5000 mile range)
- US heavy bomber bases (capable of reaching USSR with airborne refuelling)
- US nuclear and other major bases (Oct. 1962)
- strategic US fleets
- points of conflict in the Cold War
- uprisings in the Communist world

Czechoslovakia
- 1948
- 1968

East Germany
- Berlin 1948–9, 1958–62
- Berlin 1953

Estonia (E)
- 1944–55

Hungary
- 1956

Poland
- 1945–8, 1956

Lithuania (L)
- 1945–7

Ukraine (U)
- 1945–50

2 The nuclear balance, 1955–80

USSR intercontinental
- bombers
- land missiles
- sea missiles
- warheads
8,000 6,000 4,000 2,000 0
1955 1960 1965 1970 1975 1980

USA intercontinental
- bombers
- land missiles
- sea missiles
- warheads
8,000 6,000 4,000 2,000 0
1955 1960 1965 1970 1975 1980

USSR regional
- bombers
- missiles
- warheads
3,000 2,000 1,000 0
1955 1960 1965 1970 1975 1980

USA regional
- bombers
- missiles
1955 1960 1965 1970 1975 1980

capable of being launched from land silos and submarines, the odds altered: now, in the event of war, each of the two superpowers could attack the other's cities directly (chart 2).

In October 1962, this scenario was almost put to the test when, following an unsuccessful US attempt to unseat the communist regime, the USSR established nuclear missile sites in Cuba. President Kennedy proclaimed a 'quarantine' of the island and threatened that, if the missiles were fired, the US would immediately retaliate against the USSR. The Russians then agreed to their removal (map 3). In return, Kennedy agreed to remove some of the US missile sites from Turkey.

This crisis, with its real threat of nuclear holocaust, proved a turning point in the Cold War. Already both monolithic blocs had begun to show signs of strain, most seriously on the Soviet side: Hungary and Poland rebelled in 1956, and from 1960 China began to quarrel openly over territory and ideology. In western Europe, France rejected American political leadership after 1958 and left NATO. A desire to limit the spread of nuclear weapons led to the conclusion of a partial test-ban treaty in 1963 and a nuclear non-proliferation treaty in 1968, but not all nuclear or potential nuclear powers signed these agreements (notably France, China and India) while others (such as Iraq) later reneged on their commitment. The Cold War therefore continued and the superpowers created huge nuclear arsenals.

In the event, the economic and political difficulties of the USSR increased to the point where the Soviet leader Mikhail Gorbachev (1985-91) felt that only a dramatic reduction in the crushing burden of military expenditure could bring relief (page 168). First the Soviets withdrew their forces from eastern Europe (1989), then NATO and the Warsaw Pact declared that the other was no longer an enemy (1990), and finally the USSR itself began to disintegrate (1991). Further agreements on the reduction of nuclear and conventional forces soon followed, although the fate of the vast arsenal accumulated by the former USSR gave cause for concern.

Europe since 1973

In 1973 the oil-producing states almost trebled the price of oil in a year, triggering worldwide price inflation. In Europe, the crisis coincided with a general slowdown in productivity and profit growth and mounting unemployment, producing widespread labour unrest. Behind the Iron Curtain, rising oil prices caused economic performance to stagnate or decline.

In western Europe, the crisis encouraged the trend to greater economic integration. By the late 1960s, the original six members of the EEC (European Economic Community) had established themselves as the economic vanguard of the continent. In 1973 Britain, Ireland and Denmark joined, followed in 1981 by Greece, in 1986 by Spain and Portugal, and in 1995 by Austria, Finland and Sweden. In 1985, the EEC agreed to create a single market under which it would became a free-trade zone. The Maastricht Treaty of 1991 then committed members (renamed the EU, European Union, in 1995) to introduce a single currency, the Euro, by 1999 (map 1).

The combined effects of the economic slowdown after 1973 and the realization that clinging to their pre-war authoritarian governments would push them to the margins of Europe helped reintroduce democracy to Portugal (1974) and Spain (1975). Greece also embraced democracy in 1974. But these changes paled in comparison with events in eastern Europe in the late 1980s, where the disintegration of the Soviet Union and the fall of communism in every one of its satellite states produced in its wake no less than 15 new countries (page 168). The nationalist tensions released also led to civil wars in the former Yugoslavia.

Nationalist tensions also continued in western Europe. Many areas achieved a measure of devolution, often on linguistic grounds (as in Belgium) while terrorism sustained Basque separatism in Spain and Irish nationalism in Ulster. Tentative political agreements were reached in both areas in 1998, though tensions survived (map 2). Although much of Europe became freer and more prosperous by the late 1990s, political stability and economic progress could not be guaranteed across the continent.

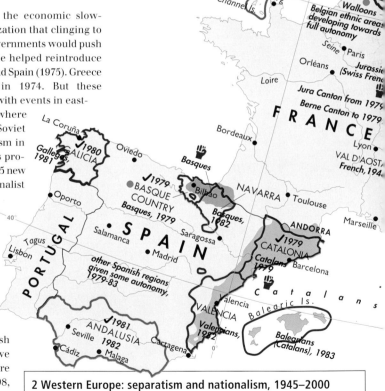

2 Western Europe: separatism and nationalism, 1945–2000

— territorial autonomy based on ethnic group, with date of autonomy

— separate administration/ autonomy for other reasons

✗ devolution rejected by referendum, with date

✓ devolution approved by referendum, with date

✊ linguistic minorities or other communities whose members have used violence in pursuit of greater autonomy or other change of political status, with areas inhabited

● ethnic or other communal based party delegated to national parliament in 1985

The success of the EU in modernizing and rationalizing European agriculture produced regular food gluts in he 1970s and 1980s. Here *(right)* Sicilian oranges have been turned, quite literally, into a food mountain. The sheer cost of maintaining farm incomes put a great strain on the European Union's budget, raising periodic calls for reform of the Common Agricultural Policy, especially urgent from the late 1990s, with the prospect of further enlargement to the east.

1 The expansion of the European Union, 1981–2000

- members of the EEC, Jan. 1981
- joined Jan. 1986
- admitted Oct. 1990
- joined Jan. 1995
- applied by June 1996 for EU membership, with date of application
- ★ countries beginning accession negotiations, 1998
- ★ countries beginning accession negotiations, 2000

The European Economic Area (EEA)
- members of the EEA, June 1996

Turkish Federated State of Cyprus, estb. 1975; "Turkish Rep. of Northern Cyprus" from 1983

ethnic distribution before 1974 — Turks — Greeks

167

The collapse of Communism since 1989

The tidal wave that swept away the communist regimes of Eastern Europe arose directly from the changes envisaged Mikhail Gorbachev, leader of the USSR (page 148). Regarding the other communist states as a drain on Soviet resources, he encouraged them to pursue economic and political reform. This policy change came at a difficult time for the Eastern bloc states, whose economic development had been adversely affected by recession in the West and by reductions in trade and aid resulting from renewed Cold War pressures. Economic modernization slowed, and provoked growing popular unrest, particularly in Poland, where a military dictatorship arose in 1981 to suppress the democracy movement. In Romania, the isolated and impoverished regime of Nicolae Ceauçescu became yet more repressive.

Although few showed enthusiasm for the old regimes, popular opposition remained muted until Gorbachev pressured his communist partners to grasp the nettle of reform in 1989. Without Soviet backing, the regimes crumbled one by one: Hungary legalized opposition parties in January; Poland established the first non-communist government since 1948 in August; demonstrations ended communist rule in Czechoslovakia, East Germany and Bulgaria in November. Violence only occurred in Romania, where an army firing squad shot Ceauçescu in December.

Throughout the Eastern bloc, multi-party elections now brought to power coalition governments committed to democratic reform and economic liberalization. In the course of 1990, East Germany voted first for currency union and then for full integration with West Germany; but other former communist countries, exposed to market pressures, soon plunged into economic decline. High unemployment and rural poverty contributed to the revival of deep-rooted ethnic and religious conflicts, conflicts that the communist regimes had only papered over for 40 years. In 1993, tensions between Czechs and Slovaks produced the partition of Czechoslovakia (map 1).

Meanwhile, in the USSR, nationalist unrest grew as the Russian-dominated republics of the USSR sensed an opportunity to emulate the Eastern European states and break free. The president of the Russian Republic, Boris Yeltsin, elected in 1990, urged Gorbachev to give the Soviet republics more independence. In August 1991, a group of hard-line communists attempted a coup and, although Yeltsin suppressed the revolt, the non-Russian republics soon declared their independence. When the Ukraine staged a referendum in December 1991 that resulted in an overwhelming vote for independence, Gorbachev bowed to reality. The USSR was dissolved on 31 December, to be replaced by a Commonwealth of Independent States (the CIS), co-operating on military and economic

issues but no longer controlled from Moscow.

With no country left to rule, Gorbachev slipped into obscurity. Russia embraced a form of presidential democracy, with Yeltsin as its first president. In 1993, hard-line parliamentary delegates hostile to further reform tried to depose Yeltsin, but he crushed them too. Re-elected as president in 1996, Yeltsin finally stepped down in 1999 and power transferred peacefully to Vladimir Putin. Meanwhile some republics – Belarus, Uzbekistan, Kazakhstan, Turkmenistan – maintained reformed communist governments while others adopted some form of democracy. In Russia itself local rulers in the constituent republics seized more power (map 2) and in the case of Chechenia sought to break away from Russia by force (page 170).

Sep. 1989: mass exodus of political refugees reach the West via Hungary; Communist leadership in crisis
Oct.–Nov. 1989: widespread demonstrations against leadership
9 Nov. 1989: Berlin Wall breached
Mar. 1990: free elections
July 1990: currency union with West Germany
Oct. 1990: reunified with West Germany

from 1985: Solidarity leads opposition to communism
June 1989: partially free elections
Aug. 1989: Solidarity-led government takes office
Jan. 1990: Communist Party dissolved
Oct. 1991: free elections

Dec. 1989: economic war between Belgrade government and Slovenia
Apr. 1990: free elections
June 1991: independence declared; Yugoslav army attempts to regain control of Slovenia
July 1991: Brioni Agreement ends fighting in Slovenia; Yugoslav army withdraws

Apr.–May 1990: free elections
Dec. 1990: Serb-inhabited areas declare independence
June 1991: independence declared; fighting in Slovenia spreads to Croatia as Serbs attempt to extend territory in Croatia and Bosnia

1987: mass strikes against wage freeze and falling living standards; growing Serb militancy against minorities
July 1990: provincial autonomies abolished
1990–1: increasing tension between Belgrade government and Slovenia and Croatia

Jan.–May 1990: democratic reforms initiated by leadership
Mar. 1991: free elections

2 The Russian Federation, 1991–8

— the Russian Federation

constituent republics within the Russian Federation, Mar. 1992

independence declared, Nov. 1991; at war with Russia from Dec. 1994 to 1996 and from Aug. 1999

The Commonwealth of Independent States (CIS)

entered close political and economic union with Russia, 2 Apr. 1996

entered close economic union with Russia, 30 Mar. 1996

other members of the CIS

60% percentage of Russians in other members of the Russian Federation

AD autonomous district

AO autonomous oblast

Map 2 labels

Arctic Ocean

FINLAND
Murmansk
POLAND
BELARUS
MOLDOVA
UKRAINE
Rostov-na-Donu
ADYGEYA 68%
GEORGIA
ARM.
AZER.
Caspian Sea
IRAN
TURKMENISTAN
UZBEKISTAN
KYRGYZSTAN
TAJIKISTAN
AFGHANISTAN
KAZAKHSTAN
St Petersburg
Moscow
CHUVASHIA 27%
MARIYEL 47%
MORDOVIA 61%
Volgograd
KALMYKIA 38%
DAGESTAN 9%
KARELIA 74%
NENETS
KOMI 58%
MORDOVIA
TATARSTAN 43%
UDMURTIA 59%
Yekaterinburg
BASHKORTOSTAN
Omsk
Novosibirsk
ALTAY 60%
KHAKASSIA
TYVA 32%
UST-ORDA BURYAT AD
BURYATIA 70%
Irkutsk
AGA BURYAT AD
Chita
KOMI-PERMYAK AD
KHANTY-MANSI AD
YAMALO-NENETS AD
TAYMYR AD
EVENKI AD
SAKHA (YAKUTIYA) 50%
FEDERATION
RUSSIAN
CHUKCHI AD
KORYAK AD
Sea of Okhotsk
JEWISH AO
Khabarovsk
Vladivostok
MONGOLIA
CHINA
ALTAY 79%

a KARACHAY-CHERKESSIA 42%
b KABARDINO-BALKARIA 39%
c NORTH-OSSETIA 30%
d INGUSHETIA (from June 1992)
e CHECHENIA
} 23% combined

Map 1 captions

Mar. 1990: Congress of Estonia formed, declares Soviet rule illegal
Mar. 1991: referendum endorses independence
Aug. 1991: independence declared
Sep. 1991: independence recognized by USSR

1989: mass anti-Communist demonstrations
Mar. 1991: referendum endorses independence
Aug. 1991: independence declared
Sep. 1991: independence recognized by USSR

1989: mass anti-Communist demonstrations
Mar. 1991: independence declared
Apr.–June 1990: economic embargo imposed by USSR
Sep. 1991: independence recognized by USSR

June 1989: Popular Front founded
Aug. 1991: independence declared
Dec. 1991: founder member of Commonwealth of Independent States

from 1988: anti-government demonstrations
Nov. 1989: mass demonstrations end Communist rule
Apr. 1990: new constitution adopted; becomes a federation
June 1990: free elections

from 1987: Communist regime relaxes control
Sep. 1989: allows East Germans to travel to the West
Oct. 1990: Communist rule ends peacefully
Mar.–Apr. 1990: free elections

Mar. 1985: Mikhail Gorbachev becomes leader of Communist Party; initiates perestroika and glasnost, loosens Soviet control of satellite states
June 1991: Boris Yeltsin elected president of Russian Federation
Aug. 1991: hard-line Communist coup against Gorbachev fails
Nov. 1991: Communist Party declared illegal
Dec. 1991: USSR dissolved

1989: opposition mass-movements emerge
Aug. 1991: independence declared
Dec. 1991: referendum endorses independence; founder member of Commonwealth of Independent States

June 1989: Popular Front wins 75% of votes in election
Aug. 1991: independence declared

Jan. 1990: state of emergency declared; Soviet troops intervene
Oct. 1991: independence declared

Nov. 1991: independence declared

Dec. 1989: mass demonstrations lead to armed uprisings and overthrow of Ceauşescu regime
June 1991: free elections
Nov. 1991: new constitution adopted

Nov. 1988: mass demonstrations against Russification
Mar. 1991: referendum endorses independence
Apr. 1991: independence declared

Sep. 1991: independence declared

Nov. 1989: President Zhivkov removed from office
June 1990: free elections
July 1991: fresh elections following adoption of new constitution

Sep. 1989: economic embargo imposed by Azerbaijan
Sep. 1991: referendum endorses independence; independence declared

Map 1 place labels

FINLAND
Baltic Sea
Tallinn
ESTONIA
Riga
LATVIA
LITHUANIA
Vilnius
RUSSIAN FED.
Minsk
BELARUS
Varsava
Kiev
UKRAINE
TRANSNISTRIA
MOLDOVA
GAGAUZIA
ROMANIA
Bucharest
BULGARIA
Sofia
Moscow
RUSSIAN FEDERATION
TATARSTAN
CHECHENIA
Grozny
GEORGIA
ARMENIA
AZERBAIJAN
NAGORNO-KARABAKH

The Polish union leader, Lech Walesa (*above*) addressing a crowd. As leader of the free trade union Solidarity, he led the resistance to communism from 1980 and became Polish president in 1990. He lost office to a former communist minister in elections in 1995.

1 The collapse of communism, 1985–91

— Soviet-dominated eastern Europe to 1989

— Soviet Union to 1991

— Yugoslavia to 1991

united with the Federal Republic of Germany, 1990

achieved independence, 1991

other former communist states, 1991

de facto independent states, late 1991, on former territory of the Soviet Union, internationally unrecognized

overrun by Yugoslav army, July–Dec. 1991

— borders, 1991

169

Civil wars in the communist successor states

The greatest casualty of the collapse of the communist bloc was Yugoslavia. Its six republics (Serbia, Croatia, Macedonia, Bosnia-Herzegovina, Slovenia and Montenegro), were held together by an overarching communist apparatus and the personal authority of Tito, the founder of communist Yugoslavia. After his death in 1980, internal divisions began to appear. The trigger for conflict was the rise of aggressive nationalism. In 1987, following the choice of the Slobodan Milosevic as leader of Serbia, tensions between the republics grew stronger. Milosevic suppressed the Albanian minority in Kosovo, and set out to expand Serbia's influence within the federation.

In 1990 multi-party elections brought nationalists to the fore in Slovenia and Croatia and paved the way for their simultaneous declaration of independence in June 1991. It also provoked a vicious seven-month war when Serb forces intervened, allegedly to protect the ethnic Serb minority in Croatia. Meanwhile another savage civil war broke out in Bosnia-Herzegovina, where Bosnian Muslims (44% of the population) and Croats (17%) pushed for independence in the face of bitter opposition from the Bosnian Serbs (31%). Each ethnic group sought to 'cleanse' the areas under its control of all opponents until by 1993 the Serbs controlled around 70 per cent of Bosnia and besieged the capital, Sarajevo, held by the Muslim-led government. At

1 The Yugoslav civil war, 1991–5

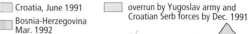

- Croatia, June 1991
- Bosnia-Herzegovina Mar. 1992
- secured by Yugoslav army and Bosnian Serb forces by Dec. 1992
- controlled by Bosnian Croat forces, Dec. 1992
- under Bosnian government control , Dec. 1992
- overrun by Yugoslav army and Croatian Serb forces by Dec. 1991
- → Croatian advances, Jan. 1993
- → Federation of Bosnia and Herzegovina advances, Oct.–Nov. 1994
- --→ Croatian and Federation of Bosnia and Herzegovina advances, spring 1995
- → Bosnian Serb advances, summer 1995
- → Croatian and Federation of Bosnia and Herzegovina advances, Aug.–Oct. 1995
- ▨ overwhelmingly or largely Muslim, 1991; no significant Muslim presence by 1996
- —— Autonomous Province of Western Bosnia, Sep. 1993–Aug. 1994
- —— remained under Serb control by Dayton Agreement Nov.1995
- ▨ returned to Croatian control in Jan. 1998 under Erdut agreement of Nov. 1995
- ⛰ UN-designated 'safe areas'

least 100,000 died during the war, which displaced half of the region's 4 million inhabitants. In 1995 a renewed Serb offensive provoked NATO intervention, leading to an uneasy peace (the Dayton Accords) which left Bosnia divided between the three ethnic groups and utterly devastated by four years of war (map 1).

3 The Caucasus, 1988–2000

- notional extent of Georgia at independence
- → advance of pro-Gamsakhurdia forces, Oct. 1993
- → Georgian advance into Abkhazia, Aug. 1992
- —— areas of Georgia under Abkhazian control, Oct. 1993
- ▨ evacuated by Georgia, Oct. 1994
- notional extent of Azerbaijan at independence
- Armenia at independence
- —— limit of Armenian control, May 1992
- → Azerbaijani advance into Karabakh, Oct. 1992
- --→ secured by Armenia and Karabakh by Nov. 1993
- Chechenia-Ingushetia at independence
- —— seceded from Chechenia, joined Rus. Fed., Mar. 1992
- ▨ claimed by Ingushetia, 1992
- → Russian advance into Chechenia by May 1995
- ⇒ mass movements of refugees
- autonomous within Russian Federation

Nov. 1991: independence declared
Dec. 1994: Russian troops invade; Grozny largely destroyed;
May 1996: Russian-Chechen ceasefire Russian troops withdraw;
Aug. 1999: Renewed Russian invasion and occupation of most of Chechenia
2000–2: continued sporadic fighting

June 1995: attacked by Chechen forces

Oct. 1992: clashes between Ossetians and Ingush; Russian troops intervene

Jan. 1990: rioting in Baku: Soviet troops intervene
Oct. 1991: independence declared
Sep. 1992: unsuccessful attempts to subjugate Nagorno-Karabakh and Armenia (to May 1994)

1989: clashes between Ossetians and Georgians
Dec. 1991 breaks from Georgia in favour of Russian Federation
Jan.-May 1992: clashes with Georgian troops; North Ossetians assist South Ossetians (Apr. 1992)

Apr. 1991: independence declared
Dec. 1991: President Gamsakhurdia overthrown
1992: Eduard Shevardnadze becomes chairman of State Council
1993: Georgia joins CIS

1990: clashes between Abkhazians and Georgians
July 1992: asserts independence from Georgia; Georgian and Russian troops intervene, North Caucasian Muslims assist Abkhazians (Aug. 1992)
May 1994: ceasefire; Russian peace-keeping troops deployed

Jan. 1990: independence declared

Sep. 1991: independence declared; Azerbaijani forces intervene; Armenian-supported Karabakh forces clash with Azeris; Armenian invasion of Azerbaijan follows May 1994: ceasefire

SLOVENIA
HUNGARY
CROATIA

Zagreb
Karlovac
Sisak
Glina
Bihać
Bosanka Krupa
UN
Sanski Most
Ključ
Maslenica
Knin
Dinaric Alps
Glamoč
Šibenik
DALMATIA
Livno
Split
Brač
Hvar
Korčula
Dubrovnik

Drava
Baranja
Osijek
Okučani
Vukovar
Sava
Prijedor
Banja Luka
Đoboj
Oraje
Brčko
Bosna
BOSNIA-
Mrkonić-Grad
Jajce
Donji Vakuf
Kupres
Travnik
Vitez
Bugojno
Gornji Vakuf
Kiseljak
Zenica
Vrbas
Maglaj
Tuzla
UN
Žepče
Olovo
Sarajevo
UN
Srebrenica
UN
Prozor
Pale
Žepa
Višegrad
UN
Goražde
UN
Jablanica
HERZEGOVINA
Mostar

YUGOSLAVIA

SERBIA
50,000 Serbs
Novi Pazar
Leposavić
refugees 61,700
Kosovska Mitrovica
Podujevo
MONTENEGRO
Istok
patriarchate of Pec
Pec
Dečani
Kosovo Polje 1389
Priština
Gračanica
Vranje
KOSOVO
Gnjilane
Uroševac
ALBANIA
refugees 405,360
Prizren
church of Bogorodica Ljeviska
refugees 197,870
Kukës
Blace
MACEDONIA (F.Y.R.O.M.)
Skopje

HUNGARY
ROMANIA
CROATIA
Novi Sad
Belgrade
BOSNIA-HERZE-GOVINA
Kragujevac
SERBIA
Niš
MONTENEGRO
Podgorica
KOSOVO
Priština
ALBANIA
Skopje
MACEDONIA

2 The crisis in Kosovo, 1999

⟶ flight of Kosovan Albanian refugees, Mar.-May 1999

✸ towns bombed by NATO forces, Mar.-June 1999

⊕ sites of religous significance to Serbs

- - - - NATO zone of occupation with nationality of occupying force

In 1998, conflict escalated in Serbia's province of Kosovo. Talks brokered by international mediators offered the Kosovo Albanians full autonomy within Serbia, but Milosevic objected. NATO responded with air strikes against Yugoslavia in March 1999 to force Belgrade to sign the peace agreement and to stop the repression of Kosovo Albanians. The Serbian security forces instead accelerated a programme of 'ethnic cleansing' against Kosovo Albanians. After more than two months of NATO bombing, Milosevic agreed in June 1999 to a peace plan that incorporated most of NATO's demands and a NATO-led peace implementation force entered the province (map 2).

Tensions within the Yugoslav Federation continued as the pro-western government of Montenegro sought to assert its independence from Belgrade until Milosevic fell from power in December 2000, after massive popular protests following his false claim of victory in presidential elections. His successor, Vojislav Kostunica, made overtures to the West and promised a return to democratic rule and in 2001 surrendered Milosevic for trial by an international tribunal, but the Federation's future remained uncertain.

The break-up of the Soviet Union, too, saw widespread ethnic and political conflict, particularly in the Caucasus region (map 3). Armenia and Azerbaijan fought over the Christian Armenian enclave of Nagorno-Karabakh; Georgia fought to keep South Ossetia within her boundaries and to prevent the independence of Abkhazia. The worst conflict occurred in Chechenia, which Russian forces invaded in 1994 and 1999 to prevent secession. Russia suffered heavy casualties in both cases and, despite occupying virtually the whole province, could not stifle a vigorous Chechen resistance.

Russia established a fragile democracy in 1992. In October 1993 hard-line parliamentary delegates hostile to further reform tried to depose President Boris Yeltsin. He ordered in tanks and special forces and bombarded the White House, the Russian parliament. On 4 October, the rebels surrendered (*left*). Yeltsin was re-elected in presidential elections in June 1996, finally stepping down in 1999 as power transferred peacefully to Vladimir Putin.

The 21ST-Century World

The 1990s saw progress in spreading democracy, in ending conflicts, in superpower disarmament and in stabilizing economic development. Yet many critical issues remained. Ecological crisis and the threat of regional wars challenged the mood of optimism in the West as it celebrated the new millennium.

The absence of global confrontation after the Cold War did not prevent regional disputes, many of which dragged in the major powers as arbiters. In 1990, Iraq invaded Kuwait, only to be expelled by United Nations forces in 1991. Thereafter, tensions persisted as Iraq and the UN argued about the terms set for the inspection and elimination of Iraqi weapons of mass destruction. In Chechenia, Russian forces fought a grim civil war against Chechen nationalists, which left the region desolate. The largest war of all involved the states that emerged from the collapse of former Yugoslavia in 1991 (see p. 170). In 1995 NATO imposed a settlement on the warring groups, but three years later fighting broke out again between Serbs and Albanian separatists in Kosovo.

Religious differences exacerbated many conflicts in the 1990s. Radical movements developed throughout the Islamic world, including the large Muslim communities now living and working in the West. The failure of western-style modernization encouraged many young

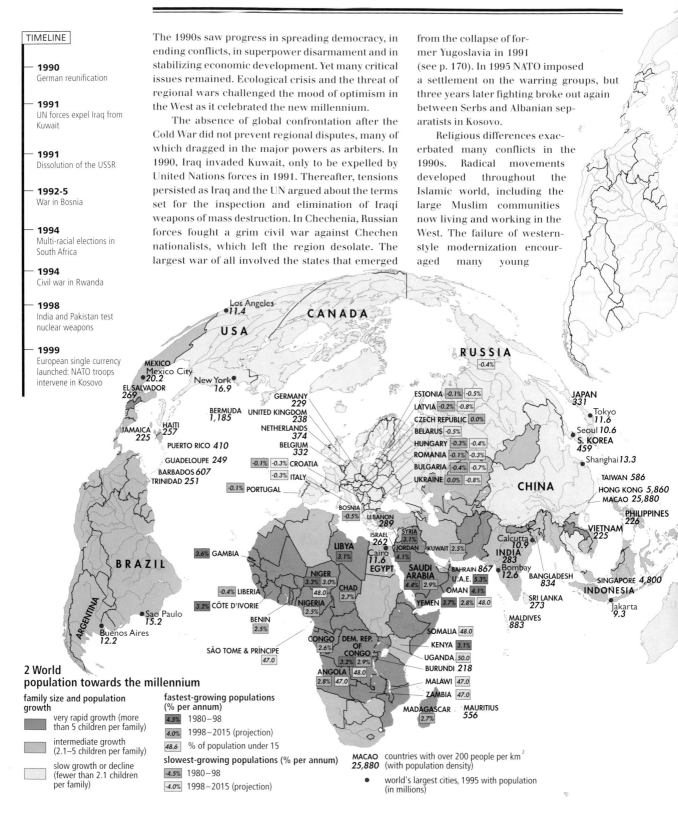

2 World
population towards the millennium

family size and population growth

- very rapid growth (more than 5 children per family)
- intermediate growth (2.1–5 children per family)
- slow growth or decline (fewer than 2.1 children per family)

fastest-growing populations (% per annum)
- 4.5% 1980–98
- 4.0% 1998–2015 (projection)
- 48.6 % of population under 15

slowest-growing populations (% per annum)
- -4.5% 1980–98
- -4.0% 1998–2015 (projection)

MACAO 25,880 countries with over 200 people per km² (with population density)

• world's largest cities, 1995 with population (in millions)

1 The revival of religious conflict

- wars and conflict with religious foundation
- areas with religious fundamentalist opposition
- states with government-sponsored fundamentalism
- ✸ sites of religious terrorism

New York (2001 terrorist attack on World Trade Centre)

civil conflict between Catholic and Protestant Christians (since 1969)

NORTHERN IRELAND

Omagh (1998 terrorist bombing)

war between Muslim minority and Orthodox Christian Serbs (1992–5)

civil war between Albanian Muslims and Orthodox Christian Serbs (since 1997)

war between Christian Armenians and Muslim Azeris (1988–94)

civil war against Islamic revolutionary forces

Algiers (1992 assasination of Boudiaf)

BOSNIA

KOSOVO

Mazar-e-Sharif (1998 massacre by Taleban)

civil war against Islamic Salvation Front (since 1992)

MOROCCO

TURKEY

NAGORNO-KARABAKH

TAJIKISTAN

BURMA

Taleban fundamentalist Sunni Muslims fight civil war against Shias and non-Muslims, 1996–2000; Taleban overthrown by US-led anti-terror campaign (2001)

ALGERIA

TUNISIA

LEBANON

SYRIA

IRAQ

IRAN

AFGHANISTAN

PAKISTAN

LIBYA

INDIA

MALAYSIA

Valley of the Kings (1997 massacre)

JORDAN

EGYPT

SAUDI ARABIA

civil war between Muslims and Christians (1975–92)

CHAD

SUDAN

YEMEN

conflict between Muslim minorities and fundamentalist Hindus; conflicts with Sikh minority over religious freedom and Sikh autonomy

conflict between Muslims and southern Christians

Tel Aviv (assasination of Israeli Prime Minister Rabin, 1995)

bombing of USS Cole (2000)

civil war between National Islamic Front government and southern Christian rebels (since 1989)

Nairobi (1998 bombing)

Dar-es-Salaam (1998 bombing)

49.0 MARSHALL IS

TUVALU 400

NEW ZEALAND

AUSTRALIA

A militiaman from Liberia (right). The civil war which began in Liberia in 1989 claimed the lives of up to 150,000 civilians and led to a total breakdown of law and order. Competing militias vied for control of the country. It was only in 1995 that the Abuja Accords began the process that led to the end of the war.

Muslims to exalt traditional values, and to seek to destroy western 'imperialism', both by driving it out of Islamic countries, and by attacking it in its heartland. This has led to civil war between Fundamentalists and Modernizers in several Muslim countries (Afghanistan, Algeria and Iran); and to terrorism against pro-Western regimes (Egypt and Saudi Arabia) as well as against the United States. Religious differences also fuelled inter-communal violence in India, Indonesia, Northern Ireland and Yugoslavia, and inter-state conflicts between Iran and Iraq and between Israel and most of her Arab neighbours (map 1).

Some of the tensions in the Middle East and in south and southeast Asia arose from rapid population growth. In these areas, people under 25 sometimes make up half the total population. Indeed students and schoolchildren played a conspicuous part in protests in India, Indonesia, Burma and in Tiananmen Square in Beijing in 1989. Young South Africans, too, played a central part in achieving democracy in 1990–4. The image of the peasant-soldier typical of the liberation movements of the 1960s gave way to chilling images of pre-teenage boys with modern weapons in their hands.

Population growth has threatened to destabilize the world system for decades. In the late 1990s the growth began to slow, though not fast enough to avert famine and the impoverishment of many developing states (map 2).

The Global economy

TIMELINE

1987
Single European Act for full economic union

1991
Russia begins programme of economic reforms

1992
Maastricht Treaty

1994
Mexico joins North American Free Trade Area (NAFTA)

1995
EEC becomes the European Union

1997-8
Financial crisis rocks east Asian economies

1999
European single currency (the 'euro') introduced

By the 1990s electronic communication and worldwide investment and marketing had created a genuinely global economy. Giant transnational companies dominated finance and production. However, world economic development still depended in part on the central management of key economic factors by groups of states, and on collaboration between them. Representatives of the largest industrial economies met regularly as the Group of Seven to co-ordinate financial and trade policies. Additionally, regional agreements sought to expand trade between small groups of states.

US$30,600   US$8,350 bn
USA
CANADA
US$590 bn

US$29,280
ICELAND

see inset map

RUSSIAN FEDERATION

BERMUDA

US$35,590

VENEZUELA

GUINEA BISSAU
US$160

ALGERIA
LIBYA
EGYPT
SAUDI ARABIA

INDIA

BRAZIL

SIERRA LEONE
US$130

NIGER
CHAD
ERITREA
US$200

US$220

US$190

ETHIOPIA

NEPAL

ARGENTINA

US$740 bn

US$200

DEMO. REP. OF CONGO
BURUNDI
US$100

US$110

US$120

MALAWI

US$190

SOUTH AFRICA

2 The world's top trading nations, 1996

millions US$ / % of world total

- Exports
- % world total

United States, Germany, Japan, China, France, UK, Italy, Canada, Netherlands, Belgium

3 Regional distribution of wealth

total world GNP 1995: US$ 27,110,768 million

Europe 32.6%   Asia 30.4%   N. America 29.7%

S. America 4.3%
Africa 1.5%
Oceania 1.5%

174

US$44,640
LUXEMBOURG

US$32,880

US$32,030

FINLAND

NORWAY

SWEDEN

DENMARK

UK

IRELAND

US$1,340 bn

NETH.

US$2,080 bn
GERMANY

Paris
OECD•

BEL.

Vienna
•OPEC
AUSTRIA

Basle
SWITZ.

FRANCE

US$1,430 bn

ITALY

US$25,970

PORTUGAL

SPAIN

US$550 bn

US$38,350
Bank for Int'l
Settlements

US$1,135 bn
GREECE

European Union (EU)

European Economic Area
(EEA)

JAPAN

US$4,080 bn   US$32,230

N A

US$980 bn

US$29,610
SINGAPORE

INDONESIA

NEW
ZEALAND

AUSTRALIA

1 The world economy and economic groupings

North American Free Trade Association (NAFTA)

Common Market of the Southern Cone (Mercosur)

Andean Community

Central American Common Market (CACM)

Economic Community of West African States (ECOWAS)

Organization for Economic Co-operation and Development
(OECD)

Organization for Petroleum Exporting Countries (OPEC)

South African Development Co-ordination Conference (SADCC)

Association of South East Asian Nations (ASEAN)

Organization of American States (OAS)

Organization of African Unity (OAU)

10 largest economies by 1999 GNP (in US$ bn)

10 largest GNP per capita (1999)

10 smallest GNP per capita (1999)

The most successful of these groupings was the European Union, which grew from the original six members of the EEC in 1957 to embrace 15 states by 1996 (page 166). Gradual economic integration culminated on 1 January 1999 in the introduction of a single currency, the euro. Economic groups elsewhere were looser associations aiming to enhance regional economic integration. In 1994, for example, the USA, Canada and Mexico joined in the North American Free Trade Association (NAFTA) (map 1 and inset).

The world's top ten trading nations in 1996 provided 61 per cent of the world's imports and 63 per cent of exports (chart 2). A high proportion of that trade took place between the top traders, rather than trade between the developed and developing world; and an increasing proportion occurred within free-trade blocs.

The fruits of the global economic success were spread very unevenly. In 1995, Europe possessed almost 33 per cent of the world's wealth, and North America a further 30 per cent (chart 3). Sustained expansion in Asia, Europe and the United States contrasted with economic decline in Africa, Latin America and the former Soviet bloc. The Russian economy in particular faced serious crisis by 1998 as the rush for capitalism failed to generate the wealth to sustain employment and welfare at the level achieved under communism. Even in east Asia, which grew faster than anywhere else in the world from the 1960s to the mid-1990s, the boom turned sour in 1997. Burdened with debt, high population growth and excessive dependence on a cluster of manufacturing exports, the new Asian economies generated a financial crisis that threatened the health of the whole global economy.

Outside the growth areas, there was persistent reliance on aid and investment from the developed world, much of it supplied by the International Monetary Fund (IMF) or the Organization for Economic Co-operation and Development (OECD). The per capita Gross Domestic Product (GDP) of the poorest states in the late 1990s was less than $300, while per capita GDP in the USA was almost $27,000. For many sub-Saharan African states, aid represented more than half of the value of total GDP. This pattern of aid-dependence altered little over the 1990s, and the gulf between the poverty of the developing world and the vast wealth of the developed industrial core remained one of the unresolved issues of global economics.

A Euro coin (above). Gradual economic integration within the European Union culminated in the introduction of a single currency, the Euro, on 1 January 1999. The Euro was beset by initial controversy, with the United Kingdom refusing to join the currency bloc and an unexpected level of weakness against the dollar. Euro notes and coins were introduced in early 2002 and national currencies within the Euro-zone were abolished entirely.

The Global environment

Until the 20th century, natural changes largely determined the environment. Now, industrialization, modern communications and mass consumption have combined to produce damaging man-made environmental change. Ecological disasters have become urgent global problems.

The onset of large-scale population growth and industrialization in the 19th century (page 100), stimulated a parallel rapid increase in man-made damage to the world's environment. Before 1945, this damage was largely localized, though very visible; the spread of industry worldwide after 1945 produced new threats to the environment which, if less visible, were nonetheless more deadly. Acid rain from waste in the atmosphere destroyed forests and eroded buildings. Pollutants in rivers and seas poisoned wildlife (map 1).

High levels of carbon dioxide released from the burning of fossil fuels raised global temperatures, while other chemicals began to weaken the ozone layer in the earth's atmosphere. Between 1800 and 1900 the level of carbon dioxide in the atmosphere increased by only 4 per cent; in the 20th century it increased by 23 per cent, with most of the change

3 Radioactive fall-out from the Chernobyl accident, 1986

∴ pattern of fall-out

occurring since the 1950s. This raised world temperatures significantly: the 1990s were the warmest decade of the millennium.

Global warming stemmed in part from a massive increase in energy consumption, most of which consisted of fossil fuels (oil, coal and natural gas). Between 1970 and 1990 energy consumption grew by 60 per cent, despite efforts to find more efficient ways of generating power and to reduce emissions. Fossil fuels released a range of chemicals

into the atmosphere which blocked the natural loss of heat and created the so-called 'greenhouse effect', leading to a global rise in temperatures (map 2).

The search for alternative sources of energy produced other types of disaster, however. In 1986, a nuclear reactor at Chernobyl in the Ukraine exploded, spreading a cloud of radioactive waste around the world (map 3). This catastrophe was but the most spectacular of many accidents in the production of nuclear power, eventually causing a reduction in its use.

Environmental issues became a central concern of the 1990s and state action produced some positive results. In Brazil, deforestation fell from a rate of 21,000 square kilometres in 1988 to only 1000 square kilometres by 1993. At Rio de Janeiro in 1992 an assembly of world leaders agreed to reduce harmful pollutants and emissions, a decision reaffirmed at a further meeting in Kyoto in 1997. The richer states also promised to subsidize industrial and agricultural projects in the developing world that respected environmental interests. In European states, political movements developed based entirely on issues of the environment, and in 1998 the environmentalist Green Party won a share of power in Germany. The future of the world ecosystem depended on the willingness of the world's richest states to accept substantial changes in consumption patterns.

MEXIC
Burmah Aga 1979

BELIZE CUBA
CENTRAL AMERICA
between 33% and 50% of rainforest destroyed

VENEZUELA
Atlantic
COLOMBIA Empress 1979
CHOCO

WESTERN
AMAZONIA

PERU

BRAZIL
10% of forest
BOLIVIA destroyed

CHILE

SOUTH
AMERICA
ARGENTINA

URUGUAY

Metula 1974

1 The crisis of the environment

deforestation: rainforests under threat

- tropical rainforest
- edge of rainforest undergoing the most rapid deforestation
- ★ threatened area with large concentrations of endangered species

ocean and river pollution: oil slicks and tar balls

- high occurrence
- low occurrence

oceanic pollution

- frequent and severe
- partial and intermittent
- 🦫 major oil tanker disaster
- ✳ oil rig blowout
- ⋮ natural seepage

river pollution

- —— severe
- —— background

CANADA

UNITED STATES

ICELAND

North Atlantic Ocean

Exxon Valdez 1989

Braer 1993

Sea Empress 1995

Amoco Cadiz 1978

Aegean Sea 1992

Jakob Maersk 1975

Sea Spirit 1990

Ellen Conway 1976

Khark 5 1989

RUSSIAN FEDERATION

NORWAY SWEDEN FINLAND

IRELAND UK

FRANCE GERMANY POLAND

PORTUGAL SPAIN ITALY

Haven 1991

GREECE

TURKEY

Independenta 1979

Nakhodka 1997

Yuyo Maru No.10 1974

NORTH KOREA

SOUTH KOREA

JAPAN

MONGOLIA

KAZAKHSTAN

Aral Sea

CHINA

TAIWAN

PHILIPPINES

PAPUA NEW GUINEA

UKRAINE

SYRIA IRAQ IRAN AFGHAN. PAKISTAN

INDIA

INDIAN SUB-CONTINENT

complete deforestation

BURMA VIETNAM

THAILAND

SOUTH EAST ASIA

nearly 50% of rainforest destroyed

NORTH WEST BORNEO

PENINSULAR MALAYSIA MALAYSIA

SRI LANKA

INDONESIA

Tadotsu 1978

Assimi 1983

SAUDI ARABIA

OMAN YEMEN

TUNISIA

ALGERIA

LIBYA

EGYPT

MAURITANIA

SENEGAL MALI

GUINEA

LIBERIA

WEST AFRICA
forest almost completely gone

NIGER CHAD SUDAN

NIGERIA

A F R I C A

CAMEROON C.A.R.

ETHIOPIA

SOMALIA

GABON

DEM. REP. CONGO

KENYA

TANZANIA

ANGOLA

Indian Ocean

QUEENSLAND

AUSTRALIA

NEW ZEALAND

ABT Summer 1991

NAMIBIA

MOZAMBIQUE

MADAGASCAR

Castillo de Bellver 1983

SOUTH AFRICA

Katina P 1992

Wafra 1971

2 Global warming

- more humid than before
- drier than before
- principal farming regions
- ● flooding through rise in sea level
- 1°c increase in surface temperature

melting ice-caps lead to heavy pack ice

c 1°C

c 3–4°C

sharp fall in grain crop yields

more destructive hurricanes

short wet winters, long dry summers

sharp fall in grain crop yields

poor rice crop

c 0.3°C–0.5°C

rise in sea level

failure of anchovy fisheries

increase in farming

millions made homeless by flooding

rise in sea level

One of the most dramatic consequences of industrial pollution was acid rain. Damage was particularly great in highly industrialized countries, such as Germany, Britain and the Czech Republic. European forest suffered particularly badly *(left)*. In Britain over 60 per cent of forests were damaged by acid rain.

Index

1 HISTORICAL PLACE NAMES

Geographical names vary with time and with language, and there is some difficulty in treating them consistently in an historical atlas, especially for individual maps within whose time span the same place has been known by different names. We have aimed at the simplest possible approach to the names on the maps, using the index to weld together the variations.

On the maps forms of names will be found in the following hierarchy of preference:

a English conventional names or spellings, in the widest sense, for all principal places and features, e.g., Moscow, Vienna, Munich (including those that today might be considered obsolete when these are appropriate to the context, e.g., Leghorn).

b Names that are contemporary in terms of the maps concerned. There are here three broad categories:

i names in the ancient world, where the forms used are classical, e.g., Latin or latinized Greek, but extending also to Persian, Sanskrit, etc.

ii names in the post-medieval modern world, which are given in the form (though not necessarily the spelling) current at the time of the map (e.g., St. Petersburg before 1914, not Leningrad).

iii modern names where the spelling generally follows that of The Times Atlas of the World, though in the interests of simplicity there has been a general omission of diacritics in spellings derived by transliteration from non-roman scripts, e.g., Sana rather than Şan'ā'.

2 THE INDEX

Where a place is referred to by two or more different names in the course of the atlas, there will be a corresponding number of main entries in the index. The variant names In each case are given in brackets at the beginning of the entry, their different forms and origins being distinguished by such words as now, later, formerly and others included in the list of abbreviations (right).

'Bizerta (anc. Hippo Zarytus)' means that the page references to that city on maps dealing with periods when it was known as Bizerta follow that entry, but the page references pertaining to it in ancient times will be found under the entry for Hippo Zarytus. Places are located generally by reference to the country in which they lie (exceptionally by reference to island groups or sea areas), this being narrowed down where necessary by location as E(ast), C(entral), etc. The reference will normally be to the modern state in which the place now falls unless (a) there is a conventional or historical name which conveniently avoids the inevitably anachronistic ring of some modern names, e.g., Anatolia rather than Turkey, Mesopotamia rather than Iraq, or (b) the modern state is little known or not delineated on the map concerned, e.g., many places on the Africa plates can only be located as W, E, Africa, etc.

Reference is generally to page number/map number (e.g. 118/1) unless the subject is dealt with over the plate as a whole, when the references have been given sub-headings where possible, e.g., Civil War 129/4. Battles are indicted by the symbol **✗**.

Though page references are generally kept in numerical order, since this corresponds for the most part with chronological order, they have been rearranged occasionally where the chronological sequence would be obviously wrong, or in the interests of grouping appropriate references under a single sub-heading.

3 ABBREVIATIONS

a/c also called	**form.** former(ly)	**obs.** obsolete
AD Autonomous District	**Fr.** French	**OT** Old Testament
Alb. Albanian	**f/s** formerly spelled	**Pers.** Persian
anc. ancient	**Ger.** German	**Pol.** Polish
AR Autonomous Region	**Gr.** Greek	**Port.** Portuguese
Ar. Arabic	**Heb.** Hebrew	**Rom.** Romanian
a/s also spelled	**Hung.** Hungarian	**Russ.** Russian
ASSR Autonomous Soviet Socialist Republic	**Indon.** Indonesian	**S** South(ern)
Bibl. Biblical	**Ir.** Irish	**s/c** sometimes called
Bulg. Bulgarian	**Is.** Island	**Som.** Somali
C Century (when preceded by 17, 18, etc.)	**It.** Italian	**Sp.** Spanish
C Central	**Jap.** Japanese	**S.Cr.** Serbo-Croat
Cat. Catalan	**Kor.** Korean	**SSR** Soviet Socialist Republic
Chin. Chinese	**Lat.** Latin	**Sw.** Swedish
Cz. Czech	**Latv.** Latvian	**Turk.** Turkish
Dan. Danish	**Lith.** Lithuanian	**Ukr.** Ukrainian
Dut. Dutch	**Mal.** Malay	**US(A)** United States (of America)
E East(ern)	**med.** medieval	**var.** variant
Eng. English	**mod.** modern	**W** West(ern)
Est. Estonian	**Mong.** Mongolian	**Wel.** Welsh
f/c formerly called	**N** North(ern)	**WW1** World War 1
Finn. Finnish	**n/c** now called	**WW2** World War 2
	Nor. Norwegian	
	n/s now spelled	
	NT New Testament	

Aachen (*Fr.* Aix-la-Chapelle *anc.* Aquisgranum) W Germany Frankish royal residence 53/1; WW1 86/2

Abkhazia autonomous region of Georgia 170/3

Abasgia region of the Caucasus 49/1

Abyssinia (*now* Ethiopia) 111/1

Achaea (*a/s* Achaia) Roman province 37/1

Acragas (*Lat.* Agrigentum *mod.* Agrigento) Sicily Greek colony 32/1

Addis Ababa Ethiopia Italian penetration 111/1

Aden S Arabia early town 81/1; Ottoman Empire 108/1; taken by British 118/1; British base 154/1

Aden Protectorate (*successively renamed* Protectorate of South Arabia, Federation of South Arabia, People's Republic of South Yemen, People's Democratic Republic of Yemen; *now part of* United Yemen)

Admiralty Islands S Pacific Japanese attack 142/1

Adowa N Ethiopia ✗111/1

Adrianople (*anc.* Adrianopolis *mod.* Edirne) W Turkey Byzantine Empire 49/1,2; Ottoman centre 71/1; occupied by Greece 136/1

Aegospotami (*Turk.* Karaova Suyu) NW Turkey ✗33/2

Aegyptus (*mod.* Egypt) Roman province 37/1

Afars and Issas, French Territory of (*form.* French Somaliland *now* Republic of Djibouti)

Afghanistan invaded by USSR 149/1, 163/1; civil war 157/3; Islamic fundamentalism 157/3

Africa early man 12/1, 14/2; cave art 15/1; agricultural origins 17/1; early cultures 27/2; early empires 58/1; slave trade 59/2; early European voyages of discovery 79/1; European expansion and trade 80-81; 18C European trade 103/2; European penetration 111/1; colonial empires 119/2; foreign investment 1914 127/1; Japanese imports 152/2; anti-colonial resistance 154/1; modern political developments 161/1; population growth 172/2; armament imports 173/1; economic groupings 174/2; economy 174/2 environment 177/1,2

Africa (*mod.* Tunisia and Libya) conversion to Christianity 34/1, 44/1; Roman province 36/1; Byzantine province 48/1

Aga Buryat AD S Siberia in Russian Federation 169/2

Aigun NE China treaty port 95/2

Ain Jalut Palestine ✗50/2

Aix (*or* Aix-en-Provence *anc.* Aquae Sextiae) S France archbishopric 53/1; *parlement* 83/2

Ajaria autonomous district of Georgia 170/3

Ajnadain Palestine ✗51/1

Aksum early empire of E Africa 27/2

Åland Islands (*Finn.* Ahvenanmaa) SW Finland neutralized 136/1

Alaska state of USA purchase from Russia 114/1

Albania Black Death 67/1; Ottoman province 108/1; principality 125/2, 137/2; annexed by Italy 145/1; Cold War 165/1; free elections 169/1; Kosovo crisis 171/2; Kosovan refugees 171/2

Albania ancient country of Caucasus 37/1

Albany (*form.* Fort Orange) NE USA seized by English 86/2

Alemannia SW Germany part of Frankish Empire 53/1

Aleppo (*anc.* Beroea *a/c* Yamkhad *Fr.* Alep *Ar.* I lalab) Syria Mitannian city 22/3; centre of European trade 103/2

Alessandria N Italy Lombard League 55/2

Aleutian Islands W Alaska to USA 114/1; attacked by Japanese 142/1; retaken by Americans 143/2

Alexandria (*Ar.* Al Iskandariyah) Egypt taken by Alexander 32/3; spread of Christianity 34/1; Roman Empire 37/1; Christian centre 45/1; Arab conquest 51/1; trade 59/2; centre of European trade 103/2

Algeria Ottoman province 70/2; French invasion 111/1; French colonization 118/1; under Vichy control 140/1; independence 154/1; Islamic fundamentalism 157/3; political development 161/1

Algiers (*Fr.* Alger *Sp.* Argel *Ar.* Al Jaza'ir *anc.* Icosium) N Algeria Ottoman rule 70/2; Habsburg Empire 93/1; Allied landing WW2 141/2

Allenstein (*Pol.* Olsztyn) W Poland acquired by Germany after plebiscite 136/1

Almanza Spain ✗83/3

Almohads Muslim dynasty and empire of North Africa 58/1

Almoravids Muslim dynasty of Morocco 58/1

Alpes Cottiae Roman province, France/Italy 36/1

Alpes Maritimae Roman province, France/Italy 36/1

Alpes Poeninae Roman province, France/Italy 36/1

Alsace (*anc.* Alsatia *Ger.* Elsass) in German Empire 55/2; acquired by French 83/2; Habsburg Empire 93/1

Alsace-Lorraine (*Ger.* Elsass-Lothringen) region of E France annexed by German Empire 116/2; ceded to France 136/1

Altay C Asia republic of Russian Federation 169/2

America, Central (a/c Mesoamerica) agricultural origins 16/1; early peoples 25/1; early civilizations 24/2; Aztec Empire 72/2; colonial expansion 87/1; 18C Atlantic economy 81/1; economy 174/1

America, North early man 14/2; early cultures 25/1; early voyages of discovery 78/1; colonial expansion 87/1; industrialization 145/1; Japanese imports 153/2; population growth 172/2; armament exports 173/2; economy 174/1; economic groupings 174/2; environment 177/1,2. See also Canada, United States

America, South early man 14/2; agricultural origins 16/1; early peoples and civilizations 25/1; Inca Empire 73/3; early voyages of discovery 78/1; colonial expansion 87/1; independence 113/1; modern politics 113/1; foreign investment 1914 126/2; Japanese imports 153/2; population growth 172/2; armament imports 173/1; economy 174/1; economic groupings 174/2; environment 177/1,2

American Samoa S Pacific 155/1 (inset)

Amoy (n/s Xiamen) S China treaty port 95/2; Japanese influence 95/2; occupied by Japanese 123/2

Amphipolis N Greece ✕33/2

Anatolia early agriculture 20/1; incipient urbanization 18/1; Hittites 22/3; Black Death 67/1; Ottoman conquest 71/1. See also Asia Minor

Ancyra (mod. Ankara obs. Eng. Angora) W Anatolia Roman empire 35/1; Byzantine Empire 44/1

Andalusia autonomous region of S Spain 166/2

Angkor Cambodia Buddhist site 35/1

Angles tribe of NW Europe, migrations 40/1

Anglo-Egyptian Sudan condominium 70/2; Ottoman territory under British control 108/1

Angola SW Africa source of slaves 59/2; Portuguese colonization 110-11; independence 154/1; political development 161/1; Cuban military intervention 149/1

Angora (anc. Ancyra mod. Ankara) W Anatolia ✕60/2

Anguilla island of West Indies independence 155/1 (inset)

Anhwei (a/s Anhui) province of E China Manchu expansion 94/1; economy 151/2

Annam N Indo-China under T'ang control 47/1; expansion and early trade 89/2

Antigua island of West Indies colony 112/1; independence 155/1 (inset)

Antioch (Lat. Antiochia mod. Antakya) NW Syria Roman Empire 37/1; archbishopric 45/1, 2; Byzantine rule 49/1

Antung (now Dandong) Manchuria treaty port 95/2

Antwerp (Fr. Anvers Dut. Antwerpen) Belgium town of Spanish Neth-erlands 92/2; WW1 132/2

Aquileia (med. Aglar) N Italy Byzantine Empire 37/1

Aquincum (mod. Budapest) Hungary Roman Empire 37/1

Aquitaine (anc. Aquitania mod. Guyenne) region of SW France Black Death 67/1

Aquitania (mod. Aquitaine later Guyenne) Roman province of Gaul 36/1; Visigothic territory conquered by Franks 52/1

Arabia maritime trading 20/1; spread of Judaism 34/1; centre of Islam 51/1; 18C European trade 103/2

Arabia Petraea Roman province of N Arabia 37/1

Arabs territorial losses to Byzantine Empire 49/1; independence from Ottomans 108/1; emigration from Israel 156/2

Arachosia (a/c Harauvatish) Afghanistan ancient province of Mauryan Empire 29/3

Aragon (Sp. Aragón) region of E Spain rural uprisings 67/1; Habsburg Empire 93/1

Arakan district of SW Burma Islamic states 64/2; British control 89/2

Archangel (Russ. Arkhangelsk) N Russia founded 83/1; Allied occupation 135/1

Arcole N Italy ✕99/2

Ardennes forest Belgium/France WW1 132/2

Arelate (mod. Arles) S France Roman Empire 36/1, 37/2

Argentina independence from Spain 113/1; political developments 159/1; industrialization and economy 126/1, 159/2

Arginusae islands of the Aegean ✕33/2

Arles medieval kingdom of S France 55/2

Armagnac region of SW France annexed to France 82/1

Armenia (anc. Urartu) country of Caucasus Roman province 37/1; Muslim conquest 51/1; Ottoman Empire 108/1; independence after WW1 136/1; independence 1991 169/1; invasion of Azerbaijan 170/2

Arras (anc. Nemetocenna) N France WW1 132/2

Arretium (mod. Arezzo) C Italy Etruscan city 32/1

Artaxata Armenia Roman Empire 37/1

Artois region of NE France Burgundian possession 82/1; province of France 83/2

Arzawans early people of Anatolia 22/3

Ashur (mod. Sharqat) Mesopotamia Assyrian Empire 22/3

Asia early man 12/1, 14/2; cave art 15/1; agricultural origins 17/1; first farmers 18-19; rise of civilization 20-21; Chinese expansion 39/1; tribal movements 41/1; early voyages of discovery 79/1, 81/1; Russian expansion 84/2; colonial empires 118/1, 119/2; foreign investment 1914 126/1; anti-colonial resistance 155/1; population growth 172/2; armament exports 173/2; economy 174/1; economic groupings 174/2; environment 177/1,2

Asia (Byzantine name Asiana) Roman province of Anatolia 37/1

Asia Minor conversion to Christianity 34/1, 45/1; Ottoman control 71/1. See also Anatolia

Asoka's Empire India 29/3

Aspern/Essling Austria ✕99/2

Assyria Empire 22/3; Roman province 37/1

Astrakhan S Russia occupied by Mongols 60/2; Tartar khanate 85/1; Bolshevik seizure 135/1

Athens (Lat. Athenae mod. Gr. Athinai) Greece Greek parent state 33/1; war with Sparta 33/2; invaded by Huns 40/1; Byzantine Empire 79/1; WW2 141/2

Augusta Treverorum (mod. Trier Eng. Treves) W Germany Roman Empire 36/1

Augusta Vindelicorum (mod. Augsburg) S Germany Roman Empire 36/1

Augustodunum (mod. Autun) C France Roman Empire 36/1

Austerlitz (mod. Slavkov) Czechoslovakia ✕99/2

Australia (originally called New Holland) early man 14/1; cave art 15/1; before the Europeans 26/1; settlement and development 106/1; emergence of Commonwealth 119/1; WW2 143/2; Pacific trade 152/2; economy 174/1

Austrasia the eastern Frankish Empire 53/1

Austria (Ger. Österreich) German settlement 55/2; Black Death 67/1; attacked by Ottomans 70/2; War of the Spanish Succession 83/3; Habsburg Empire 93/1; opposition to Napoleon 99/2; annexed by Germany 137/2; Allied occupation zones 146/1; EU 167/1

Austro-Hungarian Empire (a/c Austria-Hungary) Industrial Revolution 101/2; European alliances 124/1; WW1 133/1; dismantled 136/1

Avanti early kingdom of C India 29/3

Avars (Chin. Juan-juan) ancient people of Asia and Europe 40-41; kingdom destroyed 53/1

Avignon (anc. Avenio) S France Papal enclave 83/2

Azerbaijan (anc. Atropatene) country of the Caucasus Mongol Empire 60/1; Muslim conquest 51/1; Ottoman conquest 70/2; acquired by Russia 85/1; independence after WW1 136/1; independence 1991 169/1; invaded by Armenia 170/3

Azores (Port. Açores) islands of N Atlantic Portuguese colony 119/2

Aztec Empire Mexico 72/2

Babylon Mesopotamia Sumerian city 23/1; taken by Alexander 32/3

Bactria ancient country of SW Asia 29/3, 32/3

Badajoz SW Spain ✕98/2

Baden country of S Germany unification 116/2

Badr W Arabia ✕ 51/1

Baetica S Spain Roman province 36/1

Baffin Island N Canada discovery 78/1

Baghdad Mesopotamia Mongol attack 60/1; Mongol conquest 60/2; under Ottoman rule 70/2

Bahamas islands of N Caribbean discovery 78/1; British colony 118/2; independence 155/1 (inset)

Bahrain (f/s Bahrein Ar. Al Bahrayn) island of Persian Gulf independence 154/1

Bailén S Spain ✕98/1

Baku (n/s Baki) Azerbaijan conquered by Ottomans 70/2; British occupation 135/1

Balagansk s/c Siberia founded 84/1

Balearic Islands W Mediterranean Byzantine Empire 48/1; attacked by Saracens 54/1; to Spain 83/3

Balkans alliances 125/2; rise of nationalism 171/2

Balkh (anc. Bactra a/c Zariaspa) Afghanistan Mongol attack 61/1; conquest 51/1

Baltistan region of NW India district of Mughal Empire 63/1; tribal agency 97/3

Bandjarmasin (n/s Banjarmasin) S Borneo trade centre 64/2

Bangkok (Thai. Krung Thep) S Thailand captured by Japanese 142/1

Bangladesh (form. East Pakistan or East Bengal) 163/1

Bantam (form. Banten) Java early trade 64/2

Baqubah N Iraq oilfield 157/2

Bar region of NE France/W Germany Burgundian possession 82/1

Barbados island of West Indies British colony 112/1; independence 155/1 (inset)

Barcelona (anc. Barcino) NE Spain urban revolt 67/1

Bashkortostan (form. Bashkiria) W Russia republic of Russian Federation 169/2

Basque Country (Sp. País Vasco) autonomous region of N Spain 1979 166/2

Basque Republic N Spain autonomy 136/1

Basra (Ar. Al Başrah) Mesopotamia ✕51/1; Ottoman conquest 70/2; centre of European trade 103/2

Bassano N Italy ✕99/2

Basutoland (now Lesotho) S Africa British protectorate 119/2

Batavia (form. Sunda Kalapa, since 1949 Jakarta f/s Djakarta) Java centre of European trade 103/2; occupied by Japanese 142/1

Batum (n/s Batumi) Caucasus British occupation 135/1

Bautzen E Germany ✕99/2

Bavaria (Ger. Bayern) part of Frankish Empire 53/2; Reformation 91/1; German Empire 116/2

Bechuanaland (now Botswana) country of S Africa British protectorate 119/2

Beijing (f/s Peking) N China economy 1979-92 151/2

Belarus (a/c Belorussia) end of Communism 169/1

Belgian Congo (form. Congo Free State later Zaire now Democratic Republic of Congo) colony 111/1, 119/2; independence 154/1

Middle East (a/c Near East) Cold War 165/1

Midway island of C Pacific US base 165/1 (inset)

Milan (It. Milano anc. Mediolanum) N Italy Lombard League 55/2

Miletus W Anatolia Mycenaean city 31/1; Greek colony 33/1; Byzantine Empire 49/1

Mindanao island of S Philippines Japanese occupation 142/1; retaken by US 143/2

Ming Empire China 69/1

Min-yüeh region of S China 39/1

Mixtec States S Mexico 24/2

Mitanni ancient kingdom of Middle East 22/3

Mocha (Ar. Al Mukhā) S Yemen centre of European trade 103/2

Modena (anc. Mutina) N Italy Lombard League 55/2; unification of Italy 117/1

Moesia region of Balkans district of Byzantine Empire 49/1

Moesiae late Roman province of Greece 37/2

Moesia Inferior Roman province of the Balkans 37/1

Moesia Superior Roman province of the Balkans 37/1

Mogadishu (n/s Muqdisho It. Mogadiscio) Somalia Muslim colony 59/1; Italian occupation 110/1

Mohács Hungary ✕70/2

Moldavia (Turk. Boğdan Rom. Moldova) region of Romania/Russia Hungarian 66/2; under Ottoman control 71/1; part of Romania 125/2; independence (Moldova) 169/1

Moluccas (Indon. Maluku Dut. Molukken form. Spice Islands) islands of E Indies Muslim expansion 64/2; early Portuguese trade 81/1; Dutch control 89/2

Mondovi NW Italy ✕99/2

Monemvasia (It. Malvasia) S Greece Byzantine Empire 49/2; Ottoman conquest 70/2

Mongol Empire 60-61

Mongolia (form. Outer Mongolia) nomadic pastoralism 21/1; Mongol Empire 60-61; under Han Empire 41/1; Chinese incursions under Ming 69/1; Chinese protectorate 94/1; autonomy 95/2; Russian sphere of influence 119/2; limit of Japanese expansion 123/2

Montenegro (S. Cr. Crna Gora) region of S Yugoslavia under Ottoman rule 108/1; 19C alliances 124/2; independent state 125/2; WW1 133/1; forms part of Yugoslavia 136/1; WW2 141/2; Kosovo crisis 171/2

Montenotte N Italy ✕99/2

Montereau N France ✕99/2

Montmirail N France ✕99/2

Montreux Switzerland 1936 conference 136/1

Montserrat island West Indies British colony 155/1 (inset)

Moravia (Czech. Morava Ger. Mähren) region of C Czechoslovakia medieval German Empire 55/2; acquired by Bohemia 66/2; Hussite influence 67/1; Reformation 91/1; Habsburg Empire 93/1; forms part of Czechoslovakia 136/1

Mordovia W Russia republic of the Russian Federation 169/2

Morea (a/c Peloponnese) region of S Greece Byzantine Empire 49/2; conquered by Ottomans 71/1

Morocco (Fr. Maroc Sp. Marruecos) under Almohads 50/2; Sharifian dynasties 59/2; Spanish conquest 110/2; French and Spanish protectorates 111/1, 119/2; independence 154/1; conflict with Algeria 161/1; US bases 165/1

Morotai island N Moluccas, E Indies captured by Allies 143/2

Moscow (Russ. Moskva) W Russia early bishopric 45/2; city of Vladimir-Suzdal 57/1; captured by Napoleon 99/2; Industrial Revolution 101/2; industrial development 134/2; Bolshevik seizure of power 135/2

Mossi early states of W Africa 59/2

Mostar Herzegovina, Yugoslavia civil war 171/2

Mosul (Ar. Al Mawsil) Iraq Muslim conquest 51/1; Ottoman Empire 70/2; oilfield 157/2

Mozambique (form. Portuguese East Africa Port. Moçambique) early trade 81/1; Portuguese settlement 81/1; centre of European trade 103/2; Portuguese colony 119/2; independence 154/1; political development 161/1

Mughal Empire India 63/1

Mukden Manchuria capital of Manchuria 94/1; treaty town 95/2; Japanese occupation 123/2

Muscat and Oman (now Oman) SE Arabia British protectorate 119/2

Muscovy early principality of W Russia 85/1

Muslims minority in Bosnia and Serbia 171/2

Mwenemutapa early state of SE Africa 59/2

Mysia ancient country of W Anatolia 33/1

Muslims minority in Bosnia and Serbia 171/2

Mysore (now Karnataka) region of S India district of Mughal Empire 59/1; native state 96-97

Mytilene (a/s Mitylene) island of Aegean ceded to Greece 125/2

Nagasaki W Japan early European trade 81/1; Dutch trade 103/2; bombed by US 143/2

Nagorno-Karabakh Caucasus 169/1, 170/3

Nakhichevan region of SW Azerbaijan 170/3

Namibia (form. South West Africa earlier German South West Africa) German colony 111/1, 119/2; independence from South Africa 154/1, 161/1

Nanking (n/s Nanjing) N China Ming provincial capital 65/1; treaty port 89/2; occupied by Japan 117/2; economy 143/2

Nan-yüeh early kingdom of SW China 39/1

Nan-chao tribal kingdom of SW China 47/1

Nanning S China treaty port 95/2

Nantes NW France Scandinavian settlement 54/1

Naples, Kingdom of Black Death 67/1; to Austria 83/3; Habsburg Empire 93/1; satellite of France 99/2; unification of Italy 117/1

Narbonensis (a/c Gallia Narbonensis) Roman province of S France 36/1

Narbonne (anc. Narbo) S France Muslim conquest 50/1

Nations, Battle of the (Leipzig) E Germany ✕99/2

Naucratis Egypt Greek colony 33/1

Nauru island W Pacific independence 155/1 (inset)

Navarre (Sp. Navarra) region of N Spain/SW France conquered by France 83/2; Habsburg Empire 93/1

Navas de Tolosa S Spain ✕50/2

Neapolis (mod. Napoli Eng. Naples) S Italy Greek colony 33/1; Roman Empire 37/1

Nepal tributary state of Chinese Empire 94/1; 95/2

Nerchinsk, Treaty of 94/1

Netherlands (a/c Holland form. Dutch Republic United Provinces) Habsburg Empire 93/1; Industrial Revolution 100/2; trade with Africa and Asia 103/2; colonial power 119/2; NATO 147/4; EU 167/1. See also Belgium, Flanders, Holland

Netherlands, Austrian (mod. Belgium) revolt against Emperor 98/1

Netherlands East Indies (now Indonesia) occupied by Japanese 142/1. See also East Indies, Borneo, Java, Moluccas, Sumatra

Netherlands, Spanish (later Holland or United Provinces; and Belgium) Reformation 91/1; Dutch revolt 92/2

Neustria the Frankish lands of N France 52/1

Nevis island W Indies British colony 112/1; self-government with St. Christopher 155/1 (inset)

New Amsterdam (earlier Fort Amsterdam now New York city) colonized by Dutch 86/2

New Britain island Papua New Guinea early Melanesian settlement 27/1; retaken from Japanese 143/2; to New Guinea 155/1 (inset)

New Brunswick province of E Canada joins Confederation 1120/2

New Caledonia islands S Pacific early Melanesian settlement 26/1; French colony 119/2, 155/1; US base 142/1

Newchwang Manchuria treaty port 95/2

New England NE USA British settlement 86/2

Newfoundland province of E Canada rediscovered 78/1; British colony 86/2; British settlement 87/1; joins Dominion 120/2

New France French possessions in Canada 86/2

New Granada (mod. Colombia) Spanish colony 87/1; vice-royalty in rebellion against Spain 99/1; 18C Atlantic economy 102/1

New Guinea (now part of Papua New Guinea) early settlement 27/1; Dutch/German/British control 119/2; attacked by Japanese 142/1; retaken by Allies 143/2. See also West Irian

New Hampshire state of NE USA colony 104/1; population 121/1, Depression 138/2

New Hebrides (Fr. Nouvelles Hébrides now Vanuatu) islands S Pacific early Melanesian settlement 27/1; British/French condominium 119/2; US base 142/1; independence 155/1 (inset)

New Ireland island Papua New Guinea early Melanesian settlement 26/1; occupied by Japanese 142/1

New Jersey state of E USA colony 86/2, 104/1; population 115/3; Depression 131/2

New Mexico state of SW USA ceded by Mexico 107/1; population 121/1; Depression 138/2

New Orleans S USA French/Spanish occupation 87/1

New Sarai S Russia Mongol city 60/1

New South Wales state of SE Australia settlement and development 106/1; statehood 118/1

New Spain (mod. Mexico, C America and Caribbean) Spanish vice-royalty 78/1; early voyages of discovery 87/1; rebellion against Spain 99/1

New Territories S China acquired by Britain 95/2

New York City (1653-64 called New Amsterdam earlier Fort Amsterdam) 86/2; industry 121/1; population 121/3; economic growth 145/1

New Zealand early Polynesian settlement 27/1; settlement and development 107/2,3

Nicaea (mod. Iznik) W Anatolia Mithraic site 34/1; Byzantine Empire 49/2

Nicaragua country of C America early exploration 78/1; independence 112/1; Sandinista revolution 159/1

Nicobar Islands Indian Ocean territory of British India 119/2

Nicomedia (mod. Izmit) W Anatolia Christian centre 45/1; Byzantine Empire 49/1

Nicopolis W Greece Byzantine Empire 49/2

Niger country of W Africa French colony 111/1; independence 154/1; economy 174/1

Nigeria country of W Africa British colony 111/1, 119/2; independence 154/1; political development 161/1; economy 174/1

Nihavand (anc. Laodicea in Media) W Persia ✕51/1

Nineveh Mesopotamia early farming village 19/1; Assyrian Empire 22/3; Mitannian city 23/1

Ningpo (n/s Ningbo) E China treaty port 95/2

Ningxia (f/s Ningxia) province of N China economy 1979-92 151/2

Nippur C Mesopotamia Sumerian city 23/1

Nish (S. Cr. Niš anc. Naissus) E Yugoslavia Ottoman Empire 71/1

Nishapur (Pers. Neyshabur) W Persia Mongol conquest 61/1; Safavid conquest 63/1

Nisibis (mod. Nusaybin) E Anatolia Roman Empire 37/1

Nizhniy Novgorod (since 1932 Gorkiy) C Russia town of Vladimir-Suzdal 57/1; 1905 Revolution 115/3; Bolshevik seizure 135/1

Nomonhan (a/c Khalkin Gol) E Mongolia Russo-Japanese conflict 123/2

Nördlingen S Germany ✗93/3

Noricum Roman province of C Europe 37/1

Normandy region of N France Scandinavian settlement 54/1; French Royal domain 82/1; province of France 83/2

North Carolina state of E USA colony 86/2, 104/1; population 121/3; Depression 138/2

Northern Cook Islands (Manihiki Islands)

Northern Ireland religious divide 166/2

Northern Rhodesia (now Zambia) British colony 111/1, 119/2

North Ossetia Caucasus republic of the Russian Federation 169/2, 170/3

Northumbria early kingdom of N England 53/2

North Vietnam independence 155/1. See also Vietnam, Indo-China

North West Frontier Province N Pakistan in Indian Empire 96/2, 97/3

Norway conversion to Christianity 45/2; Black Death 67/1; Reformation 91/1; WW2 140/1, 141/2; NATO and EFTA 147/4; economy 175/1

Notium W Anatolia ✗33/2

Nova Scotia (form. Acadia) province of E Canada ceded by France 87/1; British possession 86/3, 104/1; joins Confederation 120/2; economy 120/2

Novgorod (Norse Holmegaard) NW Russia bishopric 45/2; Viking trade 57/1; WW2 141/2

Novgorod Empire NW Russia 53/2; conquered by Muscovy 851

Novgorod-Seversk early principality of W Russia 57/1

Novibazar, Sanjak of Ottoman province of Yugoslavia 124/1

Nubia region of NE Africa early settlement 27/2

Numidia Roman province of N Africa 36/1

Nupe Nigeria early Hausa state 58/1, 59/2

Nyasaland (now Malawi) British protectorate 111/1, 119/2

Oaxaca early civilization of Mexico 24/2 (inset)

Odessa S Ukraine founded 85/1; 1905 Revolution 115/3; Bolshevik seizure 135/1; WW2 141/2

Odessus (mod. Varna) Bulgaria Greek colony 33/1; Roman Empire 37/1

Offa's Dyke 53/1

Okinawa island SW Japan captured by US 143/2; reversion to Japan 163/1; US base 165/1

Olbia S Russia Greek colony 33/1

Old Calabar Nigeria 59/2

Oldenburg country of N Germany 116/2

Old Sarai S Russia Mongol city 60/1

Olmec States C Mexico 24/2

Oman region of E Arabia Muslim expansion 51/1; under Abbasid sovereignty 51/2; British sphere of influence 154/1

Ontario province of E Canada joins Confederation 120/2

Oran (Ar. Wahran) N Algeria Habsburg Empire 93/1; WW2 140/1

Orange principality of S France 83/2

Oregon state of NW USA acquired by USA 105/2; population 121/1; Depression 138/2

Orenburg (1938-57 called Chkalov) C Russia founded 85/1; Bolshevik seizure 135/1

Orissa (form. Jajnagar) region of E India district of Mughal Empire 63/1; state of modern India 97/3

Orkney islands of NE Scotland Norwegian Viking settlement 54/1

Orléanais region of C France 82/1; 83/2

Ormuz (a/s Hormuz anc. Harmozia) S Persia Portuguese control 63/1; Portuguese base 81/1

Oslo (until 1924 Kristiania a/s Christiania) Norway WW2 140/1

Otford S England ✗53/1

Ottoman Empire Mongol invasion 60/2; expansion into Europe 70-1; decline 108/1, 125/2; WW1 133/1

Oudenaarde (Fr. Audenarde) Belgium ✗83/3

Outer Mongolia (now Mongolia) Chinese protectorate 94/1; independence 131/2

Pacific Ocean early Polynesian settlement 27/1; WW2 142-43; sovereignty of islands 155/1 (inset)

Paeckche Korea early state destroyed by T'ang 47/1

Pagan C Burma Mongol attack 61/1; Buddhist site 35/1; early empire 65/1

Pakhoi S China treaty port 95/2

Pakistan independence 154/1; secession of Bangladesh 163/1; boundary dispute with India 163/1; Baghdad Pact and US alliance 165/1

Palatinate (Ger. Pfalz) historical region of W Germany Reformation 91/1; German unification 116/2

Palau (f/s Pelew) SW Caroline Islands, W Pacific occupied by US 143/2

Pale Bosnia-Herzegovina Bosnian Serb capital 171/2

Palestine (Lat. Palaestina now Israel and Jordan) Levantine cities and ports 22/1; Byzantine Empire 49/1; Ottoman province 108/1; WW2 140/1; partition between Israel and Jordan 156/1

Pamphylia ancient country of southern Anatolia 33/1, 37/1, 49/1

Panama independence 113/1; US intervention 1989 159/1; US base 165/1

Panama Canal opening 118/2

Panipat N India ✗63/1

Panmunjom Korea 1953 armistice 153/1

Pannonia C Europe Avar Kingdom 53/2

Pannonia Inferior Roman province of C Europe 37/1

Pannonia Superior Roman province of C Europe 37/1

Panticapaeum (mod. Kerch) Crimea Greek colony 33/1; Roman Empire 37/1

Papal States C Italy Black Death 67/1; Reformation 91/1; unification of Italy 117/1

Paphlagonia ancient country of N Anatolia 33/1; 49/1

Papua New Guinea SW Pacific independence 155/1. See also New Guinea

Parhae (Chin. Pohai) early Korean state 47/1

Paris N France parlement 83/2; ✗99/2; Industrial Revolution 100/2

Parma N Italy Roman Lombard League 55/2; unification of Italy 117/1

Passchendaele NW Belgium WW1✗ 132/2

Pearl Harbor Hawaii bombed by Japanese 142/1

Pechenegs tribe of Ukraine, 48/2, 56/2, 57/1

Pecsaete tribe of early England 53/1

Pegu early state of S Burma, Buddhist site 35/1; early trade 89/2

Peking (form. Mong. Khanbalik, Chin. Beijing) N China Ming capital 69/1; Japanese occupation 123/2; economy 151/2

Peloponnesian War 33/2

Peninsular War 98/2

Pennsylvania state of E USA colony 86/2, 104/1; population 121/1; Depression 138/2

Pereyaslav early principality of Ukraine 57/1

Pergamum (Gr. Pergamon Turk. Bergama) W Anatolia Roman Empire 37/1

Périgord region of C France annexed to France 82/1

Perm (1940-57 called Molotov) C Russia founded 85/1; Bolshevik seizure 135/1

Persepolis Persia taken by Alexander 32/3; Muslim conquest 51/1

Persia (now Iran) Mongol invasion 61/1; campaigns of Alexander 32/3; Zoroastrianism 34/1; attacked by White Huns 40/1; under Abbasid sovereignty 51/2; Safavid Empire 63/1; Islamic state 157/3

Persian Gulf (a/c Arabian Gulf or The Gulf) Iran-Iraq War 157/2

Peru Spanish colonization 87/1; 18C Atlantic economy 102/1; independence 113/1

Petrograd (before 1914 St. Petersburg since 1924 Leningrad) WW1 133/1; Russian Revolution 135/1

Petsamo (Russ. Pechenga) NW Russia Russian conquest from Finland 141/2

Phazania (mod. Fezzan) region of S Libya 37/1

Philadelphia E USA founded 86/2

Philippines early trade 81/1; Spanish conquest 89/2; occupied by Japanese 123/2, 142/1; retaken by Americans 143/2; independence 155/1; political development 163/1; US bases 165/1

Philippine Sea ✗143/2

Philippopolis (mod. Plovdiv Turk. Filibe) Bulgaria Byzantine Empire 49/1; Ottoman Empire 71/1

Philomelium (mod. Akşehir) C Anatolia Byzantine Empire 49/2

Phnom Penh Cambodia 65/1, 89/2; Vietnam war 162/3

Phocaea W Anatolia Greek colony 33/1

Phoenicia at time of Greeks 33/1

Phoenicians move into Africa 27/2

Phrygia ancient country of W Anatolia 33/1; Byzantine Empire 49/1

Picts early tribe of Scotland 40/1

Piedmont (It. Piemonte) region of N Italy 117/1

Pigs, Bay of Cuba CIA invasion 164/3

Pisidia ancient country of C Anatolia 49/1

Podolia region of S Ukraine acquired by Lithuania 66/2

Pohai (Kor. Parhae mod. Manchuria) NE China early state 47/1

Poitiers (anc. Limonum) C France 17C seat of intendant 77/2

Poitou region of W France province of France 83/2

Pola (mod. Pula) N Yugoslavia Roman Empire 37/1

Poland conversion to Christianity 45/2; union with Lithuania 66/2; Black Death 67/1; acquired by Russia 85/1; Reformation 91/1; revolt against Russia 98/1; WW1 133/1; WW2 140-41; territorial changes 146/1; Warsaw Pact and Comecon 138/3, 165/1; end of Communist rule 169/1

Polish Corridor 136/1

Polynesia islands of C Pacific early settlement 27/1

Pomerania (Ger. Pommern Pol. Pomorze) region of N Europe medieval German Empire 55/2; Reformation 91/1; unification of Germany 116/2

Pomerelia (Ger. Pommerellen) region of N Europe occupied by Teutonic Knights 66/2

Pondicherry (Fr. Pondichéry) SE India French enclave 97/3

Pontus district of N Anatolia 33/1; Roman province 37/1,2; Byzantine Empire 49/1

São Tomé and Príncipe islands W Africa united as independent republic 154/1

Saracens invasion of S Europe 54/1

Saragossa (*anc.* Caesaraugusta *mod.* Zaragoza) N Spain bishopric 44/1; ✗98/1; captured by French 98/1

Sarajevo C Yugoslavia captured by Ottomans 71/1; WW1 133/1; WW2 140/1; civil war 171/2

Saratoga NE USA ✗104/1

Sardinia (*It.* Sardegna) island W Mediterranean Roman empire 36/1; Byzantine Empire 48/1; Muslim conquest 50/1; Saracen attacks 54/1; Habsburg Empire 93/1; Kingdom 99/2, 117/2

Sardis (*a/s* Sardes) W Anatolia Roman Empire 37/1; Byzantine Empire 49/2

Sarkel S Russia ✗56/2

Sarmatians (*Lat.* Sarmatae) tribe of Caucasus and S Russia 33/1, 37/1

Sarmizegetusa Romania Roman Empire 37/1

Sasanian Empire Western Asia 41/1

Saudi Arabia Gulf War 157/3

Savoy (*Fr.* Savoie *It.* Savoia) region of France/Italy medieval state 55/2; Calvinism 91/1; Habsburg Empire 93/1; ceded to France 117/1

Saxon March 53/2

Saxony region of N Germany Frankish Empire 53/2; Black Death 67/1; Reformation 91/1

Scandinavia (*anc.* Scandia) Viking invasions of Europe 54/1. See also Denmark, Sweden, Norway

Scapa Flow N Scotland WW1 133/1

Schleswig-Holstein region of N Germany unification of Germany 116/2

Scotland (*anc.* Caledonia) Scandinavian settlement 54/1; Black Death 67/1; Reformation 91/1; Devolution 166/2

Scupi (*mod.* Skoplje *Mac.* Skopje *Turk.* Üsküb) Byzantine Empire 49/1

Scythians ancient tribe of S Russia 33/1

Sebastopol (*Russ.* Sevastopol) Crimea. S Russia 1905 Revolution 115/3; WW1 133/1

Sedan N France ✗116/2; WW2 140/1

Selinus (*mod.* Selinunte) Sicily Greek colony 32/1, 33/2

Seljuks Turkish Muslim dynasty of Middle East 49/2, 51/2

Senegal W Africa French colony independence 154/1

Senegambia region of W Africa source of slaves 59/2; slave trade 102/1

Seoul (*Jap.* Keijo) S Korea Korean war 153/1

Septimania ancient region of S France, part of Frankish Empire 52/2

Serbia (*now part of* Yugoslavia) country of SE Europe conversion to Christianity 45/2; Byzantine Empire 49/2; empire under Stephen Dushan 66/2; Black Death 67/1; Ottoman province 71/1; Industrial Revolution 108/1; WW1 133/1; independence 136/1; WW2 141/2; Kosovo crisis 171/2

Serdica (*a/s* Sardica *mod.* Sofia) Bulgaria Roman Empire 37/1; Byzantine Empire 49/1

Seringapatam S India ✗97/1

Sevastopol (*Eng.* Sebastopol *med. Turk.* Akhtiar) Crimea acquired by Muscovy 85/1

Seville (*Sp.* Sevilla *anc.* Hispalis) S Spain Emirate of Cordoba 50/1

Shaanxi (*f/s* Shensi) province of N China economy 1979-92 151/2

Shakas early dynasty of N India 29/4

Shanghai E China treaty port 95/2; occupied by Japanese 123/2; Nationalist control 130/1; industry 131/2; economy 151/2

Shansi (*n/s* Shanxi) province of N China Ming province 69/1; Manchu expansion 94/1; economy 151/2

Shan State(s) Burma part of India 97/3

Shandong (*f/s* Shantung) province of E China economy 1979-92 151/2

Shantou (*f/s* Swatow) S China special economic zone 151/2

Shantung (*n/s* Shandong) province of E China under Ming 69/1; Manchu expansion 94/1; Japanese influence 130/1; economy 151/2

Shanxi (*f/s* Shansi) province of N China economy 1979-92 151/2

Shensi (*n/s* Shaanxi) province of N China under Ming 69/1; Manchu expansion 94/1; economy 151/2

Shenzhen S China special economic zone 151/2

Shetland (*form.* Hjaltland) NE Scotland Norwegian settlement 54/1

Shias Muslim minority of S Iraq 147/3

Siam (*now* Thailand) spread of Buddhism 64/2; conquests 89/2; under Japanese influence 123/2; occupied by Japanese 142/1

Sian (*n/s* Xi'an) China Ming provincial capital 69/1

Siberia cave art 15/1; Russian expansion 79/2

Sichuan (*f/s* Szechwan) province of W China economy 1979-92 151/2

Sicily (*Lat.* and *It.* Sicilia) island C Mediterranean Greek colonization 32/1; Byzantine Empire 49/1; Saracen raids 54/1; German attacks 55/2; to Savoy 83/3; Habsburg Empire 93/1; Kingdom of the Two Sicilies annexed to Piedmont/Sardinia 117/1; WW2 141/2

Sidon (*mod.* Saïda *Ar.* Sayda) Lebanon Phoenician city 33/1; taken by Alexander 32/3

Sierra Leone country of W Africa slave trade 102/1; British settlement 111/1; British colony 119/2; independence 154/1

Sikkim country of Himalayas British protectorate 95/2 dependency of India 96/3; annexed to India 155/1

Silesia (*Ger.* Schlesien *Pol.* Śląsk) region of Germany/Poland medieval German Empire 55/2; Habsburg Empire 93/1; unification of Germany 116/2; divided between Germany and Poland 136/1

Silla (*Eng.* Korea *Kor.* Koryo) occupied by T'ang 47/1

Singapore (*earlier* Tumasik) S Malaya early trade 89/2; occupied by Japanese 142/1; independence 155/1; economy 175/1

Sinkiang (*n/s* Xinjiang) province of NW China part of Han Empire 95/2; cession of territory to Russia 95/2; economy 151/2

Sinope (*mod.* Sinop) N Anatolia Greek colony 33/1; Roman Empire 37/1; Byzantine Empire 49/1

Slovakia forms part of Czechoslovakia 136/1; occupied by Hungary in WW2 141/2

Slovenia in Yugoslavia 128/1; independence 169/1

Smolensk W Russia bishopric 45/2; principality 57/1; acquired by Lithuania 66/2; captured by Napoleon 99/2; Bolshevik seizure 135/1

Smyrna (*mod.* Izmir) W Anatolia Roman Empire 37/1; Byzantine Empire 49/1,2; Ottoman Empire 71/1; centre of European trade 103/2

Socotra island Arabian Sea acquired by Britain 119/2

Sofala Mozambique Portuguese settlement 59/2; early trade 81/1

Sofia (*anc.* Serdica *a/s* Sardica *med.* Sredets) Bulgaria Ottoman control 71/1; WW2 141/2

Sogdiana (*a/c* Sogdia, Suguda) ancient region of C Asia Chinese protectorate 46/1

Solferino N Italy ✗117/1

Solomon Islands SW Pacific British protectorate 119/2; occupied by Japanese 142/1; retaken by Allies 143/2; independence 155/1 (inset)

Somalia (*form.* British and Italian Somaliland) independence 154/1; political development 161/1

Somaliland divided between British, Italians and French 119/2

Somme river NE France WW1 offensive 124/2

Songhay (*a/s* Songhai) early empire of W Africa 58/1

Soochow E China treaty port 95/2; industry 131/2

Sopron (*Ger.* Ödenburg) Hungary to Hungary after plebiscite 136/1

Sorbs Slavic tribe of C Europe 53/2

South Africa Union 119/2; Republic 154/1; political development 161/1

South Carolina state of SE USA colony 86/2, 104/1; population 121/1; Depression 138/2

South-East Asia early civilizations 29/1; Mongol attacks 61/1; post 1945 conflicts 163/1

Southern Rhodesia (*now* Zimbabwe *f/c* Rhodesia) British colony 111/1, 119/2

South Ossetian Caucasus 170/3

South Tyrol (*Ger.* Südtirol *It.* Alto Adige) region of Austro-Hungarian Empire acquired by Italy 136/1

South Vietnam independence 155/1; war 162/3. See also Vietnam, Indo-China

South Yemen (*also called* People's Democratic Republic of Yemen *form.* Federation of South Arabia *earlier* Protectorate of South Arabia *earlier* Aden Protectorate) independence 154/1; union with north Yemen 154/1

Spa Belgium 1920 Conference 136/1

Spain (*anc.* Hispania) early invasions 40/1; conversion to Christianity 44/1; Muslim conquest 50/2; Umayyad caliphate 50/2; Reformation 91/1; War of the Spanish Succession 83/3; colonial empire 119/2; opposition to Napoleon 98/1; Industrial Revolution 100/2; 18C Atlantic economy 103/2; 19C alliances 124/1; US bases 165/1

Spanish Guinea (*now* Equatorial Guinea) W Africa colony 118/1

Spanish March 52/2

Spanish Sahara (*a/c* Western Sahara *includes* Rio de Oro) NW Africa 103/2; Spanish colony 111/1; partition between Morocco and Mauritania 154/1, 161/1

Spanish Succession, War of the 83/3

Sparta (*a/c* Lacedaemon) S Greece Peloponnesian War 33/2; Roman Empire 37/1

Spartalos N Greece ✗33/2

Sphacteria S Greece ✗33/2

Srebrenica NE Herzegovina UN safe area 171/2

Srinagar N India capital of Kashmir 97/3

Srivijaya E Indies early empire 65/1

Stalingrad (*until 1925* Tsaritsyn *since 1961* Volgograd) S Russia WW2 141/2

Stresa N Italy 1935 Conference 136/1

Styria (*Ger.* Steiermark) province of SE Austria acquired by Habsburgs 66/2; Habsburg Empire 93/1

Sudan (*form.* Anglo-Egyptian Sudan) Mahdist state 111/1; Anglo-Egyptian condominium 111/1, 119/2; independence 154/1, 161/1; Islamic fundamentalism 157/3

Sudetenland C Europe German annexation 137/2

Suez Canal N Egypt Egyptian-Israeli war 156/1

Suifen NE China treaty port 95/2

Sukhothai C Thailand Buddhist site 35/1; major political centre 65/1

Sumatra (*Indon.* Sumatera) E Indies spread of Buddhism 35/1; Dutch possession 119/2; occupied by Japanese 142/1

Sumerians ancient people of Mesopotamia 23/1

Sung Empire China Mongol conquest 61/1

Süntel N Germany ✗53/2

Surabaya (*Dut.* Soerabaja) Java trading centre 89/2; occupied by Japanese 142/1

Swabia (*Ger.* Schwaben) province of medieval German kingdom 55/2

Swakopmund SW Africa German settlement 111/1

Swatow (*n/s* Shantou) S China treaty port 95/2; Japanese occupation 123/2; 151/2

Picture credits

Picture credits